D0161517

Insurgency, Terrorism, and Crime

International and Security Affairs Series
Edwin G. Corr, General Editor

Also by Max G. Manwaring

(ed. with Court Prisk) *El Salvador at War: An Oral History of Conflict from the 1979 Insurrection to the Present* (Washington, D.C., 1988)

(ed.) *Uncomfortable Wars: Toward a New Paradigm of Low Intensity Conflict* (Boulder, 1991)

(ed.) *Gray Area Phenomena: Confronting the New World Disorder* (Boulder, 1993)

(ed. with Wm. J. Olson) *Managing Contemporary Conflict: Pillars of Success* (Boulder, 1996)

Spain and the Defense of European Security Interests: A Military Capability Analysis (Boulder, 1997)

(ed. with John T. Fishel) *Toward Responsibility in the New World Disorder: Challenges and Lessons of Peace Operations* (Portland, 1998)

(ed. with Anthony James Joes) *Beyond Declaring Victory and Coming Home: The Challenges of Peace and Stability Operations* (Westport, Conn., 2000)

(ed.) *Deterrence In The Twenty-first Century* (Portland, 2001)

(ed.) *Environmental Security and Global Stability: Problems and Responses* (Lanham, Md., 2002)

(ed. with Edwin G. Corr and Robert H. Dorff) *The Search for Security: A U.S. Grand Strategy for the Twenty-first Century* (Westport, Conn., 2003)

(with John T. Fishel) *Uncomfortable Wars Revisited* (Norman, 2006)

INSURGENCY, TERRORISM, AND CRIME

Shadows from the Past and Portents for the Future

Max G. Manwaring

Foreword and Afterword
by Edwin G. Corr

University of Oklahoma Press : Norman

Library of Congress Cataloging-in-Publication Data

Manwaring, Max G.
Insurgency, terrorism, and crime : shadows from the past and portents for the future / Max G. Manwaring ; foreword and afterword by Edwin G. Corr. — 1st ed.
p. cm. — (International and security affairs series ; 5)
Includes bibliographical references and index.
ISBN 978-0-8061-3970-8 (hbk. : alk. paper) 1. Asymmetric warfare. 2. Counterinsurgency—Case studies. 3. Insurgency—Case studies. 4. Gangs—Case studies. 5. Crime and globalization. 6. Terrorism—Prevention. 7. National security—United States—21st century. I. Corr, Edwin G. II. Title.
U163.M2688 2008
355.02'13—dc22

2008012870

Insurgency, Terrorism, and Crime: Shadows from the Past and Portents for the Future is Volume 5 in the International and Security Affairs Series.

The paper in this book meets the guidelines for permanence and durability of the Committee on Production Guidelines for Book Longevity of the Council on Library Resources, Inc. ∞

1 2 3 4 5 6 7 8 9 10

Contents

- Euro LA centric
  No Malaysia [illegible] Vietnam
  No neg lesson [illegible]
  No Africa [illegible]
- Non physical determination of democ = window dressing
  w/out true rule of laws a [illegible] [illegible] at all
  [illegible] in the process
  partial state collapse of state-area & state writ is geog narrow

good point

- corruption
- objective wealth disparity not addressed

p65
p70 [illegible] that NSC is supposed to do ?
p73 corruption
Ideal [illegible] over fact & analysis
p93

Foreword

EDWIN G. CORR

In this important volume, Max G. Manwaring has done it again! *Insurgency, Terrorism, and Crime* is yet another broad leap forward in U.S. national security thinking. Manwaring, who holds the General Douglas MacArthur Chair of Research and is a professor of military strategy at the Strategic Studies Institute of the U.S. Army War College, admirably blends theoretical research with practical applications in his many publications.

For Max's first major book on this subject, *Uncomfortable Wars: Toward a New Paradigm of Low-Intensity Conflict* (1991),[1] I wrote in the foreword that I wished the book had been written prior to my tours as the U.S. ambassador in Peru, Bolivia, and El Salvador, where I led U.S. efforts against narcoterrorism and insurgencies. (I also served in Southeast Asia during the Vietnam War, but not as ambassador.) During the decade and a half following the end of the Central American insurgencies and civil wars, Manwaring and his colleagues produced a dozen more books and twice as many articles elaborating on the Manwaring Paradigm, and their concepts were incorporated into U.S. armed forces field manuals. In 2006, John Fishel and Max Manwaring published *Uncomfortable Wars Revisited*,[2] which synthesized this body of literature. I wished then that the book had been available to top leaders of the United States before their decisions and planning for the invasion of Afghanistan and Iraq and for the occupation of those countries and support of the new governments there.

I now strongly recommend that our top decision makers in the areas of foreign policy and national security read *Insurgency, Terrorism, and Crime* and act in accordance with the principles and theories laid out herein to restructure foreign policy, national security thinking, the organization of our national security bureaucracy, and policy implementation. As still the world's most powerful country in the post–cold war era, we must organize ourselves and have a national strategy to cope successfully with threats to our national security and to that of our partner nations in the present and emerging global security arena.

The American people at the time of the publication of this book are so engrossed with our nation's involvement in the wars of Iraq and Afghanistan—plus humanitarian disasters, such as Darfur—that we may have difficulty in concentrating on and thinking about our medium- and longer-term global foreign policy interests and national security. Yet we must! The failure of our top foreign policy and national security decision makers to have a realistic approach, a better understanding of the world, and a viable overarching security strategy (similar to the policy of containment during the cold war) is in large part the explanation of how and why the United States finds itself now unhappily embroiled in Iraq.

For more than two decades, Manwaring and his colleagues have been developing and proposing a national security strategy for the United States' relations with the turbulent and less-developed areas of the world that threaten global security and development. In many of these countries, the lack of effective governance and public order manifests in insurgencies, terrorism, and crime, which inevitably spill over into or become intentionally directed at other nations of the world. This dangerous situation has been greatly intensified by the rise of militant Islam in the form of asymmetric warfare led by Al Qaeda, a nonstate organization that now threatens the nation-state system and the world.

Irregular war, guerrilla war, insurgency war, asymmetric war, partial war, postmodern war, contemporary conflict, international narco-terrorism—whatever we choose to call it—is the by-product of weak or collapsing nation-states. War has changed. The predominance of asymmetric war waged by nonstate actors and the growth of a parallel nonstate global system now challenge the four-hundred-year-old state-centric world system. Al Qaeda most vividly illustrates this.[3] Adversaries in conflict have changed, motives for conflict have expanded and become mixed, and wars have changed and continue to change. War is conducted not only by states but also by nonstate groups, such that it now involves everybody and everything. The United States and its partner countries need to adopt new strategies and means to defeat the new enemies, even while continuing to draw upon time-tested principles about war and conflict, such as those of Sun Tzu and Carl von Clausewitz.

In this book, Manwaring provides some of the strategies and methods that should be very seriously considered in such an endeavor. The case studies in this book present numerous forms of national security threats, including the presence of multiple nonstate actors simultaneously challenging a single nation-state, the use of proxies, the ruthless application of terror, and the decreasing differences between criminal organizations and insurgents. Some of the case studies also demonstrate means of preventing or defeating an insurgency by applying the Manwaring Paradigm and through the creation of effective governance. The abandonment of violence by an insurgency and transformation into an accountable government is another possible outcome exemplified by these case studies of contemporary conflict. All can be analyzed in light of the seven strategic-level dimensions of the Manwaring Paradigm through which success or failure is determined in asymmetric warfare. The analytic generalizations, or key points and lessons, that Manwaring derives from these case studies through the use of his paradigm and Robert K. Yin's "suspense approach" serve as a framework upon which readers can build a better understanding of the reality of modern asymmetric conflict.

The United States needs a citizenry and leadership that are informed about the world we live in, with knowledge about how to protect our nation and advance its interests. In *Insurgency, Terrorism, and Crime,* Max Manwaring makes another significant contribution to this endeavor. I plead to our citizens and leaders to read and digest the lessons of this book.

Preface

This book is the result of two separate research incentives. First, it follows several previous works aimed at stimulating strategic thinking on "uncomfortable" contemporary unconventional, irregular, and asymmetric conflicts. For that, I must thank General John R. Galvin, U.S. Army (retired), and former ambassador Edwin G. Corr, who have steadfastly encouraged that initiative for over twenty years. Second, this book is the direct result of a U.S. Army War College Faculty Research Grant, 2006–2007, that allowed me to examine lessons learned from cases that are useful in illustrating models of harbinger types of insurgencies (irregular, asymmetric conflicts) and counterinsurgencies. For that, I must thank Douglas C. Lovelace, Jr., director of the Strategic Studies Institute at the U.S. Army War College, and Major General David H. Huntoon, Jr., commandant at the U.S. Army War College.

The commonality that links the two sets of research efforts noted above is the concern that strategic civilian and military leaders and opinion makers in the United States tend to think of the long-past Vietnam and current Iraqi insurgencies and counterinsurgencies as the only examples of unconventional conflict worth considering. Moreover, there has been too much operational-tactical crisis response to specific situations and too little strategy applied to a war as a whole. Thus, the relevance of this book lies in its transmission of hard-learned lessons of the past and present to current and future leaders. These leaders will need to solve the next big set of global security problems in the twenty-first century. To achieve success, they must think about these problems from multiple angles, on multiple levels, and in varying degrees of complexity. As we reflect on the present and future global security situation and the well-being of future generations, we have the opportunity to adjust our mindset and to profit from the mistakes of the past. But we must begin now.

Before we rush into change for the sake of change, however, a word of caution is in order. First, "lessons learned" may not be consistent with the popular wisdom and therefore are more difficult to assimilate into policy and budgets. It is not just a matter of learning from past errors or successes. The question is, Are we willing to deal with a given issue even though doing so may be unpopular or politically incorrect? Second, "lessons learned" can be erroneous if too literally applied to a seemingly similar situation. The honest way to face the first problem is to examine personal conscience, priorities, and ethics; a quick look back into history can provide an illustration and solution to the second problem. For example, in the year 1415, a superior French force was defeated at Agincourt by the English under Henry V, as a result of adapting to erroneous lessons learned.

Sixty years earlier, in 1346, the English under Edward III severely defeated the forces of Philip VI of France at Crécy. Edward chose a defensive position close to the center of a narrow valley and on the downslope of a small hill. There he placed his men-at-arms and knights. He then located his longbow archers as legs of a vee on each flank of the valley. French men-at-arms, followed by mounted knights and crossbowmen, attacked with superior numbers in successive waves through the valley floor. But the French knights, following the men-at-arms, could never break through the mass in the middle or take advantage of the mobility of their horses. Instead, they fell to a rain of arrows from the English longbows. There were many lessons for the French to learn: don't attack piecemeal; don't fight longbows with crossbows; don't attack in a defile that limits maneuver room. But one lesson remembered by the French, who left 1,500 knights among the thousands of dead in the valley of Crécy, was that the English men-at-arms and the English knights were dismounted on the front slope of the hill.

At Agincourt, a vastly superior French force of approximately 20,000, with 12,000 men-at-arms, blocked Henry V's return to England. This time, the French chose the battlefield. It was a narrow front along a road with forest on both sides. The English took up positions on a small hill in the center of the defile—upon and in front of which Henry placed his dismounted knights and men-at-arms. Again, the longbow archers were positioned in a vee radiating out from the center of the hill just inside the edges of the forest. Impatiently, the French unsuccessfully attacked the archers along the wooded flanks with light cavalry while the main body charged the middle position. This time, the French demonstrated that they had learned their lesson. The men-at-arms and the knights—wave after wave—attacked the English dismounted! The French lost 10,000 of their 20,000-man force. Henry sailed home with almost all of his army—and another victory.

The French had studied the battle of Crécy well. The minutiae were completely understood. But there apparently had been no strategic analysis, no appreciation of the entire situation, and consequently no valid lessons learned. In drawing conclusions about the experiences noted above, readers and planners must strive to note the archers, the general capabilities of the force, the layout of the valley, and the whole strategic scene rather than focusing only on the obvious—the dismounted knights on the front slope of the hill. We have William Shakespeare to thank for preserving these "lessons learned," although I must credit one of my mentors, Colonel Court Prisk, U.S. Army (retired), for these insights.

I would like to thank a few other people whose knowledge, experience, analytical powers, wisdom, and patience have helped make this book possible. It is not possible to name every person individually, but a few of the most influential must be acknowledged. They include Lieutenant Colonel John T. Fishel, U.S. Army (retired), who has been coauthor, mentor, and friend; General Fred F. Woerner, Jr., U.S. Army (retired); former ambassador Frank McNeil; and my colleagues Gabriel Marcella, William J. Olson, and Kim Fishel. They have been thoughtful strategists and constant inspirations and supporters.

In this context, I respectfully dedicate this book to Colonel Robert M. Herrick, U.S. Army (retired), who has led the effort of virtually all those individuals named above in taking turns at various times and on different occasions to beat me about the head and shoulders and prod me on.

This book should not be construed as reflecting the official positions of the U.S. Army War College, the Department of the Army, the Department of Defense, the Department of State, or the U.S. government. I, alone, am responsible for any errors of fact or judgment.

Insurgency, Terrorism, and Crime

Introduction

Whatever it is called—irregular war, guerrilla war, insurgency war, asymmetric war, partial war, or postmodern war—contemporary war (conflict) is the product of weak or collapsing nation-states and the emergence of new organizing principles. The sociology of war, of war making, and of those who are able to make it have changed. One major characteristic of the so-called postmodern era is the emergence of asymmetric nonstate actors and the growth of a nonstate global system parallel to the traditional state-centric international system.[1] This new system is playing an increasingly significant role in creating new subnational, national, regional, and global political-security realities.

Osama bin Laden and Al Qaeda abruptly and violently contradicted the traditional ideas that war is the purview of the state and that nonstate and irregular ways and means of conducting contemporary war were aberrations.[2] In these terms, Al Qaeda demonstrated that a nonstate actor could effectively challenge a traditional nation-state—and indeed the symbols of power in the global system—and pursue its strategic objectives without conventional weaponry or manpower. At the same time, Al Qaeda illustrated that nonstate actors and their actions can be protean and constantly mutating. As a result, adversaries in conflict have changed, motives for conflict have changed, means to pursue war have changed, and war has changed—and continues to change.

In this new global security environment, war is no longer merely an instrument of state policy but also serves as an instrument of personal whim or grudge. War is no longer only an instrument of state action; it is also an instrument of small groups and individual (nonstate) actors. War is no longer so costly that only a wealthy nation-state can afford to become involved in such a methodology to bend an adversary to its will. Rather, war, the power to make war, and the power to destroy or significantly change nation-states are now within the reach of small self-appointed groups and even individuals. War is now without frontiers or enforceable controls. War now involves everybody and everything. War is unrestricted.[3]

The logic of the situation argues that the conscious choices made by civil-military leadership in the international community and in individual nation-states about how to deal with the contemporary nontraditional security environment will define the processes of national, regional, and global security, stability, and well-being far into the future. This requires a new insurgency/counterinsurgency paradigm in which the traditional state military and police security organizations continue to play major roles—but in ways that should be closely coordinated with all the other instruments of national power under the control of the civil authority. Thus, the strategic imperative of this book is the transmission of hard-learned lessons of the past and present to current and future civilian and military leaders. These leaders will be solving the next big set of security problems in the twenty-first century, and they must think about these problems from multiple angles, on multiple levels, and in varying degrees of complexity.

Several cases are useful in illustrating models of harbinger types of insurgency (irregular war). These cases indicate very different approaches to power when their theoretical aspects are analyzed in general terms and in terms of a "suspense approach," as suggested by case study methodologist Robert K. Yin.[4] This combined analysis yields strategic (macro-level) commonalities pertaining to the ongoing insurgency/irregular war situation that are, along with their attendant recommendations and the conceptual framework, likely to remain relevant for decision makers, policy makers, and opinion makers for a long time to come.

GENERAL METHODOLOGY

Case study methodology does not require the testing or demonstration of hypotheses. Thus, there is no need for sophisticated statistical computations, testing, and analysis; the necessary elements are ingenuity, flexibility, and sensitivity to the need to collect relevant evidence with minimal expenditure of time, effort, and money. The research purposes are to answer the fundamental "who," "what," "why," "how," and "so what?" insurgency/counterinsurgency questions that are important in policy, practical, and theoretical terms; gain greater familiarity with the complex political-social insurgency phenomenon; gain sharper and more relevant insights; and develop generalizations that may, with further research, become theoretical propositions.[5]

The Cases

To satisfy these research purposes, I concentrate on the most likely forms of insurgency war for now and the future, as postulated by Ian F. W. Beckett and Thomas A. Marks, noted authorities on insurgency and counterinsurgency;[6] the seven explanatory case situations that make up the individual chapters of this book are analogous to conducting an equal number of experiments on related topics.[7] Each case illustrates one or more of Beckett's and Marks's postulates: multiple nonstate actors simultaneously challenging a single nation-state (Colombia); the use of a variety of legal and illegal approaches and the use of proxies (Venezuela); the employment of a multidimensional paradigm along with a ruthless application of terror (Al Qaeda); an increasing lack of differentiation between gangs, other transnational criminal organizations, and insurgents (Central America, El Salvador, and Mexico); the highly politicized nature of insurgencies, including "preventive" or "preemptive" insurgencies (Portugal); adaptive and innovative thinking (Uruguay); and a creative "best practices" counterinsurgency strategy that resulted in the failure of a impressive terrorist insurgency strategy (Italy).

It must be remembered in this context that the common-denominator objective of all insurgencies is to bring down, radically change, or control a targeted government. Thus, this research approach leads to an enhanced policy and practical understanding of the architecture of successful or unsuccessful strategy—or best/worst practices—in dealing with the insurgency/irregular war phenomenon.[8]

The first case demonstrates that an insurgency may involve multiple conflicts between multiple players. The Colombian state has experienced and continues to experience conflicts with four different nonstate actors—the Revolutionary Armed Forces of Colombia (FARC), the National Liberation Army (ELN), the paramilitary "self-defense" organizations, and the so-called narco-terrorists. These groups are different in terms of motive (ideological and commercial) and method of operations, but they maintain a precarious "marriage of convenience" as they wage war, sometimes against each other and sometimes against the Colombian state. As a consequence, Colombia must deal with at least three major wars within the general insurgency/drug war. Additionally, this case shows the absolute need for state institutions that are strong enough to deal strategically with multiple adversaries with multiple objectives, methods, and means of operations. This case also demonstrates that, while instability is a threat, the ultimate threat is that of state failure. Clearly, this case is an example of an increasing lack of differentiation between insurgents and international criminals and of the increasingly complex political-psychological-economic-social-security implications of contemporary conflict around the globe.

Second, the Venezuelan case reflects the fact that indirect (that is, asymmetric or fourth-generation) methods and means including a combination of social-economic-informational-political-psychological-military ways and resources may be more effective than direct military-related ways and resources in achieving contemporary Bolivarian supranational revolutionary political objectives. This case also supports Walter Laquer's assertion that contemporary war is not simply the purview of groups of nonstate militants. State-sponsored interstate and intrastate war is quietly flourishing. As a matter of fact, Laquer asserts that contemporary fourth-generation wars are modern substitutes for the great wars in Europe and elsewhere in the eighteenth and nineteenth centuries because traditional state-versus-state wars have become too expensive and too politically and militarily risky.[9] In any event, fourth-generation war requires more than weaponry and technology; it also requires lucid and incisive thinking, resourcefulness, determination and time, and a certain disregard for convention. In these terms, the kind of war being pursued by Hugo Chavez's Venezuela stresses ideas and images and appeals to public opinion, rather than traditional military confrontation. This, then, is a model with a great deal of appeal in the world today. One important, and very violent, variation on that paradigm is being carried out by Al Qaeda.

Third, the ongoing case of Al Qaeda in Spain and throughout the West is interesting and instructive. The ruthless application of terror within the context of irregular war demonstrates that Al Qaeda bombings in London, Madrid, and elsewhere in Europe as well as the destruction of the World Trade Center in New York can accomplish at least three things. First, over the short term, terrorists can psychologically dominate a populace; and second, they can change government policy in favor of their immediate objectives. Over the long term, the achievement of many short-term, or limited, objectives can effectively render a targeted government or institution strategically incapable of opposition—as a result of "death by a thousand cuts." As a consequence, the long-term application of Al Qaeda's tactics and strategy appears to be a complex, multidimensional example of fourth-generation war as a substitute for conventional war.[10] At the same time, however, the ruthless application of terror can generate a backlash of national and governmental will and the development of relatively effective countermeasures. In any event, terror—depending on how it is used—can be a strategic and tactical "force multiplier" for the aggressor as well as for the defender. This situation emphasizes the fact that terror and counterterror tactics and strategies are highly political-psychological acts that can be performed by a small number of dedicated and well-trained people and do not rely on a large popular army of liberation to force fundamental political change.

Fourth, the mutation of protean street gangs and transnational criminal organizations (TCOs) into insurgents illustrates that insurgents need not be ideologically oriented, the traditional revolutionary fighters emerging from the mountains and jungles to take down or control a government. Rather, they may have specific commercial money-making motives and can emerge out of the *favelas, callampas, villas miseries,* and *pueblas jovenes* (city slums) not so much to replace governments as to gain very lucrative freedom of movement and action within a supposedly sovereign nation-state. Also, mature second- and third-generation street gangs have been known to act as proxies and mercenaries for traditional nation-states that want to maintain plausible deniability; gang members may act as mercenaries for warlords, organized criminal organizations, or drug-trafficking cartels that on certain occasions need additional firepower. The instability and lack of individual and state security generated by street gangs and TCOs and their nefarious allies are also known to lead to radical change or failed-state status. In these terms, gangs are no longer a singular law enforcement issue. As crime and war become more and more indistinguishable, gangs must be considered a larger national security issue—even as, paradoxically, they must be viewed as a local concept.

Fifth, the Portuguese case demonstrates that a nation's armed forces may act as an unorthodox kind of insurgency: a preemptive or preventive insurgency. Rather than conducting a simple traditional coup, the agents of the Portuguese Revolution of 1974 generated a fundamental change of government from that of the civilian dictator, Antonio de Salazar, to that of a liberal democracy. Additionally, this case illustrates that a military-led insurgency need not be a bloody conflict or result in a military dictatorship. Rather, the Portuguese used patience; the instruments of "soft power"; and the words, images, and ideas of fourth-generation war to alter the political-psychological factors that were the most relevant in that culture. This experience also demonstrates that in internal conflict, the centers of gravity are not enemy military forces. They are, as the great military theorist Carl von Clausewitz warned, public opinion and leadership.[11] The Portuguese Revolution of 1974 was a precocious forerunner of the several peaceful transitions from authoritarianism to democracy, most notably in Eastern Europe.

Sixth, the Uruguayan case illustrates adaptive and innovative thinking in terms of making a sea change in a violent revolutionary war paradigm. That radical change led to a benign political-psychological approach to achieving power. The Uruguayan case, 1962–2005, is a prime harbinger example of such dramatic political change. In that connection, the Tupamaro leadership made a set of unorthodox decisions to move from a violent military approach to a nonviolent and nonmilitary approach. That, in turn, led to free and fair elections in 2005 that gave the militarily defeated Tupamaro insurgency group control of the Uruguayan government in 2006. This case has not gone unnoticed. Interestingly, the Irish Republican Army (IRA), the Provisional Irish Republican Army (PIRA), the Spanish Basque Independence Movement (ETA), and the Nicaraguan Sandinista movement would appear to have recently made similar decisions to enable their respective political objectives.

Seventh, and last, the Italian case (late 1960s–early 1980s) is instructive, serving as a good example from which to learn how governments might ultimately control—or succumb to—the strategic challenges of irregular insurgency war. In that connection, the Italian experience clearly illustrates the effective "best practices" through which to reverse the impetus toward a hostile takeover and failing- or failed-state status. Even though every conflict situation is specific, it is not completely unique; there are analytical commonalities at the strategic level. The paradigm demonstrated in the Italian case has power and virtue in part because of the symmetry of its application. That is, it is adaptable both for a besieged government and for a violent internal nonstate challenger. In these terms, no successful strategy—on either side of the conflict spectrum—has been formulated over the past fifty years that has not explicitly or implicitly taken into account all the strategic dimensions (factors) applied in the Italian counterterrorist experience.[12]

This purposive sample of seven cases was chosen for three specific purposes: first, to familiarize readers with the diversity and complexity of the phenomenon; second, to provide confirmation or denial of the existence of a relationship between the outcome of a conflict/war (success or failure), the environment within which the irregular war takes place, and the various activities undertaken to either conduct or counter it; and third, to articulate proven paths toward good governance and ultimate success. In this context, the environment and the activities serve as independent variables, and the end result as the dependent variable. With this information, strategic analytical commonalities and recommendations can be determined that are relevant to each specific type of insurgency war explored and to the larger, general global security phenomenon.

The "Suspense Approach"

Although a considerable literature on insurgency and counterinsurgency, low-intensity conflict, and terrorism exists, each work generally provides a unique situational account of specific unfolding events. To my knowledge, no one has yet rationalized the development of a holistic and workable strategy to confront the phenomenon effectively. Thus, a major objective of this book is to answer a set of questions and thereby draw conclusions regarding various facets of a causal argument pertaining to the kinds of unconventional/asymmetric/irregular conflict that the United States and other national powers and international organizations face now and are likely to face well into the future. As a consequence, this volume eschews addressing the unfolding of a unique singular contemporary security issue and instead addresses a set of analytical commonalities that would be the basis for a successful multidimensional counterinsurgency/irregular/asymmetric war strategy likely to remain relevant for a long time to come.

This objective is achieved through a "suspense approach." Yin defines that approach as the inversion of the traditional linear-analytic approach to case studies. That is, "the direct 'answer' or outcome of a case study is, paradoxically, presented in the initial section. The remainder of the case study—and its most suspenseful (interesting) parts—is then devoted to the development of an explanation of the unsuccessful or successful outcome (consequences and countermeasures) of the effort. That will, in turn, lead to analytic generalizations."[13] A minimum level of generalization is needed to predict how potentially hostile forces may behave in a given situation: "If two or more cases are shown to support the same theory, replication may be claimed, and one can aim for 'level two inferences.'"[14]

In following this approach, I examine the ways and means by which the overarching objective of "success" (the dependent variable) was achieved in this purposive sample of cases. The SWORD model (also known as the Manwaring Paradigm or the "Max Factors") that John Fishel and I developed suggests seven strategic-level dimensions (independent variables) through which ultimate success or failure may be determined. These factors, which may be considered "wars within the general war," include (1) the type of general war and kind of enemy being faced; (2) the "legitimacy war," attacking or defending the moral right of a given regime to govern; (3) "wars" to isolate belligerents from their internal support; (4) "wars" to isolate belligerents from their external support; (5) the closely related "war to stay the course"; (6) intelligence and information "wars"; and (7) "wars" to unify multidimensional, multilateral, and multiorganizational elements of state and international power into a single effective effort.[15]

Additionally, the model acknowledges that insurgencies and counterinsurgencies operate on two levels—long term, or offensive; and short term, or defensive. The long-term offensive component deals with the political-economic-social-psychological and military conditions that are the root causes of the conflict. The short-term defensive level addresses the immediate efforts and actions that must be taken to render the insurgents (or the targeted government) ineffective. Altogether, these offensive and defensive actions focus primarily on aggressive political and subtle military means, as explicitly illustrated in the Portuguese case.

A statistical analysis of over forty cases indicates that the SWORD model predicts at an impressive 89 percent (almost 20 percent higher than the next-best-performing model tested), and the chances of mispredicting a case using this particular set of variables is 1 in 1,000. The statistical analysis of this model indicates that the better balanced the operationalization of these closely related independent variables (that is, dimensions) is, the better the chances for success.[16]

The nexus between the SWORD model (or Manwaring Paradigm) and the suspense approach lies in the close interrelationship between those seven dimensions and the major components of Yin's suggested format. That is, these factors incorporate the contextual, political, civil, and military dimensions of the suspense approach at the strategic level. A useful way to organize these dimensions within the format of the following chapters is to adopt a matrix approach. The matrix may be viewed as having four sets of elements: context ("What" questions); protagonists' organization, motives, and objectives (fundamental "Who," "Why," and "How" questions); consequences and countermeasures (more-profound "What" and "How" kinds of questions); and outcome ("So what" questions). These elements are closely linked and overlapping in that they are mutually influencing and constitute the cause-and-effect dynamics of a given conflict situation.

In that connection, the intent is to help political, military, and opinion leaders think strategically about explanations for the outcomes of some forerunners of the many irregular wars that this country and others face now and will continue to face in the future.[17] Hundreds of studies and papers provide long "laundry lists" of measures of effectiveness at the tactical and operational levels of contemporary conflict. That kind of information is necessary but not sufficient to move from winning battles to winning "the war." Civilian and military leaders need a firm grip on the complex nature of contemporary insurgency challenges, a more precise understanding of strategies, and a strategic-level architecture (conceptual framework) for achieving better results than in the past. Within this context, the primary intent of this "suspense effort," especially as evidenced by the last three (Portuguese, Uruguayan, and Italian) cases, is to postulate a strong coherent conceptual framework from which understanding, policy, strategy, doctrine, organization, hard and soft power, civil-military force structure, and effective response might flow. Another intent of this effort is to achieve theory-building level-two inferences.

POINT OF DEPARTURE: TOWARD THE FUTURE

War is changing. It is no longer limited to using military violence to bring about fundamental and radical political change. Rather, all means that can be brought to bear on a given situation must be used to co-opt, urge, and compel an adversary to do one's will.[18] Superior firepower is no panacea, and technology may not give one a knowledge or information advantage. The astute modern warrior will tailor the campaign to the adversary's political-economic-psychological vulnerabilities and to the adversary's political-psychological perceptions. This represents a sea change in warfare and requires nothing less than a paradigm change in how conflict is conceived and managed.

This book, then, provides an important and interesting perspective on the contemporary and future irregular/asymmetric war situation. It is also a beginning point from which civilian and military leaders might generate holistic civil-military success against persistent nontraditional threats and turn that success into long-term political victory. As Sun Tzu reminds us, "War is a matter of vital importance to the State; the province of life or death; the road to survival or ruin. It is mandatory that it be thoroughly studied."[19]

CHAPTER 1

A Multiple Conflict Syndrome

The Colombian Insurgency

Reports regarding the demise of the ongoing insurgency in Colombia are greatly exaggerated. Generally speaking, things are going in favor of the Maoist Revolutionary Armed Forces of Colombia (FARC) and the other nonstate actors involved in the conflict. Yes, they have lost a few combatants, but no one who cannot be easily replaced. Yes, these insurgents have lost territory and control of some supply and attack corridors, but—again—nothing really important. Yes, these revolutionary insurgents have lost a few battles, but not the war. And yes, at least two of the various insurgent organizations have been reported to be interested in peace negotiations with the Colombian government, but not as an admission of weakness. Rather, in classic revolutionary style, they are interested in negotiations as a means of gaining time and allowing political forces to come together to allow ultimate victory. Remember, in this kind of conflict, anything except total political-military defeat is victory!

People concerned with insurgency, irregular war, asymmetric war, or terror war (whatever "guerrilla war" might be called at the moment) are not exempt from feelings of hopeful expectancy. One way to deal with this—and to avoid false expectations and susceptibility to wishful thinking—is to understand some of the fundamental "What," "Why," "Who," and "How" questions (that is, adopting a matrix approach) concerning the kind of ongoing revolutionary war that has been fought in Colombia over the past forty to fifty years. The various elements are mutually influencing and constitute the "cause and effect" dynamics of a given conflict situation. The primary issues in this multiple-conflict syndrome case include context; the major protagonists' organization, motives, and objectives; consequences and responses; and key points and lessons.

CONTEXT

Within the past three or four decades, the nature of insurgencies has changed dramatically throughout the world, with what Steven Metz, an expert on military strategy, calls "commercial insurgency and the search for wealth."[1] One of the most far-reaching transformations began in the 1970s with the growing involvement of insurgent forces with narcotraffickers in the Middle East and Asia (Lebanon and the Golden Triangle come quickly to mind).[2] Thus, the narco-insurgent connection is not new, and it is not confined to Latin America. The question, then, is not whether there might be an alliance between the illegal drug industry, the insurgents, and the paramilitaries—the main protagonists—in Colombia, for that has been understood and admitted since the 1980s.[3] The question now is whether these political actors' threats to the state warrant real concern and a serious strategic response.

Theoretical Context

The contemporary use of political-psychological efforts (rather than military resources) as the primary means of achieving the control or overthrow of an existing government has been termed "political war."[4] It may be combined with military violence, economic pressure, subversion, and diplomacy, but its chief aspect is the use of words, images, and ideas. It is also a natural means of expression and self-assertion for extremist political actors, terrorists, and insurgents. The more messianic or wealth-oriented the vision, the more likely the nonstate actor is to remain committed to the use of violent political-psychological measures to achieve the desired objectives.[5]

Rebellion has always existed. It is a simple, violent effort to force an incumbent government to redress grievances. For a rebellion to become an insurgency, a much stronger political component must be added to the equation, that is, the "authoritative allocation of values in a society," or essentially "who gets what"—to include resources, rights, and privileges.[6] Thus, an insurgency is a political war in support of a goal in which the power of the state to allocate is at stake. Even those revolutionary movements that are not explicitly political (such as radical Islam) ultimately must attain political power to implement the changes and reforms they demand. The insurgent political intent, then, is to force a radical socio-economic-political restructuring of a nation state—and its governance.[7]

The difference, then, between rebellion and insurgency is that rebellion requires only redress of grievances, whereas insurgency requires the achievement of control of or overthrow of the incumbent government.[8] The stakes in insurgency war are therefore not limited; they are total from the standpoint of both the eventual winners and the eventual losers. Ultimately, it is a question of survival. Thus, we come back to where we began: in studying terror war, guerrilla war, irregular war, limited war, or any other common term for subnational conflict, we find that these expressions mischaracterize the activities of armed nonstate organizations attempting to gain political control of the state. Such organizations involved in this kind of effort are engaged in a highly complex political act—political war. To emphasize this fact, "insurgency" and "political war" are used as synonymous or compound terms in this chapter.

Political and military leaders of the United States and other world leaders have been struggling with the "new" political aspect of unconventional (irregular) war since the end of World War II, particularly since the ending of the cold war. Yet the nature of the unconventional war dilemma still is not well understood. Unfortunately, the strategic theory of political war has played little part in the debate. Yet the type of conflict that is likely to challenge U.S., Western, and global leadership over the near to long term must be informed by an understanding of insurgency as political war. Understanding the nature of a given conflict, according to Carl von Clausewitz, is "the first of all strategic questions and the most comprehensive."[9] In that context, ample evidence indicates that the highly respected Brazilian theorist of insurgency war, Abraham Guillen, was right when he explained that "revolutionary war is never decided by arms, but rather by winning the political support of the people."[10]

One can take an important step toward understanding the insurgencies in our midst by examining an example case. That may be done in abstract theoretical terms, or it may be accomplished by remembering some of the hard-learned—and sometimes unpopular—lessons of the past, such as the diverse but premier set of lessons from Colombia from 1948 to the present. What makes this conflict significant beyond its domestic political context is that it has been and is a harbinger of much of the subnational political chaos emerging from the cold war's end. This case stresses (1) the problems of counterinsurgency as well as insurgency; (2) that subnational (i.e., intrastate) conflict may involve multiple protagonists—to include Colombian social-political elites—challenging the effective sovereignty and security of the state at any given time; (3) that motives are likely to be commercial as well as ideological, and orientations may go beyond traditional revolutionary motivations and methods; (4) that insurgents may be more interested in human terrain than in physical terrain; (5) that objectives are normally more political-psychological than military; (6) the pervasive and protean nature of contemporary insurgency; and (7) that regardless of motive and method and time and space, there are salient analytical lessons at the strategic level. Thus, examining this case is a logical point from which to garner lessons to begin to understand how governments might ultimately control—or succumb to—multiple insurgency threats inherent in subnational nonstate political war.

Political-Historical Context

In the 1930s and 1940s, chronic political, economic, and social problems created by a self-serving civilian oligarchy began to create yet another crisis in the long list of internal conflicts in Colombian history. In 1930, Liberal reformists came to power and deprived Conservatives of the control of the central government and extensive local patronage. The Liberals also initiated an ambitious social agenda that generated increasing civil violence between Conservative and Liberal partisans.[11]

The catalyst that ignited the eighteen-year period called *la violencia* (i.e., the violence) in April 1948 was the assassination of Liberal populist Jorge Eliecer Gaitan. That murder sparked a riot known as the Bogotazo that left much of the capital city destroyed and an estimated 2,000 dead. Although the government was able to contain the situation in Bogotá, it could not control the violence that spread through the countryside. Rural violence became the norm as an estimated 20,000 armed Liberal and Conservative combatants settled old political scores. Over the period from 1948 to 1966, la violencia claimed the lives of over 200,000 Colombians.[12] During those years, the various Colombian governments dealt with the violence on an ad hoc basis. There was no strategic-level plan. There was no adequate or timely intelligence. There was no consensus among the political, economic, and military elites regarding how to deal with the armed opposition. And there was no meaningful cooperation, coordination, or communication between the civil governments and the armed forces.[13]

In this unstable environment of virtually uncontrolled violence, rural poverty, political disarray, and central government weakness, the illegal drug industry began to grow and prosper. That prosperity, in turn, provided resources that allowed insurgent organizations such as FARC to grow and expand. Later, as the Colombian government proved less and less effective in controlling the national territory and the people in it, the vigilante (or self-defense) paramilitary groups emerged.[14] The thread that permitted these violent nonstate actors to develop, grow, and succeed was (and still is) adequate freedom of movement and action over time. The dynamics of this destructive "Hobbesian Trinity" of illegal-drug-trafficking, insurgent, and paramilitary organizations have substantially expanded freedom of movement and action for those organizations, while correspondingly eroding that of the state.[15]

THE MAIN PROTAGONISTS IN COLOMBIA'S THREE WARS (PLUS ONE)

The problem in Colombia is that that country, and its potential, is deteriorating because of three ongoing, simultaneous, and interrelated wars involving the illegal drug industry, various insurgent organizations (primarily the Revolutionary Armed Forces of Colombia—FARC), and paramilitary/vigilante groups (the United Self-Defense Groups of Colombia—AUC). This unholy trinity of third generation–type gangs and other transnational criminal organizations (nonstate actors) is perpetrating a level of corruption, criminality, human horror, and internal (and external) instability that, if left unchecked at the strategic level, can ultimately threaten Colombia's survival as an organized democratic state and undermine the political stability and sovereignty of its neighbors. The critical point of this argument is that the substance, or essence, of the long-continuing Colombian crisis centers on the general organization, activities, and threats of what James Rosenau calls the major violent "sovereignty free" (nonstate) actors at work in that country today.[16]

The "Who" Question

Narcos

The illegal drug industry in Colombia can be described as a consortium that functions in much the same way as virtually any multinational Fortune 500 company. Products are made, sold, and shipped; bankers and financial planners handle the monetary issues; and lawyers deal with the legal problems. The consortium is organized to achieve superefficiency and maximum profit. It has chief executive officers and boards of directors (called *capos*), councils, a system of justice, public affairs officers, negotiators, project managers—and enforcers. And it operates in virtually every country in the Western Hemisphere and Europe.[17]

Additionally, the illegal drug industry has at its disposal a very efficient flat organizational structure, the latest in high-tech communications equipment and systems, and state-of-the-art weaponry. With these advantages, decisions are made quickly that can ignore or supersede laws, regulations, decisions, and actions of the governments of the nation-states in which the organization operates. Narcos have also assassinated, bribed, corrupted, intimidated, and terrorized government leaders, members of the Congress, judges, law enforcement and military officers, journalists, and even soccer players. As such, the illegal drug industry is a major agent for destabilizing and weakening the state governmental apparatus.[18]

At the same time, narco cosmetic patronage to the poor, creation of their own electoral machinery, open participation in traditional political parties, the financing of friendly election campaigns, and assassinations of elected officials deemed uncooperative have facilitated even greater influence over the executive, legislative, and judicial branches of the Colombian government by demonstrating the utility and urgency of meeting narco expectations and demands. Finally, all this mitigates against responsible government and against any allegiance to the notion of the public good and political equality. In that process, the consortium has achieved a symbiotic relationship with the state and in a sense is becoming a virtual state-within-the-state.[19]

The Insurgents

The FARC insurgents are essentially a *foco*—an insurrectionary armed enclave—in search of a mass base. Because of the general lack of appeal to the majority of the Colombian population, the insurgents have developed a military organization designed to achieve the armed colonization of successive areas within the Colombian national territory. The intent is to "liberate" and mobilize the disaffected and dispossessed population into an alternative society. That is, FARC responded to the lack of popular support, as did the communists in Vietnam, by attempting to take control of the human terrain. In this effort, FARC has proved every bit as ruthless as the Vietcong. Torture and assassination—to say nothing of kidnapping, extortion, intimidation, and other terrorist tactics—are so common as to go almost without comment except in the most extreme cases. Strategically, operationally, and tactically, the FARC approach to taking control of the state is the Vietnamese approach.[20]

These terrorist activities, designed to dominate the human terrain more than the physical terrain, would have probably remained more or less out of sight and out of mind of mainstream Colombia had they been confined to underpopulated and underconsidered rural areas of the country—and had the insurgents not become involved in the illegal drug phenomenon. In 1982, a decision was taken by the Seventh Conference of the FARC to develop links with the Colombian drug industry that would provide the money and manpower necessary for the creation of a "true Bolivarian democracy."[21] As a result, FARC expanded from approximately 2,000 guerrilla fighters in 1982 to over seventy company-sized units with approximately 18,000–22,000 fighters in 2005. This illicit funding has provided FARC with the capability of confronting regular Colombian military units up to battalion size and of overrunning police and military installations and smaller units. At the same time, insurgent presence spread from 173 municipalities in 1985 to 622 in 1995. In 2005, FARC was reported to maintain an armed presence in every department throughout Colombia and to control approximately 40 percent of the national territory.[22]

Even though the insurgents do not have the sympathy of the major part of the Colombian population, FARC's myriad local bodies have access to a virtually inexhaustible pool of marginalized youth living at the seams of society. To recruit them, FARC has utilized all of the methodologies (e.g., initiatory rites, indoctrination, strong discipline, and unremitting proof of loyalty) associated with youth gangs in the United States and elsewhere in the Western Hemisphere. As a result, sufficient combat power can be developed to allow the major urban areas of the country to be isolated and finally captured.[23] Thus, Colombian insurgents have maintained control of large portions of the countryside and placed themselves in positions throughout the country from which to eventually move into or dominate the major population centers. The stated intent is to create an army of 30,000 with which to stage a "final offensive against the regular armed forces and to do away with the state as it now exists in Colombia."[24] By controlling large parts of the Colombian national territory outside the major cities and significant portions of the human terrain throughout the country, the insurgents are challenging state authority in parts of the country reportedly still under government control.

The Paramilitaries

The AUC "self-defense" organizations are semiautonomous regional alliances relatively independent of each other. Nevertheless, a central organization exists, primarily to develop a national coordinated strategy against the insurgents. Additionally, the AUC national front organization provides guidance, training, and other help to member organizations as necessary. The strategy and tactics of AUC, interestingly, mirror those of the insurgents: the paramilitary groups seek to expand their control of grassroots levels of government—municipalities or townships and rural areas—and to exercise political influence through the control, intimidation, or replacement of local officials. And like the insurgents, the paramilitaries profit from drug trafficking.[25]

These vigilante groups began as self-defense organizations for the protection of family, property, and the law and order of a given geographical area. Because of the AUC's orientation against the insurgents and willingness to provide fundamental justice and personal security to those defined as noncollaborators with the insurgents, these vigilante groups have consistently improved their standing in Colombian society. For example, the number of AUC groups increased from 273 to more than 400 at the height of their power, with an estimated current total of 8,000–10,000 active combatants. At present, AUC groups are estimated to maintain an armed presence in about 40 percent of the municipalities of the country. Moreover, the paramilitaries have organized, trained, and equipped "shock brigades" that, since 1996, have become capable of successfully challenging insurgent military formations.

Despite paramilitary success against insurgents where the state has been absent or ineffective and despite growing popular support, the Colombian government has disavowed the AUC. President Alvaro Uribe has made a considerable effort to demobilize the AUC and is claiming success. An estimated 13,000 of the AUC's fighters have reportedly been disbanded, but one must temper this reduction in membership numbers with the following realities: the hard-core AUC members are not giving up, and they continue to fight; the various AUC units have become increasingly autonomous; demobilized members are operating in an outsourcing mode as subsidiaries or pseudo-paramilitaries for the AUC or—as gangs—"renting" their criminal services to the highest bidder; and reportedly, the Colombian Congress "is awash in AUC cash . . . to insure that their influence remains strong at the highest levels of government."[26] In this way, the paramilitaries comprise a third set of competing nonstate actors challenging the authority of the state and claiming the right to control all or a part of the destabilized national territory.[27]

The "Plus One" War Involving the Social-Political Elites

The dissident actions of the upper classes of Colombian society further complicate the intranational conflict mosaic of mutual and conflicting interests and exert a substantial negative force in Colombia's effort to strengthen its institutions and conduct a successful intrastate war. The country's elites have traditionally shown very little interest in the military and have never supported the idea or reality of a strong central government or strong state institutions. The power to control insurgents is also the power to control the virtually autonomous elites; as a result, the burden of fighting Colombia's three wars falls primarily on the poorly supported military and the hapless peasantry. The Constitutional Court has ruled that only professional (i.e., volunteer) soldiers—not conscripts—can be ordered into combat. Subsequent attempts to introduce a lottery system of conscription in 2004, which would possibly draft children of the elites and bring them into the war, failed to get a final reading in the Congress.[28]

The military has always felt that it has been fighting the narco-insurgency war alone. In the 1960s and the 1970s, when military victory was thought to be within the grasp of the armed forces, politicians acting as elite surrogates were said to have essentially "pulled the rug out from under them," preventing the successful conclusion of the war. The same feelings are being privately expressed again. In sum, the argument from the military is that the controlling elites fundamentally distrust and historically fail to provide sufficient resources to the armed forces.[29]

This takes us back to the broader assertion that the Colombian elites have not supported and do not now support strong government or strong institutions. As a consequence, as Douglas Porch has observed, "State institutions do not work. Impunity and corruption are rife. The legal system does not work, so people take the law into their own hands and have no fear of legal consequences."[30] In historian David Bushnell's assessment, "The political structure and elites simply accommodate violence, absorb it, while the population makes the necessary psychological adjustments, as if it were a normal condition, like rain."[31]

In these conditions, the Maoists and other insurgents in Colombia can look forward to the possibility that the correlation of forces will sooner or later come to favor those who would violently take control of the state. A possible scenario would include at least four elements: a possible diminishing of U.S. aid to the Colombian government; renewed political, economic, and social instability and a resultant economic downturn; President Uribe's becoming a lame duck and the subsequent election of a "not-so-hardliner"; and the further diminishing of the capability of the state to conduct its legitimizing security and governance responsibilities.

Triple Threat

The three wars, plus one, in Colombia have generated a triple threat to the state. First, through murder, kidnapping, intimidation, corruption, and other means of coercion, the violent internal insurgents undermine the ability of the government to perform security, development, governance, and other legitimizing functions. Likewise, through impunity, corruption, and legal maneuvering, the nonviolent elites undermine the ability of the state to perform legitimizing functions. Second, by violently imposing their will on the elected government, members of the armed opposition compromise the exercise of the authority of the state. Likewise, by nonviolently imposing—but still imposing—their will on the elected government, the social elites compromise the exercise of the authority of the state. Third, by taking control of large portions of the national territory, the narcos, FARC, and the paramilitaries are directly performing the tasks of government and acting as sovereign entities within the state. Yet, legally and ironically, this set of wars within the general insurgency war remains a law enforcement issue or a socioeconomic reform issue rather than being seen as a threat to Colombian national security and sovereignty.

The "Why" Question

Motives and Linkages

The motives for the narco-insurgent-paramilitary alliance are straightforward: accumulation of wealth, control of territory and people, freedom of movement and action, and legitimacy. Together, these elements represent usable power—power to allocate values and resources in a society.

The equation that links illegal narcotics trafficking to insurgency and to the paramilitaries in Colombia (and elsewhere) turns on a combination of need, organizational infrastructure development, ability, and the availability of sophisticated communications and weaponry. For example, the drug industry possesses cash and lines of transportation and communication. Insurgent and paramilitary organizations have followers, organization, and discipline. Traffickers need these to help protect their assets and project their power within and among nation-states. Insurgents and paramilitaries are in constant need of logistical and communications support—and money.[32]

Together, the alliance has the economic and military power equal to or better than that of most nation-states in the world today. This alliance also has another advantage; all three groups possess relatively flat organizational structures and sophisticated communications systems that, when combined, create a mechanism that is considerably more effective and efficient than any slow-moving bureaucratic and hierarchical governmental system. That combined organizational advantage of the nexus is a major source of power in itself.

Internal Objectives

The narco-insurgent-paramilitary nexus is not simply individual or institutional intimidation for financial or criminal gain. Nor is it merely the use of insurgents and AUC groups as hired guns to protect illegal drug cultivation, production, and trafficking. These are only business transactions. Rather, the long-term objective of the alliance is to control or substantively change the Colombian political system.[33]

Narcos may not seek the overthrow of government as long as the government is weak and can be controlled to allow maximum freedom of movement and action.[34] The insurgents, however, seek the eventual destruction of the state as it exists. Whether or not the insurgents are reformers or criminals is irrelevant; their avowed objective is to take direct control of the government and state.[35] Likewise, the paramilitaries want fundamental change. They appear to be interested in creating a strong state that is capable of unquestioned enforcement of law and order. Whether the vigilante groups are democratic or authoritarian is also irrelevant. Out of self-preservation, they have little choice but to take direct or indirect control of the state.[36] The common narco-insurgent-paramilitary government change or overthrow effort, therefore, is directed at the political community and its institutions. In this sense, the nexus is not simply criminal in nature but is a major political-psychological-moral-military entity. The countryside ceases to be a simple theater for combat and becomes a foco, or base, from which to build or destroy (depending on what side of the equation one is on) substantive power.

The Latin American security dialogue tends to refer to the narco-insurgent-paramilitary alliance not in terms of individual identities (in the sense of a business organization striving to control the price of drugs, weapons, or general protection) but rather as a whole entity that is significantly greater than the sum of its parts. The security dialogue is concerned with a political-economic-military force that has become a major national and transnational nonstate actor. That actor threatens the stability, development, and the future of the democratic system not simply in Colombia but throughout the Western Hemisphere.[37] To be sure, this is a loose and dynamic merger subject to many vicissitudes, but the "marriage of convenience" has lasted and appears to be getting stronger. The logic is simple—if all else fails, the nexus may be able to outresource the Colombian government and, through the purchase of high-tech military equipment and "guns-for-hire," buy its way to victory.[38]

External Objectives

The narco-insurgent-paramilitary alliance appears to have developed a political agenda for exerting leverage in the international as well as the Colombian national arena. The perceived goal of a given national agenda is to promote an egalitarian social revolution that will open up opportunities for everybody—and give the organization the legitimate basis for controlling some sort of nationalistic narcocracy. The objectives of the international political agenda are to establish acceptance, credibility, and de facto legitimacy among the sovereign states with which the general organization must negotiate.[39]

In that connection, the spillover effects of the illegal drug- and arms-trafficking industry have inspired criminal violence, corruption, and instability throughout Latin American in general and Caribbean transit countries in particular. For some time, the illegal drug industry has operated back and forth across Colombia's borders and adjacent seas. Colombian insurgents and paramilitary groups have made frequent incursions into the neighboring countries of Brazil, Ecuador, Panama, Peru, and Venezuela. The resulting destabilization is acknowledged to undermine the security, well-being, and effective sovereignty of these countries.[40] Throughout Latin America, the situation in Colombia has led to the addition of a new term to the Spanish lexicon: *Colombianizacion*. That term defines a political-social situation generated by narcotrafficking and insurgency. "Colombianization" refers to the disintegration of national institutions, a massive decay of civil society, and a permanent state of violence.[41]

Clearly, nonstate criminal-terrorist organizations such as those that constitute the Colombian narco-insurgent-paramilitary nexus are significant political actors with the ability to compromise the integrity and sovereignty of individual nation-states.[42] This takes us back to the idea that the Hobbesian Trinity is effectively becoming, or has become, a state-within-the-state as well as a state among states. As early as 1994, journalist Robert Kaplan warned that the alternative to the creation of a new state-within-a-state was criminal anarchy.[43] But the narco-insurgent-paramilitary alliance does not pose a mere criminal violence challenge. It has developed a sophisticated political agenda and is a clear and present danger to the existence of Colombia and to several other states in the Western Hemisphere, as we now know them.[44]

THE "HOW" QUESTION: FARC'S PROGRAM FOR ACHIEVING STATE POWER

Virtually any political actor with any kind of resolve can take advantage of the instability that is engendered by the ongoing Colombian crisis. The tendency is that the best-motivated and best-armed organization on the scene will eventually control that instability for its own narrow purposes. Given that FARC is considered to be the best organized, best armed, and best positioned of the Hobbesian Trinity, that Maoist-oriented organization is also considered to be the most likely insurgent entity in Colombia to seize state power.

The struggle between insurgents and the nation-state is always for political-moral legitimacy, that is, the moral right to govern a society. The armed opposition's possibilities for success also depend on a good design and the careful implementation of its program of action. In the Colombian case, FARC retains the strategic and operational initiative whatever its tactical setbacks. Strategically, no element of its combat power has been seriously degraded. Operationally, despite government reports to the contrary, FARC domination of the rural space to isolate the urban areas continues apace.[45]

Tactically, FARC operates in small units with political, psychological, and military objectives—in that order. Examples of these activities include assassinations, kidnappings, more-general terrorism, destruction of transportation and communications nets, and reconstitution of its bases for the reestablishment of control and governance within specific areas. FARC will continue to jab and probe and enforce its will against carefully selected (i.e., weak) targets, but direct or large-scale confrontations with the regular Colombian armed forces are unlikely. The strategic-political objective to which these tactical and terrorist operations must contribute is to remind the Colombian people and the rest of the world that the Colombian government is elitist and foreign dominated and does not have the moral right—or physical capability—to govern the country. At the same time, these tactical operations must contribute to the creation of the political space necessary to politically, psychologically, and physically isolate urban areas from rural communities.[46]

At the operational level, FARC continues to prepare for a "long war" because the insurgent organization is substantially inferior (militarily and politically) to its governmental opponent and success requires taking the time to build its military and political capabilities. FARC considers this to be an offensive effort. Doctrinally and in dialectical terms, antithetical activities generally considered defensive in nature are pursued in the offensive at all levels. This is a case in point. FARC continues to develop cadres to staff the expanding political, military, and support components of the organization; to maintain psychological and organizational efforts with the masses; and to consolidate its position in Colombia's interior and poor districts in the major cities.[47]

The thesis in FARC's current offensive strategy at the operational level includes, first and foremost, "armed propaganda." The primary purpose of this part of the armed struggle is to convince the Colombian people that FARC is and will be the real power in the country and that it continues to work to provide the freedom of movement that is necessary to establish a nationalistic Bolivarian democracy. Additionally, the purpose of the present operational effort is to augment and improve the ways and means of isolating the major urban areas. This is accomplished through the insertion of mobile warfare units to dominate rural space. What makes such terroristic actions effective in the rural areas is the virtual absence of anyone else to turn to for security. In such a vacuum, a few armed men and women can establish or reestablish FARC presence and begin to build a statelike sovereign infrastructure.[48]

At the strategic level, tactical and operational efforts continue with FARC taking a low military profile, increasing sabotage and terrorism in rural areas and city slums, and waiting for the time when its rural bases of support are established well enough to make decisive strikes within the cities. The intent now (as in the past) is to focus the primary attack psychologically and politically on the Colombian government's right and ability to govern. In the meantime, FARC waits until it is strong enough to make serious attacks on the capital city of Bogotá feasible. Then and only then will FARC attempt to seize the power of the state.[49]

Thus, FARC is pursuing an integrated political, psychological, and military approach to power. In a sense, FARC is a giant foco. But it is a different and more dangerous foco than that envisioned by Che Guevara. Guevara died arguing that a strictly military effort would literally bring revolution from the barrel of a gun. In contrast, FARC recognizes that the political and psychological mobilization of the masses—not just the recruitment of a few armed combatants—will generate combat power adequate to enable the isolation and capture of the urban areas. As a consequence, political-psychological action is the first and primary instrument needed to achieve power. Nevertheless, in true Maoist fashion, the final military phase of the FARC program will gradually replace the political-psychological phases, becoming first dominant and then decisive.[50]

Experience shows that if carefully done, the long-term combined use of indirect political-psychological influences, organizational development, viable security measures, and direct military violence techniques can eventually undermine the position and legitimacy of an incumbent government by breaking the bonds uniting a people, its political leadership, and its protective security organizations. These "persuasive and coercive/terrorist" political activities cannot be considered simple legal and law enforcement problems. Neither can they be considered problems requiring mere socioeconomic reform. They are real and substantive threats to the national security and sovereignty, and they must be addressed as such.

THE "SO WHAT" QUESTION: WHERE THE HOBBESIAN TRINITY LEADS

Threats from the Hobbesian Trinity at work in Colombia and the rest of the hemisphere today come in many forms and in a matrix of different kinds of challenges, varying in scope and scale. If they have a single feature in common, it is that they are systemic and well-calculated attempts to achieve political ends.

The Erosion of Colombian Democracy

The policy-oriented definition of democracy that has been generally accepted and used in U.S. foreign policy over the past several years is probably best described as procedural democracy. This definition tends to focus on the election of civilian political leadership and perhaps on a relatively high level of participation on the part of the electorate. Thus, as long as a country is able to hold elections, it is considered a democracy—regardless of the level of accountability, transparency, corruption, and ability to extract and distribute resources for national development and protection of human rights, liberties, and security.[51]

In Colombia, important paradoxes confound this simple definition. Elections are held on a regular basis, but leaders, candidates, and elected politicians are regularly assassinated; hundreds of governmental officials considered unacceptable by the nexus have been assassinated following their election. Additionally, intimidation, direct threats, and the use of relatively minor violence on individuals and their families play an important role prior to elections. As a corollary element, although the mass media is free from state censorship, journalists and academicians who make their anti-narco-insurgent-paramilitary opinions known through the press—or too publicly—are systematically assassinated.[52]

Consequently, it is hard to credit Colombian elections as democratic or free. Neither competition nor participation in elections can be complete in an environment where armed and unscrupulous nonstate actors compete violently with the government to control the government—before and after elections. Moreover, it is hard to credit Colombia as a democratic state as long as elected leaders are subject to control or vetoes imposed by vicious nonstate actors. As a consequence, Ambassador David Jordan argues that Colombia is an "anocratic" democracy. That is, Colombia is a state that has the procedural features of democracy but retains the features of an autocracy, whereby the ruling elites face no scrutiny or accountability. Professor Eduardo Pizarro describes Colombia as a "besieged democracy" and writes about the "partial collapse of the state." And Ambassador Curtis Kaman states "without fear of contradiction" that about 70 percent of the Colombian Congress "is bent."[53] In any event, the persuasive and intimidating actions of the narco-insurgent-paramilitary alliance in the electoral processes have pernicious effects on democracy and tend to erode the ability of the state to carry out legitimizing functions.

The Partial Collapse of the State

The Colombian state has undergone severe erosion on two general levels. First, the state's presence and authority is questionable over large geographical portions of the country. Second, the idea of the partial collapse of the state is closely related to the nonphysical deterioration of democracy. Jordan argues that corruption is key in this regard and is a prime mover toward "narco-socialism."[54]

The notion of partial collapse of the state refers to the fact that state institutions are absent from or only partially present in many of the rural areas and poorer urban parts of the country. Even in those areas that are not under the direct control of narco, insurgent, or paramilitary organizations, institutions responsible for protecting citizens—notably, the police and judiciary—have been coerced to a point at which carrying out their basic functions becomes difficult. Indicators of this problem can been seen in two statistics: the murder rate in Colombia is among the highest in the world (75 per 100,000 people), yet the proportion of homicides that end with a conviction is less than 4 percent.[55] These indicators of impunity strongly confirm that the state is not adequately exercising its social-contractual and constitutional-legal obligations to provide individual and collective security within the national territory.

The nonphysical erosion of the state centers on the widespread and deeply entrenched issue of corruption. As one example, in 1993 and 1994 the U.S. government alluded to the fact that former president Ernesto Samper had received money from narcotics traffickers. On the basis of that information, the U.S. withdrew Samper's visa in 1996 and decertified Colombia for not cooperating in combating illegal drug trafficking. Subsequently, the Colombian Congress absolved Samper of all drug charges by a vote of 111 to 43.[56] In that connection, and not surprisingly, another indicator of government corruption at the highest levels is found in the Colombian Congress. For example, the Senate—in a convoluted legal parliamentary maneuver—decriminalized the issue of "illicit enrichment" by making it a misdemeanor that could be prosecuted only after the commission of a felony.[57] Clearly, the reality of corruption at any level of government favoring the illegal drug industry mitigates against responsible governance and the public well-being. Indeed, the reality of corruption brings into question the reality of Colombian democracy and the reality of effective state sovereignty.

Internal and External Responses to Armed Nonstate Threats

Colombia, the United States, and other countries that might ultimately be affected by the destabilizing consequences of the narco-insurgent-paramilitary alliance in Colombia have tended to deal with the problem in a piecemeal and ad hoc fashion, or even ignore it. In Colombia, this has been done within an environment of mutual enmity between the civil government and the armed forces.[58]

With the promulgation of the social-political-military Plan Colombia in 2000 and subsequent policies such as Democratic Security in 2002 and plans such as Libertad Uno in 2003 and Plan Patriota in 2004–2005, there is now the basis of a coherent political-military project—but not the kind of game plan advocated by Ambassador Myles Frechette.[59] Frechette calls for a holistic, long-term national capability–building plan that would include taxing the upper elements of society that presently pay few or no taxes.[60] Additionally, there is no apparent quest for improved governmental legitimacy; no serious effort to implement a viable unity of civil-military effort; no coordinated, long-term plan to isolate the armed protagonists from their various sources of support; and no commitment to the country or to allies to "stay the course of the war." Additionally, the intelligence and information wars within the war leave much to be desired.[61] In all, Colombia appears to be simply muddling through and, after nearly fifty years, either adapting to the situation or hoping for the problem to go away.

The United States has tended to ignore the insurgency and paramilitary problems in Colombia, except for making rhetorical statements regarding the peace process, terrorist activities, and human rights violations. The United States has instead focused money, training, and attention almost entirely on the counterdrug campaign; a rapid but limited infusion of military hardware, a rigorous program designed to transform the Colombian military into a more aggressive combat force, and badly needed financial assistance have allowed the Colombian government under President Uribe to recover some of the political ground and national territory ceded to FARC during the 1990s. Nevertheless, the United States has tended to see the Colombian crisis in limited terms: the number of hectares of coca eradicated, the number of kilos of coca that have been detected and destroyed, and the number of narcotraffickers jailed. Thus, even though the United States and Colombia have achieved a series of tactical successes against the narco-terrorists, Colombia's violent nonstate actors remain relatively strong and ever more wealthy. At the same time, Colombia becomes more and more fragile.[62]

The other countries in the Western Hemisphere that are affected by the nefarious activities of the narco-insurgent-paramilitary nexus tend to do little more than watch, wait, and debate about what, if anything, to do regarding the seemingly new and unknown Hobbesian phenomenon. As a consequence, positive political sovereignty, democracy, socioeconomic development, territory, infrastructure, stability, and security are quietly and slowly destroyed—and tens of thousands of innocents continue to be displaced and die.

KEY POINTS AND LESSONS

- Colombia faces not one but a potent combination of three different armed threats to its democracy and its very existence.
- Each set of violent, stateless actors that constitute the loose "Hobbesian Trinity" has its own specific motivation; the common denominator is the political objective of effectively controlling or radically changing the Colombian government and the existing state.
- The narco-insurgent-paramilitary alliance utilizes a mix of aggressive, widespread, and violent political-psychological, economic-commercial, and military-terrorist strategy and tactics primarily to control human (but also physical) terrain in Colombia and other countries in which it operates. The generalized result of the intimidating and destabilizing activities of this alliance of violent nonstate actors is a steadily increasing level of manpower, wealth, and power that most nation-states of the world can only envy.
- The Hobbesian Trinity represents a triple threat to the effective sovereignty of the Colombian state and to its hemispheric neighbors: undermining the vital institutional pillars of regime legitimacy and stability, challenging the central governance of countries affected, and taking effective political control of large portions of "ungoverned" national territory.
- Despite some outside concern regarding the fact that the FARC insurgent leadership is getting old and may not live to see the fruition of the Maoist revolutionary efforts, that leadership appears to be unconcerned with speeding up or limiting the deliberate plan of action to seize the power of the state.

- The FARC leadership appears to think of time being on its side in the general revolutionary struggle. Moreover, the leadership argues that an increasing number of the "young and the restless" who are not being incorporated into the Colombian state will provide the necessary manpower to topple the elitist, foreign-dominated, capitalistic government.
- The Colombian and U.S. response to the narco-insurgent-paramilitary nexus has been ad hoc, piecemeal, and without a holistic strategic civil-military campaign plan. As a consequence, Colombia and its U.S. ally have not really addressed the war that is taking place in the hemisphere. That war continues to fester and grow toward the ultimate objective of controlling or deposing the Colombian state.

The Colombian insurgency (and its associated TCO phenomenon) has been ongoing from at least the mid-1940s to date. In that time, violence and destruction have varied like a sine curve from acute to tolerable. However, just because a situation improves to the point of being tolerable does not mean that the problem has gone away or should be ignored. Sun Tzu reminds us that "there has never been a protracted war from which a country has benefited."[63]

CHAPTER 2

Transforming War into "Superinsurgency"

Hugo Chavez and Fourth-Generation Warfare

War no longer exists. Confrontation, conflict, and combat undoubtedly exist all around the world—most noticeably, but not only, in Iraq, Afghanistan, the Democratic Republic of the Congo, and the Palestinian Territories—and states still have armed forces that they use as a symbol of power. Nonetheless, war as cognitively known to most noncombatants, war as a battle in a field between men and machinery, war as a massive deciding event in a dispute in international affairs: such war no longer exists.[1] The author of this statement, British general Sir Rupert Smith, has the experience and understanding to explain further: "The old paradigm was that of interstate industrial war. The new one is the paradigm of war amongst peoples."[2] This new paradigm involves strategic confrontation among a range of combatants, not all of which are armies. In these terms, war among peoples reflects some hard facts:

- Combatants are not necessarily armies; they tend to be small groups of armed soldiers who are not necessarily uniformed, not necessarily male but also female, and not necessarily adults but also children;
- These small groups of combatants tend to be interspersed among ordinary people and have no permanent locations and

no identity that clearly differentiate them from the rest of a given civil population;

- There is no secluded battlefield far away from population centers upon which armies engage;
- Armed engagements may take place anywhere, including in the presence of civilians, against civilians, and in defense of civilians;
- Combatants use differing types of low-tech weapons that are sometimes improvised yet always effective;
- Combat or confrontation uses not only coercive military force but also co-optive political and psychological persuasion;
- Conflicts are conducted at four levels—political, strategic, operational (theater), and tactical—with each level sitting within the context of the other in descending order from the political;
- Contemporary conflict is now lengthy and evolves through two or three or more noncoercive organizational stages before serious coercion and confrontation come into play;
- Even then, military operations are among the many instruments of power employed by the combatants;
- Conflict is often transnational, in that combatants use legal political frontiers and other countries' territories for sanctuary, staging areas, and rest and recuperation;
- The major military and nonmilitary battles in modern conflict take place among the people, and when they are reported, they become media events that may or may not reflect social reality;
- All that is done is intended to capture the imaginations of the people and the will of their leaders, thereby winning a trial of moral (not military) strength; and
- The struggle is total, in that it gives the winner absolute power to control or replace an entire existing government or other symbol of power.[3]

These are the principal characteristics of what President Hugo Chavez of Venezuela calls fourth-generation war (4GW), asymmetric war, *guerra de todo el pueblo* ("war of all the people"), the people's war, or war among peoples.[4] Chavez asserts that this type of conflict has virtually unlimited possibilities for a superinsurgency against the United States in the twenty-first century. Chavez's revolutionary (Bolivarian) ideas appear to be developing and maturing, and he and Venezuela may, at a minimum, be developing the conceptual and physical capabilities to challenge the status quo in the Americas. This straightforward challenge translates into a constant, subtle, ambiguous struggle for power that is being insinuated into political life in much of the Western Hemisphere.[5]

In pursuit of his Bolivarian dream, Chavez has stirred the imaginations of many Latin Americans, especially the poor. Additionally, he has aroused the imaginations of many other interested observers around the world. Chavez is now providing political leaders—populists and neopopulists, New Socialists and disillusioned revolutionaries, and submerged *nomenklaturas* worldwide—with a relatively orthodox and sophisticated Marxist-Leninist-Maoist model for the conduct and implementation of a successful, regional 4GW "superinsurgency."[6] As Colonel Thomas X. Hammes reminds us, this is the only kind of war that the United States has ever lost.[7]

Thus, the conscious choices made by civil-military leadership in the international community and individual nation-states about how to counter Hugo Chavez—or anyone else intending to engage in contemporary, asymmetric 4GW—will define the processes of national, regional, and global security, stability, and well-being far into the future. As a consequence, until we recognize the need to change our fundamental thought patterns (mindsets) and organizational structures to deal effectively with this overwhelming reality, we will make little substantive progress toward achieving success in our current confrontations and conflicts.[8]

BROADENING THE CONCEPT OF THREAT

The legal-traditional concept of threat to national security and sovereignty primarily involves the protection of national territory, citizens, and vital interests abroad against external military aggression.[9] Accordingly, the legal-traditional concept tends to define threats to national security and sovereignty in relatively narrow, obvious, nation-state and military terms, whereas the more contemporary, nontraditional security dialogue tends to define threats in broader, subtler, more-ambiguous terms that enhance real and popular perceptions of relative stability and well-being. Stability and well-being tend to refer to the use of a variety of means—only one of which is military—in the pursuit of political, economic, and social objectives. Enemies can thus be traditional nation-states; nontraditional, external nonstate actors (small groups and individuals) or proxies; and violent nontraditional intrastate actors that might threaten the achievement of those broader objectives and the vitality of the state. As a result, the enemy is not necessarily a recognizable military entity that has an industrial / technical capability to make war. The enemy thereby becomes any individual or group, state or nonstate political actor who plans and implements (1) the kinds of violence that create or exploit instability, (2) actions that inhibit legitimate governmental control of the national territory and the people in it, and (3) other threats to national well-being. As a result, threats to national security and sovereignty are now being defined in more-complex, ambiguous, and multidimensional terms.[10]

Where the Complex, Ambiguous, and Multidimensional Threat Environment Leads

Contemporary threats to national stability, sovereignty, and well-being are not necessarily direct attacks on a government. They are, however, proven means for weakening governing regimes. These new threats reflect a logical progression from the problems of institutional and state weaknesses and, in turn, move the threat spectrum from traditional state to nontraditional nonstate actors.[11] That progression leads to the inference that several small, weak states in the Caribbean and Latin America are at serious risk of failure to perform sovereign governance and security functions. The Revolutionary Armed Forces of Colombia (FARC), Peru's Sendero Luminoso, and other insurgents call activities that facilitate or accelerate the processes of state failure and generate greater freedom of movement and action for themselves "armed propaganda," while drug cartels operating in the Andean Ridge of South America and elsewhere call these kinds of activities "business incentives." Thus, in addition to helping to provide wider latitude to further their causes, insurgent and other violent nonstate actors' armed propaganda and business incentives are aimed at lessening a regime's credibility and capability in terms of its ability and willingness to govern, to develop its national territory and populace, and thus to provide general well-being.[12] The problems of governance take us to the real threat engendered by personal and collective insecurity together with diminishing national stability and sovereignty—that is, state failure.

The state failure (destabilization) process tends to move from personal violence to increased collective violence and social disorder to kidnappings, bank robberies, violent property takeovers, murders/assassinations, personal and institutional corruption, criminal anarchy, and internal and external population displacements. In turn, the momentum of this process of violence tends to evolve into more-widespread social violence, serious degradation of the economy, and diminished governmental capabilities of providing personal and collective security and guaranteeing the rule of law to all citizens. Then, using complicity, intimidation, corruption, and indifference, an irregular political actor or nonstate group can quietly and subtly co-opt politicians, bureaucrats, and security personnel to gain political control of a given piece of the national territory. The individual or nonstate group that takes control of a series of networked pieces of such ungoverned territory can then become a dominant political actor (warlord) and destabilizer, if not a state-within-a-state or a group of states.[13]

Somewhere near the end of the destabilization process, the state will be able to control less and less of its national territory and fewer and fewer of the people in it. Nevertheless, just because a state fails does not mean that it will simply go away. The diminishment of responsible governance and personal security generate greater poverty, violence, and instability—and a downward spiral in terms of development and well-being. It is a zero-sum game in which nonstate or individual actors (such as insurgents, transnational criminal organizations, and corrupt public officials) are the winners and the rest of the targeted society are the losers. Ultimately, failing or failed states become dysfunctional states, dependent on other states or international organizations, tribal states, rogue states, criminal states, narco-states, "new people's republics," draconian states (military dictatorships), or neopopulist states (civilian dictatorships). Moreover, failing or failed states may dissolve and become parts of other states or may reconfigure into entirely new entities.[14]

If misguided political dreams were to come true, Osama bin Laden would see the artificial boundaries of the Muslim Middle East and North Africa turn into caliphates reminiscent of the glory days of the twelfth and thirteenth centuries,[15] and Hugo Chavez would witness the metamorphosis of fifteen or twenty Latin American republics into one great American nation.[16] Experience demonstrates, however, that most of these political dreams never come true. Ultimately, the international community must pay the indirect social, economic, and political costs of state failure. Accordingly, the current threat environment in the Western Hemisphere is not a traditional security problem, but it is no less dangerous. The consistency of these kinds of experiences throughout the world and over time inspires confidence that these lessons are valid.[17]

Linking Security, Stability, Development, Responsible Governance, and Sovereignty

In terms of national security and sovereignty equating national well-being, it is helpful to examine the linkage among security, stability, development, democracy, and sovereignty. This linkage involves the circular nature of the interdependent relationships among security, stability and development, governance and peace, and effective sovereignty. Finding solutions to this set of issues takes the international community or individual intervening actors beyond providing some form of humanitarian assistance in cases of human misery and need. It takes international political powers beyond traditional monitoring of bilateral agreements or protecting a people from another group of people (nonstate actor) or from a government. It takes nation-state actors and international organizations beyond compelling one or more parties to a conflict to cease human rights abuses and other morally repugnant practices or repelling some form of conventional military aggression.

An elaboration on the security-insecurity process accomplishes two goals. First, it clarifies the fact that some issues now considered singular law enforcement problems are broader threats to the nation and its sovereignty. Second, such an analysis provides a logical foundation for an examination of the nontraditional notion of conflict. Solutions to the problems of stability and well-being as derived through such an examination relate directly to five highly interrelated and reinforcing lessons that the international community should have learned by now.[18]

The Relationship of Security to Stability

Security begins with the provision of personal protection to individual members of the citizenry. It then extends to protection of the collectivity from violent internal nonstate actors and external nonstate and state enemies (including organized criminals, self-appointed reformers, vigilante groups, and external enemies) and, in some cases, from repressive local and regional governments. Additionally, security depends on the continued and expanded building of a country's socioeconomic infrastructure. Then, in the context of socioeconomic development, facilitated by the establishment and maintenance of legitimate law and order (political development), a governing regime can deliberately begin to build the political-social-economic infrastructure that will generate national well-being and stability. In turn, through providing personal and collective security to the citizenry, the state can begin to exercise de facto as well as de jure sovereignty (the effective legal authority over a body politic).[19] The reasoning is straightforward: the security that enables political and economic development has a decisive bearing on establishing internal order, enhancing national well-being and stability, developing national and regional power, and, therefore, securing internal and external peace.[20]

The Relationship of Stability to Development

In the past, developed countries generally provided economic and financial aid to developing countries, under the assumption that personal and collective security and political development would automatically follow. That has not happened. Experience teaches that coherent, long-term, multilevel, and multilateral capability-building measures must be designed to create and strengthen human and state infrastructure. At the same time, these measures must generate the technical, professional, and ethical bases through which competent and honest political leadership can effectively provide individual and collective well-being. In the context of political-social-economic development, facilitated by the establishment of legitimate law and order, a responsible governing regime can begin to develop sustainable peace and prosperity.[21]

The Relationship of Development to Responsible Governance

The relationship of sustainable development to responsible governance relies on morally legitimate government. Legitimate government is essential for generating the capability to manage, coordinate, and sustain security, stability, and development effectively. This capability implies the presence of competent, honest leaders who can govern responsibly and have the political competence to engender a national and international purpose to which citizens can relate and support. Clearly, the reality of corruption at any level of government favoring any special interest militates against responsible governance and the public well-being. Unless and until a population perceives that its government deals with issues of personal security, well-being, and development fairly and effectively, the potential for internal or external forces to destabilize and subvert a regime is considerable. Regimes that ignore this lesson often find themselves in a "crisis of governance," facing increasing social violence, criminal anarchy, terrorism, insurgency, and the potential for being overthrown.[22]

The Relationship of Responsible Governance to Sovereignty

Responsible democracy and political legitimacy are based on the moral right of a government to govern and the ability of the regime to govern morally. The operative term here is "to govern morally." This depends on the culture and mores of the community of people being governed and, basically, on peoples' perceptions. Globally, when people perceive their governments to be corrupt and their countries' socioeconomic conditions as disenfranchisement, poverty, lack of upward social mobility, and lack of personal security, those governments have limited rights and abilities to conduct the business of the state. As a government loses the right and ability to govern fairly and morally—according to the local culture—it loses legitimacy. In turn, the loss of moral legitimacy leads to the degeneration of de facto state sovereignty. That is, the state no longer exercises effective control of the national territory and the people in it.[23]

From Sovereignty Back to Security

Again, a fundamental societal requirement for acceptance and approval of state authority (sovereignty) is that a government must ensure individual and collective security. The security problem ends with the establishment of firm but fair control of the entire national territory and the people in it, which takes us back to the concept of sovereignty. That is, without exercising complete control of the national territory, a government cannot provide the elements that define the notion of effective sovereignty. In this context, a government's failure to extend an effective sovereign presence throughout its national territory leaves a vacuum in which gangs, drug cartels, leftist and religious insurgents, the political and narco-right, warlords, and various alternative governments and nonstate actors may all compete for power—and contribute substantially to the processes of state failure. A government's failure to control the national territory precludes its ability to protect citizens against violence, conduct an effective judicial system, uphold the rule of law, plan long-term development, carry through responsible political processes, and maintain sustainable peace.[24]

Linking the various elements of stability and sovereignty is a matter of combining different efforts whose only common trait is that they cannot be resolved by a single instrument of state power or even by a single government. This analysis gives substantive meaning to the argument that contemporary conflict (such as Chavez's 4GW) is more than a military-to-military confrontation such that all instruments of state and international power must be utilized to achieve a result or end state that equates to sustainable peace. In this new global security environment, war can be everywhere and can involve everybody and everything. This represents a sea change in warfare and requires nothing less than a paradigm shift in how conflict is conceived and managed.

THE TRANSFORMATION OF THE NOTION OF CONFLICT

Osama bin Laden and Al Qaeda abruptly and violently contradicted the traditional ideas that war is the purview of the state and that nonstate and irregular ways and means of conducting contemporary war were aberrations.[25] Al Qaeda demonstrated both that a nonstate actor could effectively challenge a traditional nation-state (and, indeed, the very symbols of power in the global system) and pursue strategic political objectives without conventional weaponry or manpower and that nonstate actors and their actions can be constantly mutating. As a result, adversaries in conflict have changed, purposes and motives of conflict have changed, and means to pursue conflict have changed. Moreover, as the means of conducting war (conflict) change, the battlefields expand, overlap, move about, and become increasingly complex and anarchical. Thus, conflict is now without frontiers or enforceable controls. Additionally, the center of gravity no longer consists of an enemy's military formation or the industrial-logistical ability to conduct conflict; instead, it is public opinion and leadership, a lesson from Clausewitz.[26] This takes us to General Smith's conclusion that conflict, the power to conduct conflict, and the power to destroy or radically change nation-states are based less on military power than on political and psychological power.[27] Former lieutenant colonel Chavez understands all this—and more. Other strategic leaders should become equally conversant with this new sociology of conflict.

Adversaries Have Changed

Conflict is no longer merely an instrument of state action, but is also employed by small groups and individual actors (nonstate actors). Thus, an aggressor may not necessarily be a traditional nation-state that has forcefully moved into the national territory of another; the enemy may instead be a nonstate actor or a surrogate or proxy that plans and implements the kind of direct or indirect, lethal or nonlethal, or military or nonmilitary activity that exploits instabilities within its own country or between its country and other countries. Many of the "wars of national liberation" and "people's wars" that were fought all over the world during the cold war are good examples of this phenomenon. Today, in this context, the international community should consider the implications for national stability, security, and sovereignty, given the high probability of state and nonstate entities (including transnational criminal organizations) providing money, arms, technology, training, sanctuaries, and other assets to radical populist movements and to insurgent, terrorist, or criminal groups throughout Central and South America and the Caribbean. At the same time, we should consider the implications of all kinds of weaponry becoming more and more available and less and less expensive to anyone with a will to use violence against a given political target.[28]

Purpose and Motive Have Changed

The circular logic that links stability to development and to sovereignty and societal peace takes us back to purpose and motive. Combatant enemies are no longer opponents who pose absolute and clear threats to the national territory or society in recognizable military formations. One can no longer take, hold, or destroy a geographical objective or an enemy military formation. Enemies now conceal themselves among the population in small groups and maintain no fixed address. Thus, the nontraditional, contemporary purpose of becoming involved in a conflict is to establish conditions for achieving a political objective. Irregular enemies now also seek to establish conditions that drain and exhaust their stronger opponents. In striving to establish these conditions, opponents' political objectives center on influencing public opinion and political leadership. Ultimately, the primary motive is to impose one's will on the other.[29]

In this new global security environment, secondary and tertiary motives for conflict have changed dramatically from the traditional goals of (1) gaining or denying access to populations, markets, resources, territories, choke points, or lines of communication or (2) compelling adherence to an ideology. Newly recognized motives include attaining commercial advantage and gaining wealth.[30] To be sure, ideological motives for pursuing conflict have not gone away; as but one example, Al Qaeda's Osama bin Laden represents a militant, revolutionary, and energetic commitment to a long-term approach to a renewal of an extremist interpretation of Islamic governance, social purpose, and tradition.[31]

In the final analysis, the central idea in contemporary conflict is to influence and control people. Thus, the primary center of gravity (the hub of all power and movement) is not military; it is public opinion and leadership.[32] In these terms, public opinion and leadership provide the basic architecture from which to develop a viable ends, ways, and means strategy. The intent of such a strategy is to capture the will of the people and their leaders and, by that means, win the trial of moral strength.[33]

Means Have Changed

The ways and means of achieving one's purposes / motives have changed from primarily military means to a combination of all available methods of conducting conflict. Generally, that suggests (1) military and nonmilitary, (2) lethal and nonlethal, and (3) direct and indirect ways and means. As only a few examples, combinations of military, transmilitary, and nonmilitary operations would include the following:

- Conventional war / network war / sanctions war
- Guerrilla war / drug war / media war
- Biochemical war / intelligence war / resources war
- Terrorist war / financial war / ideological war
- Limited atomic war / diplomatic war / trade war[34]

Utilizing combinations of operations broadens the ability of a nation-state (or a hegemonic nonstate actor) to employ all available instruments of national and international power to protect, maintain, or achieve its vital interests. Regardless of what form a given conflict may take—from indirect financial war, to indirect media war, to direct military war—war is war, or conflict is conflict. Any of the above types of operations can be combined with others to form completely new ways and means of conducting conflict. There is no instrument of power that cannot be mixed and matched with others. The only limitation would be one's imagination; self-interest would be the only constant. That is why Qiao Liang and Wang Xiangsui call this type of conflict "unrestricted war."[35] One must remember, however, war (conflict), regardless of the form it takes, is still the means to compel an enemy to accept one's will.

Battlefields Have Changed

As the purposes, parties, and means that pertain to contemporary conflict have changed, so have the battlefields. Steven Metz and Raymond Millen argue that four distinct yet highly interrelated battle spaces exist in the contemporary security arena: (1) traditional, direct interstate war; (2) unconventional nonstate war, which tends to involve gangs, insurgents, drug traffickers, other transnational criminal organizations, and warlords who thrive in the ungoverned spaces between and within various host countries; (3) unconventional intrastate war, which tends to involve direct versus indirect conflict between state and nonstate actors; and (4) indirect interstate war, which entails aggression by one nation-state against another through proxies.[36]

Regardless of the analytical separation of the different battlefields, all state and nonstate actors involved are engaged in one common political act—political war, to control or radically change a government—to institutionalize the acceptance of one's will.[37] Additional strategic-level analytical commonalities in the modern battlefields include the absence of formal declarations or terminations of conflict, the lack of an easily identified human foe to attack and defeat, the lack of specific territory to be attacked and held, the absence of a single credible government or political actor with which to deal, and the lack of a guarantee that any agreement between or among contending actors will be honored.[38] In this fragmented, complex, and ambiguous political-psychological environment, conflict must be considered and implemented as a whole. The power to deal with these kinds of situations is no longer combat firepower (or the more benign police power) but is instead the multilevel, combined political, psychological, moral, informational, economic, social, police, and military activity that can be brought to bear holistically on the causes and consequences—as well as the perpetrators—of violence.[39] That kind of response will generate security and protect the individual and collective well-being, which can lead to durable societal peace.[40]

RETHINKING THREAT AND RESPONSE

The military transformation necessary to begin to achieve this kind of holistic approach to the use of power is not merely a modernization of technology and firepower; it also requires changes in doctrine and force structure and the development of new forms of indirect confrontation (combat). Clearly, in rethinking threat and response in contemporary irregular conflict, vastly more important than manpower, weaponry, and technology are the following leadership capabilities: lucid and incisive thinking, resourcefulness, determination, imagination, and a certain disregard for convention. In this context, one must remember this kind of holistic conflict is based on perceptions, beliefs, expectations, legitimacy, and the political will to challenge an opponent. In short, this kind of conflict is based primarily on words, images, and ideas. It will not be won simply by militarily seizing specific territory or destroying specific buildings, cities, or industrial capabilities. This kind of conflict is won by altering (indirectly and directly) the political-psychological factors that are most relevant in a targeted culture in one's own favor.[41]

This is the contextual beginning point for understanding where Hugo Chavez intends to go and how he expects to get there. This is the starting point from which to understand the first-, second-, and third-order effects that will shape the security environment with which Latin America and much of the rest of the world must struggle over the next several years. This is also the point from which to develop the strategic vision to counter radical populism, *caudillismo,* and the purposeful oppositionist (revolutionary) instability, violence, and chaos that those movements engender. It is also the starting point from which to develop strategies and principles of action that either will support or attempt to counter an unconventional 4GW superinsurgency policy; in other words, insurgency and counterinsurgency are two sides of the same proverbial coin.

IMPLICATIONS: LATIN AMERICAN SECURITY AND SOVEREIGNTY UNDER SIEGE

President Chavez is encouraging his Venezuelan and other Latin American followers to pursue a confrontational, "defensive," populist, and nationalistic agenda that will supposedly liberate Latin America from economic dependency and the political imperialism of the North American "Colossus" (the United States).[42] Chavez argues that liberation, New Socialism, and Bolivarianismo (the dream of a Latin American liberation movement against U.S. hegemony) will be achieved only by radically changing the traditional politics of the Venezuelan state to that of direct (totalitarian) democracy,[43] conducting a superinsurgency or war of all the people (people's war) to depose the illegitimate external enemy (North America), and building a new Bolivarian state, beginning with Venezuela and extending eventually to the whole of Latin America (thereby destroying the North American hegemony throughout all of Latin America).[44]

The Radical Restructuring of the Venezuelan State

The political, economic, social, informational, and security bases for the achievement of President Chavez's Bolivarian state are ambitious, vast, and amorphous but include four concepts or programs.

Political-Economic Concepts

The system of power on which internal and external Bolivarian objectives will be achieved is based on the concept of direct democracy. The main tenets dictate that (1) the new authority in the state must be a leader who communicates directly with the people, interprets their need, and emphasizes "social expenditure" to guarantee the legitimate needs and desires of the people; (2) elections, Congress, and the courts will provide formal democracy and international legitimacy but will have no real role in governance or in controlling the economy; (3) the state will own and control all the major means of national production and distribution; and (4) the national and regional political-economic integration function will be performed by the leader (Hugo Chavez) by means of his financial, material, and political-military support of "people's movements."[45]

Social Programs

To strengthen his personal position and internal power base, President Chavez is spending large amounts of money on the amorphous Plan Bolivar 2000, for building and renovating schools, clinics, day nurseries, roads, and housing for the poor. Additionally, the president is developing education and literacy outreach programs, agrarian reform programs, and workers' cooperatives. At the same time, he has established Mercal, a state company that provides subsidized foodstuffs to the poor. Chavez has also imported 16,000 Cuban doctors to help take care of the medical needs of the Venezuelan underclasses. Clearly, these programs offer tangible benefits to the mass of Venezuelans who were generally neglected by previous governments.[46]

Communications and Information

The intent, in this effort, is to generate mass consensus. Bolivarianismo will require maximum media (radio, TV, and newspapers / magazines) support to convey ideas, develop public opinion, and generate electoral successes. Ample evidence exists that Chavez-controlled media are using emotional arguments to gain attention, to exploit real and imagined fears of the population and create outside enemies as scapegoats for internal failures, and to inculcate the notion that opposition to the regime equates to betrayal of the country. President Chavez's personal involvement in the communications effort is also clear and strong. Statements by, speeches of, and interviews of Chavez are broadcast throughout Venezuela, the Caribbean basin, and large parts of Central and South America every day on the state-owned and controlled Television del Sur.[47]

The Military / Security Program

The Venezuelan Constitution of 1999 provides political and institutional autonomy for the armed forces, under the centralized control of the president and commander in chief. President Chavez has also created an independent national police force (outside the traditional control of the armed forces) that answers to the president. At the same time, efforts have gone forward to establish a 1.5-million-person military reserve and two additional paramilitary organizations—the Frente Bolivariano de Liberación (Bolivarian Liberation Front) and the Ejercito del Pueblo en Arms (Army of the People in Arms). The armed forces and the police perform traditional national defense and internal security missions, within the context of preparing for what President Chavez calls the war of all the people. The military reserve and the paramilitary are charged to protect the country from a U.S. or Colombian invasion (or resist such an invasion with an Iraqi-style insurgency) and to act as armed, antiopposition forces. The institutional separation of the various security organizations ensures that no one institution can control the others, but the centralization of those institutions under the president ensures his absolute control of security and "social harmony" in Venezuela.[48]

Venezuelan security forces are being trained for their mandated roles and are conducting maneuvers that demonstrate their proficiency at repelling an external invasion force and their capability to conduct irregular war: the Chinese are training Venezuelan commandos, and the regular Venezuelan military is training unconventional forces in counter-invasion resistance tactics.[49] In addition, light arms, ammunition, air and naval transport, and other equipment appropriate for 4GW and armed propaganda are being purchased from Russia, Spain, and other countries at a reported cost of over $3 billion.[50]

The Combination of Programs

All these programs together provide the president of Venezuela with the unified political-economic-social-informational-military instruments of power of the nation-state. That unity of effort can allow him the singular pursuit of his political-strategic objectives. At a minimum, then, Venezuela may be becoming capable of helping to destabilize large parts of Latin America. The political purpose of any given destabilization effort would be to prepare the way to force a radical restructuring of a target country's government and economy—and bring it under Venezuelan political-economic influence.

Hugo Chavez understands that war is no longer limited to using military violence to bring about desired political-economic-social change. Rather, all means that can be brought to bear on a given situation must be used to compel a targeted government to do one's will. He will tailor his campaign to his adversaries' political-economic-cultural-military vulnerabilities and to their psychological precepts. This is the basis of Chavez's instruction to the Venezuelan armed forces, and their invited foreign guests, at the "1st Military Forum on Fourth Generation War and Asymmetric War" in 2004. The charge to the forum was to develop a doctrinal paradigm change from conventional military to people's war. Chavez said, "I call upon everybody to start an . . . effort to apprehend . . . the ideas, concepts, and doctrine of asymmetric war."[51]

Irregular Fourth-Generation War and Superinsurgency

Since 1648 and the Treaty of Westphalia, a more realistic definition of aggression and war has been developed that allows a way out of the intellectual vise-lock imposed by Westphalian legalism. This new, broader concept of conflict takes us toward a full spectrum of closely related, direct and indirect, lethal and nonlethal, military and nonmilitary, national, subnational, and individual sovereignty and security concerns (threats). In the broadest possible terms, whoever impinges on state control of national territory and the people in it is a threat to that country's national sovereignty and security. Whatever the specific threat, its logical conclusion can lead either to violent radical political change or to the failure of a traditional nation-state.[52]

Former lieutenant colonel Chavez knows this. Lacking the conventional power to challenge the United States or practically any one of his immediate neighbors, Chavez understands that irregular asymmetric warfare is the logical means for his Bolivarian expression and self-assertion. As a result, in May 2005, he provided all Venezuelan military officers (and others who wanted it) with a new book written by a Spanish Marxist-oriented New Socialist, named Jorge Verstrynge Rojas. Entitled *La guerra periférica y el Islam revolucionario* (Peripheral [Indirect] War and Revolutionary Islam),[53] this book provides a theoretical and doctrinal basis for the conduct of indirect, irregular, political-psychological war in the twenty-first century. Nothing in the book is really new, but it is a well-conceived and well-written piece of work by an experienced practitioner and oppositionist. It reminds the reader of the indirect applications of *Unrestricted Warfare,* written by Qiao Liang and Wang Xiangsui, two Chinese colonels, in 1999.[54]

The main themes that run through these books stress the use of all available networks—political, economic, social, informational, and military, through direct and indirect means—to dominate the nontraditional human terrain (rather than simply the conventional geographical terrain). By using the full spectrum of the multidimensional components of indirect and unrestricted (or total) war, a protagonist can produce what Qiao and Wang call a "cocktail mixture" of unconventional ways and means of confronting a stronger opponent. This kind of irregular war—based on the notion that the human terrain is the main contemporary center of gravity—is based primarily on words, images, and ideas (although unrestricted war does not preclude direct military operations). The only ethics are those that contribute directly to the achievement of the ultimate political objective of forcing a stronger opponent to acquiesce to the weaker adversary's will. The only rule is that there are no rules.[55] However, this form of warfare did not arise in a vacuum; Chavez's superinsurgency, or fourth-generation war, illustrates his understanding of the paradigm shift in the concepts of threat and conflict.

First- through Third-Generation Conflict

First-generation war is characterized by the low-tech attrition war that has been the principal means of conducting conflict from the beginning of human civilization. The basic idea is that the more opponents killed or incapacitated relative to one's own side, the better. Historically, attrition war appears to serve only those protagonists with the largest numbers of human resources. When facing a numerically superior opponent, warfighters have needed to find other means to compensate for numerical inferiority.[56]

The result was second-generation warfare, in which the basic concept is to employ surprise, speed, and lethality to bring pressure to bear on an enemy's weak spots. In essence, the military force that can "move, shoot, and communicate" more effectively relative to the opponent has the advantage and is more likely to prevail.[57] The German blitzkrieg of World War II and the American "shock and awe" approach in the Persian Gulf and Iraq wars exemplify second-generation warfare.

Third-generation conflict moved from the blatant use of physical force toward the employment of brainpower to achieve success against an enemy. This entails a transition from hard power to a combination of hard and soft power. In addition to using first- and second-generation methods, third-generation conflict methodology tends to take advantage of intelligence, psychological operations, other knowledge-based means, technologies, and cultural programming (manipulation) as force multipliers. The basic intent of soft power is to provide more-effective and more-efficient means than hard power through which to paralyze enemy action.[58] However, even though the use of soft brain power is less bloody than the use of hard-power assets (such as infantry, artillery, armor, and aircraft), the ultimate objective of war remains the same: to force the enemy to accede to one's own interests.

Strategic Characteristics

Rather than thinking of each generation of conflict as an independent form of warfare, one should consider them as parts within the concept of unrestricted and peripheral (indirect) war.[59] In essence, because fourth-generation warfare is a methodology directed by the weak against the strong, the primary characteristic is asymmetry (the use of disparity between contending opponents to gain relative advantage), as Lieutenant Colonel Chavez well knows. Moreover, he understands that contemporary nontraditional (peripheral) war is not a kind of lesser or limited appendage to the more comfortable attrition and maneuver warfare paradigms but is, instead, a great deal more.[60]

First, the "battlefield" is everywhere. Second, twenty-first-century conflict is intended to resist, oppose, gain control of, and/or overthrow an existing government or symbol of power.[61] Third, Chavez understands that although battles are won at the tactical and operational levels, wars are won at the strategic level.[62] In that context, the most salient strategic-level characteristics of 4GW include the following elements.[63]

Primarily Political-Psychological. Experience and the data show that the moral right of an incumbent regime or challenger regime to govern is the most important single dimension in contemporary conflict. The principal tool in achieving and maintaining the right to govern is legitimacy. Legitimacy of cause and behavioral rectitude on one hand and the illegitimacy of the opponent on the other are key. In nearly any conflict situation, the opposition claims to offer a redress of real or perceived grievances and a better way of life.[64] On the behavioral side of the Latin American situation, President Chavez is putting forward the idea of liberation from the politically and economically dominating and exploitive "Colossus of the North." Under these terms, he is persuading and co-opting people rather than coercing them. The primary instruments of power now include dialogues on ideology, debates on Latin American versus North American cultural values, the attempt to influence through the example of compassion, and the Bolivarian appeal to the potential of Latin American *grandeza* ("greatness"). Military instruments of power are used to achieve political and psychological objectives, rather than purely military objectives.[65]

Lengthy. Because insurgency-rooted conflict is generally political-psychological, the protagonists must understand that significant amounts of time must elapse in which to change people's minds and prepare them for phased, progressive moves toward short- and midterm as well as long-term objectives. Clearly, the better one protagonist is at that persuasive effort, the more effective that protagonist will be relative to the opposition, but this takes time.[66] Mao and his Chinese communists, for example, fought for twenty-eight years (1921–49); the Vietnamese communists fought for thirty years (1945–75); the Nicaraguan Sandinista insurgents fought for eighteen years (1961–79); and the Peruvian Sendero Luminoso insurgents claim that they are prepared to fight for seventy-five years (1962–?) to achieve their revolutionary goals.[67] A Dutch colonel in Afghanistan describes the lengthiness of contemporary conflict in terms that are less precise yet quite accurate and realistic: "We are not here to fight the Taliban. We're here to make the Taliban irrelevant."[68] President Chavez knows that the key function of an irregular 4GW protagonist is to sustain the fundamental ideas and organization—and outlast the opponent. As a consequence, anything except defeat in detail is victory.[69]

Belligerents with Varying Levels of Responsibility to Their Constituents. This aspect of superinsurgency equates not only to the issue of responsibility but also to organizational effectiveness. Challenger protagonists in this type of war generally hold decision-making power in their self-appointed hands. These leaders do not normally have to consult with constituents before making decisions and do not have to explain their actions after the fact. No formal officials have to be elected, no national laws or boundaries must be respected, and no responsibility is owed to anyone outside the organization. Thus, the principal tool in this situation is organization to generate as complete a unity of effort as possible, and as a result, nonstate organization for unity of effort is flatter, smaller, and more effective than most governmental and traditional military bureaucracies. Decisions can be made and implemented faster than those of traditional governmental opposition, and the asymmetric protagonist can be generally proactive while forcing the foe to be merely reactive.[70] President Chavez's centralization of the Venezuelan government and creation of what is essentially a one-party state—with himself at the head of it all—demonstrates a clear sense of the utility and continuity of organizational unity of effort. That centralizing reorganization of the Venezuelan government also clarifies the purpose of Chavez's moves to change the constitution to allow his continuation in office.[71]

Transnational Dimensions and Implications. At least three transnational aspects are associated with contemporary 4GW conflict. First, experience and the data show that insurgencies require resources that they cannot produce for themselves: money, equipment, training, and political-psychological support at regional and international (supranational) levels. As a result, these implementing resources and support must be provided by other actors, whether state or nonstate. Second, most (if not all) successful insurgency-rooted movements have had access to sanctuaries across international borders to recuperate, reequip, retrain, and maintain their offensive capabilities. Third, insurgents constantly cross borders to evade pursuit and to expand their freedom of action and movement.[72]

The principal tools in this situation include foreign alliances; public diplomacy at home and abroad; intelligence, information, and propaganda operations; and cultural manipulation measures to influence or control public opinion and decision making in a targeted country and abroad. Accordingly, several cases—from the Algerian War (1954–62), the Salvadoran insurgency (1980–89), and the (Russian) Afghan War (1979–89) to the past and present situations in the former Yugoslavia—provide examples of this phenomenon.[73] Again, Hugo Chavez understands these things. This wise competitor knows exactly what General Vo Nguyen Giap meant when he said, "If the people's war of liberation [in Vietnam] ended in a glorious victory, it is because we did not fight alone. That victory cannot be isolated from the sympathy and support of progressive peoples throughout the world."[74] This reality takes us back to the centrality of behavioral rectitude and moral legitimacy.

Total War. Fundamentally, people want things that may be divided into "freedom from" and "freedom to." They want freedom from fear, intimidation, hunger, poverty, and uncertainty. They want freedom to prosper and do what they reasonably want to do. And they want a society and political structure that they can understand and relate to. They will attribute moral legitimacy to and follow the political or military leader who (given the circumstances) is considered to be the most likely to provide these things.[75] By transforming the emphasis of war from military violence to the level of a struggle for moral legitimacy, the insurgents can strive for total objectives—the control or overthrow of a government. The use of indirect moral and other nonlethal force permits a protagonist to engage in a secret and prolonged war while purporting to pursue altruistic purposes. Accordingly, war is not an extension of politics: war is politics. Because it is a zero-sum game, there can only be one winner. It is, as noted above, total war.[76]

The Chavez Program for the Liberation of Latin America

Hugo Chavez consistently identifies the origins of the Bolivarian revolution and defines the central strategic problem in Latin America as the lack of legitimacy of the U.S.-dominated governments in the region. He further identifies the primary objective of the revolution as power. This is an example of power being generated by an intelligent, motivated, and disciplined leader and his organization for achievement of direct democracy, coupled with a promise of regional greatness. Chavez is therefore pursuing a superinsurgency with a confrontational, defensive, populist, and nationalistic agenda that is intended eventually to liberate Latin America from U.S. economic dependency and political domination. That is a Herculean task, but he appears to be prepared to take his time, let his enemies become accustomed to a given purposeful action, and then slowly move toward new stages of the revolution in a deliberate manner, conducted in phases. By staying under his opponents' "threshold of concern," Chavez says that he expects to "put his enemies to sleep—to later wake up dead."[77]

This is not the rhetoric of a madman. It is the rhetoric of an individual who is performing the traditional and universal Leninist-Maoist function of providing a strategic vision and the operational plan for gaining revolutionary power. Chavez is planning for a protracted struggle, using a long-term, three-stage, multiphase program for gaining power. His notional three stages use different terminology but are similar to those of Lenin and Mao.

Stage 1: Establishment of an Organization (Lenin: Development of a Cadre; Mao: Strategic Defensive)

This is the essential first effort. It requires taking the time necessary to lay the strongest possible organizational foundations for the subsequent political-psychological-military struggle. In this stage, the revolutionary leadership must concentrate on doctrine and leadership development, expansion of the organization's relationship with other political movements, and generally, the creation of a receptive political-psychological environment for the revolutionary movement. More specifically—as one of Chavez's mentors, Abraham Guillen, teaches—the Bolivarian leadership must propagate Latin American nationalism; educate and prepare several hundred professionals for combat, organizational duties, and governance, thereby enabling them to lead the masses through a revolution and into the proverbial halls of power; and create a popular front not just of "a few true believers but [comprising] a combination of Christians, Socialists, trade unionists, intellectuals, students, peasants, and the debourgeoised middle class who will march together to defeat sepoyan (regional) militarism and U.S. imperialism."[78]

Guillen, a strong advocate of contemporary urban insurgency, argues that from these beginnings, the revolutionary Bolivarian leadership must expand organizational and training efforts from the urban centers into the countryside and begin to mobilize the energy of all the people of Latin America. But he advocates waiting for economic and social crises to discredit incumbent Latin American regimes rather than fighting them militarily, because defeating sepoyan security forces will not resolve all problems. Moreover, he believes that revolutionary politics must not be sectarian, dogmatic, or intolerant but must instead be flexible, freed from semantic "-isms" and operating in the name of the general interest: "[Revolutionary leadership] must formulate its own program . . . which stresses whatever unites rather than divides [the people]." The intent, according to Guillen, is to win the support of and awaken the admiration of the vast majority of the targeted population (which is the concept of human terrain).[79]

Stage 2: Development of Political and Military Power (Lenin: Create Political Infrastructure and Form and Deploy a Military Arm; Mao: Strategic Stalemate)

As with the organizational stage, the second stage of the revolution is preparatory and long term. Again, the leadership must take the time necessary to develop and nurture popular support while increasing the size of the organization and simultaneously establishing and defending liberated zones. This kind of effort allows the consolidation and expansion of political and logistical support bases, the extension of influence throughout the various Latin American countries, and the establishment of de facto control in areas uncontrolled or abandoned by the state.

More specifically, the political effort requires the formation and nurturing of ancillary multinational organizations, of which the most important are a united anti-imperialist political party (or front), a united central trade union organization, a united Latin American youth federation, a united Labor Party, and a united army of unity and liberation. The general purposes of these organizations would be to continue to raise the level of direct popular action against "indigenous feudalism, aboriginal capitalism, sepoyan militarism, and *yanqui* imperialism." These organizations would also provide leadership experience and human skills that will be necessary when the time comes to form a direct government of the people and install a socialist mode of production and distribution.[80]

As might be expected, Guillen and other contemporary revolutionary theorists argue that the military effort that they advocate is more political and psychological than military, for their revolutionary war does not propose to decide anything by means of battles or by occupying foreign soil. Nevertheless, an army of national liberation must eventually be formed in each Latin American country, with a central Latin American strategic command. The army would be further organized into local militias that fight only in their own zones, provincial or district militias that fight in their own zones, and an army that fights in all parts of the country, with the cooperation of local and provincial militias.[81]

Operations to further a Bolivarian superinsurgency would consist of scattered surprise attacks at the enemy's weakest points undertaken by quick and mobile units superior in arms and numbers. The army and the militias would be able to cede territory and human terrain if necessary but would be required to continually harass the enemy until the enemy's morale is broken. The popular army would also coordinate mass actions (demonstrations), strikes, mutinies, occupation of factories, and seizures of schools and universities. Additionally, the army would coordinate sabotage, kidnapping, robberies, terrorist acts, and armed propaganda throughout the country. In the latter phases of Stage 2, the military arm of the revolutionary movement would entice the enemy into territory where the population is supportive, such that the enemy would be exhausted, demoralized, and ultimately defeated in a prolonged struggle. Finally, in Maoist terms, a national liberation army would prepare for Stage 3 of the revolution by becoming organized, trained, and equipped to confront directly but gradually a demoralized conventional enemy force and bring about the final military collapse of its adversary. Again, the intent is not to destroy but to wear down the enemy over time, until the enemy's resolve is gone. As a result, "political and moral factors are more decisive for victory than [are] heavy armament and ironclad units."[82]

Stage 3: Capture of a Targeted Government (Lenin: Capture of a Targeted Government; Mao: Strategic Offensive)

This stage of the liberation process (revolution) is reached only when the enemy is completely demoralized, and it requires the efforts of a relatively small military force to finalize the total collapse of the state. This collapse will be the result of no single spectacular action but of several small, deadly, and successive actions. Theoretically, the collapse will not be allowed to take place until interior and urban support bases are consolidated, the Bolivarian leadership cadre is sufficiently prepared and large enough to administer and govern the state effectively, and the revolutionary organization is prepared both to hold its ground against a concerted "imperialist" counterattack from outside the country and to move against the next targeted state in a subsequent subphase of the general Latin American liberation effort.[83]

Conclusions: Chavez's Progress

At present, Chavez is only in the beginning phases of his first organizational stage of the long-term program for the liberation of Latin America. The culmination of Stage 1 is still a long time away, so Stages 2 and 3 must be several years down the revolutionary path. At the strategic level, then, President Chavez appears to be consolidating his base position in Venezuela through the establishment of personal political control through the totalitarian mechanisms of direct democracy, taking a relatively low revolutionary profile, and waiting for a propitious time to begin the expansion of the revolution on a supranational Latin American scale. He will likely continue to focus his primary attack on the legitimacy of the U.S. economic and political domination of the Americas, as well as on that of any other possible rival. And he will likely continue to conduct various rhetorical attacks on adversaries; cultivate diverse allies in Latin America, the Middle East, and Asia; and continue to engage in organizational "seeding operations" for the creation of a receptive political climate throughout Latin America.[84] Until the last moment in Stage 3—when the targeted government is in the process of collapsing—every action is preparatory work and not expected to provoke much immediate concern from the enemy.[85]

The seriousness of this final stage and the preliminary organizational stages of Chavez's 4GW program to liberate Latin America cannot be dismissed as too difficult, too ambiguous, or too far into the future to deal with. In 2005, I emphasized this adaptation of 4GW and summarized its consequences by taking a page from a Harry Potter adventure—calling it "Wizard's Chess" (and characterizing Chavez as a master of this deadly game), as a metaphorical example of contemporary asymmetric conflict. The analogy is still instructive and sobering:

> In that game, protagonists move pieces silently and subtly all over the game board. Under the players' studied direction, each piece represents a different type of direct and indirect power and might simultaneously conduct its lethal and nonlethal attacks from differing directions. Each piece shows no mercy against its foe and is prepared to sacrifice itself in order to allow another piece the opportunity to destroy or control an opponent—or to checkmate the king. Over the long term, however, this game is not a test of expertise in creating instability, conducting illegal violence, or achieving some sort of moral satisfaction. Ultimately, it is an exercise in survival. Failure in Wizard's Chess is not an option.[86]

This cautionary tale reminds us that irregular asymmetric 4GW is the only type of conflict that a modern power has ever lost.[87] The fact that the world's only remaining superpower does not have a unified strategy and a multidimensional, interagency organizational structure to deal with 4GW superinsurgency is surprising and dismaying.

RETHINKING THREAT AND RESPONSE

Moving from a Military to a Populace-Oriented Conflict Model

In rethinking threat and response in the new global security environment, one must realize that the United States, Europe, and those other parts of the global community most integrated into the interdependent world economy are embroiled in a complex security arena that, although possibly less bloody in soft-power terms, is ultimately no less brutal. Given this reality, failure to prepare adequately for present and future irregular contingencies is unconscionable. The first organizational step in developing an appropriate response to contemporary conflict is to become aware of global disequilibrium and popular sovereignty and to begin to deal with the relationship of instability to legitimate governance. The cognitive second step is to realize, whether one likes it or not or whether one is prepared for it or is not, that a populace-oriented model most accurately describes the contemporary security arena.[88] Taking these steps would set the foundation for a better understanding of and a more effective response to contemporary irregular, people-oriented, asymmetric conflict.

A Populace-Oriented Model

A populace-oriented extension of the SWORD model for taking responsibility for unconventional intranational, nonstate, and indirect interstate conflicts—going beyond "declaring victory and coming home" —depicts the activities and efforts of the various players involved (see figure 1).[89] This model portrays the allegiance of a population as the primary center of gravity. Persuasive, co-optive, and coercive measures of ensuring personal security will determine success or failure in the achievement of a just civil society and a durable peace. Thus, both the government (and its external allies) and the internal illegal opposition (and its external allies) can coerce, co-opt, and persuade the populace into actions on behalf of either side. In addition, the people can coerce and persuade the government or opposition to change the conditions in society to meet their demands and to undertake the types of behavior and actions that the citizenry perceives to be legitimate. The application of this model for contemporary irregular populace-oriented conflict requires additional conceptual and organizational efforts such as the following.

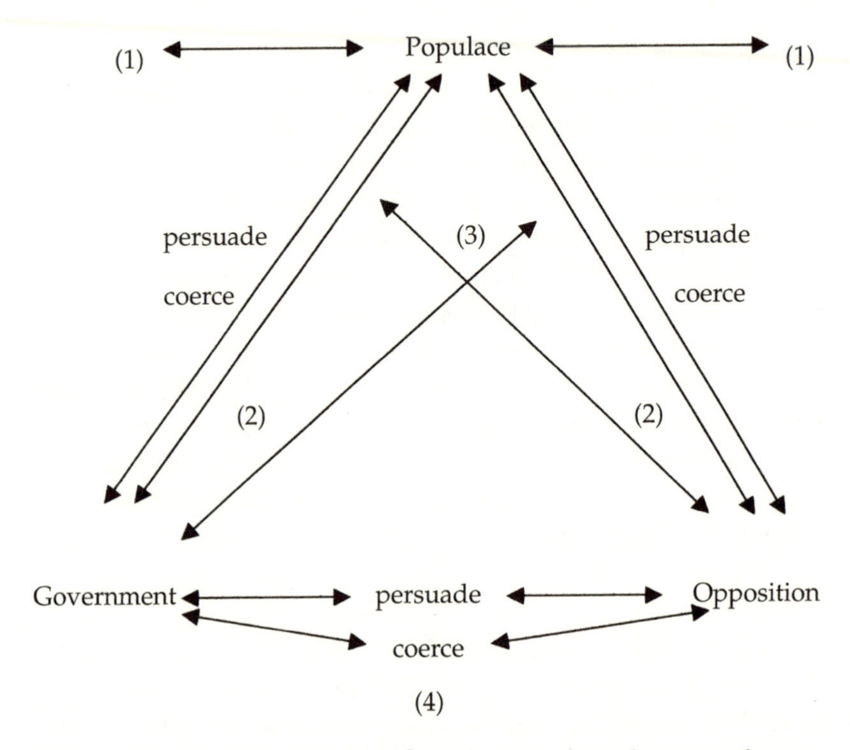

Figure 1. Populace-oriented model of the movement of popular support between an incumbent government and an illegal internal foe. (1) Overall goal: gain popular support. (2) Development and other activities designed to gain popular support. (3) Indirect activities designed to isolate government and opposition forces from the populace. (4) Direct attacks by the government and opposition on each other, intended to discourage popular support for the other.

A New Concept of Center of Gravity

Rethinking the notion of center of gravity intrudes on the comfortable, conventional vision of war in which an obvious enemy military formation poses a clear threat to national boundaries, resources, and other interests. As mentioned earlier, Clausewitz reminds us that in places subject to internal strife (intranational, indirect international, and nonstate conflicts), the hub of all power and strength (center of gravity) is the people.[90] Thus, in contemporary unconventional conflict, the primary center of gravity changes from a familiar military concept to an ambiguous, unconventional, and uncomfortable populace-oriented paradigm.

This analysis helps to explain, for example, what happened in Vietnam. Americans thought they were fighting a limited war of attrition against a traditional military enemy—whose uniform was funny-looking black pajamas. However, the threat that the South Vietnamese government and the United States had to deal with was not limited, conventional, or comical. Rather, the Vietcong enemy was making unconventional, coercive, populace-oriented, political-psychological preparations to take complete control of the state.[91] That nontraditional enemy focused its primary political-psychological attack on the legitimacy of the corrupt, U.S.-dominated South Vietnamese government. The main military effort was conducted in support of that objective in the form of armed propaganda. That terrorist strategy was conducted not to win the war but to convince the people of Vietnam, other parts of the world, and even the United States that the South Vietnamese government and its foreign ally could not and would not provide the security and other legitimizing functions that responsible government is supposed to provide its people.[92]

A major implication here is the necessity for correctly determining and aggressively attacking the primary sources of an enemy political actor's physical, psychological, and moral strength. In that connection, centers of gravity must be attacked—and defended. This reflects the two sides of the insurgency-counterinsurgency struggle. Thus, for the attacking side to take the necessary measures in defending its own centers of gravity is as important as dealing with those of its opponents. In this context, U.S. leadership failed to defend American public opinion against the full-scale media war that was conducted by North Vietnam and its external allies throughout the world and thereby exhibited their failure to understand that the streets of Peoria and the halls of Congress were more decisive in determining the outcome of a war thousands of miles away than were the military battlefields in Vietnam.[93]

A New Concept of Deterrence

Deterrence is not necessarily military—although that is important. It is not necessarily negative or directly coercive—although that, too, is important. Deterrence is much broader than any of these elements. Deterrence can be direct or indirect, political-diplomatic, socioeconomic, psychological-moral, and militarily coercive. In its various forms and combinations of forms, it is an attempt to influence how and what an enemy or potential enemy thinks and does. That is, deterrence is the creation of a state of mind that either discourages one thing or encourages something else. Motive and culture thus become crucial.[94] In this context, political-military communication and preventive diplomacy become vital parts of the deterrence equation.

As a result, the deterrence rule of thumb must move from U.S.-centric values and determine precisely what a hostile leadership values most, then identify exactly how that cultural value (whatever it is) can realistically be manipulated and held at risk. Conversely, a new deterrence rule of thumb must also consider what a hostile leadership values most and—as opposed to the proverbial stick—identify precisely what carrots might also be offered. In these terms, we must think of ourselves not so much as warfighters as war preventers.[95]

Thus, it is incumbent upon the United States and the rest of the global community to understand and cope with the threats imposed by contemporary, nontraditional actors; think outside the conventional box; and replace the old nuclear theology with a broad deterrence strategy, as it applies to the chaos provoked by the diverse state, nonstate, intrastate, and transnational nuclear and nonnuclear threats and menaces that have heretofore been ignored or wished away. The deterrence task, then, is straightforward. Culturally effective ways and means must be found to convince nontraditional players that it is not in their interests to continue to engage in negative behavior.[96]

An Unconventional Strategic Objective and Redefinition of Power, Enemy, and Victory

Given that the enemy is no longer an easily identified military entity and given the essentially political-psychological-moral-coercive nature of the linkages among security, stability, development, legitimate governance, and sovereignty, the contemporary security environment requires a new strategic objective. In the past, the strategic objective has been defined variously as "unconditional surrender," "peace with honor," "doing the right thing," "drawing a line in the sand," "showing we mean business," "being credible," and "rendering the enemy powerless."[97] Also, in the past, U.S. leadership found that dealing with tactical- and operational-level nodes of vulnerability was easier than taking a broader approach.[98] Yet data and experience continually reinforce the political, strategic, holistic, and multidimensional aspects of contemporary conflict.[99]

Power is no longer simply combat firepower directed at a uniformed soldier or an enemy's military or industrial complex. Power is multilevel and combines political, psychological, moral, informational, economic, social, military, police, and civil-bureaucratic activities that can be brought to bear appropriately on the causes as well as the perpetrators of violence. And victory is no longer the obvious and acknowledged destruction of military capability, to be followed by unconditional surrender. Victory or success is now—more frequently, with perhaps with a bit of spin control—defined as the achievement of peace. What the world appears to be looking for and what the populace-oriented model can lead to is a sustainable peace with justice.[100]

Analysis of the problems of generating a sustainable peace with justice takes us beyond providing some form of humanitarian assistance or refugee assistance in cases of human misery and need. The core strategic problem is responsible political leadership in the post–cold war world. Foreign policy and military asset management must address this central issue.[101] Additionally, the enormity and the logic of the establishment of a durable and just peace demand a carefully thought-out, phased, long-term planning and implementation process. General Smith reminds us that contemporary combatants must seek to establish conditions that create a conceptual space for diplomacy, economic incentives, political pressure, and other measures to create a desired political end state: otherwise, as he observes, "our military forces—and the force they apply—will lack utility."[102]

End-State Planning and an Integrated Strategic Implementing Process

The key to the implementation of a viable political stability strategy and strategic clarity is planning. This depends on a clear strategic vision, based on the populace-oriented model as a starting point. A viable strategy also depends on an organizational management structure and adequate resources to apply the vision on the basis of realistic calculations of ends, ways, means, and long-term timing. This takes us to end-state planning, unity of effort, and strategic clarity.

End-state planning starts with the truism that conflict is a continuation of politics by other means—but with two qualifying arguments. First, military violence is required only when the conditions or changes sought cannot be achieved through political-diplomatic, social-economic, or informational-psychological ways and means.[103] Second, end-state planning advocates synchronization of all national and international civilian and military instruments of power so that the most synergism can be gained from the interaction of the variables selected for action.[104] The end-state planning argument concludes that if the United Nations or the United States or any other international player is going to succeed in future conflicts, then civil and military forces must be structured and employed in ways that respond to the dynamic political, economic, social, and military variables at work in the stability-peace paradigm. Additionally, as logic and experience demand, the interagency community must base its decisions on a clear, mutually agreed definition of what ultimate success looks like—that is, share a vision of strategic clarity.[105]

Attempts to achieve political and strategic objectives cannot be based on the ad hoc use of national and international instruments of power. Without organizations that can establish, enforce, and continually define a holistic plan and generate consistent national and international support, authority is fragmented and ineffective in resolving the myriad problems endemic to survival in contemporary conflict—as a result, operations can become increasingly incoherent. Requiring a high level of planning and coordination is not a matter of putting the cart before the horse. It is a matter of knowing where the horse is going and precisely how it is going to get there. Decision makers, policy makers, and planners should never lose sight of that bigger unity of effort picture.[106]

Implementation of a Populace-Oriented Conflict Model

These cooperative and cognitive efforts will not be easy to implement. However, they should prove in the medium to long term to be far less demanding and costly in political, economic, military, and ethical terms than to continue an ad hoc, business-as-usual, reactive crisis management approach to hemispheric and global security.

WHAT MUST BE DONE—FIRST

The political-strategic paradigm outlined above acknowledges that the ultimate outcome of any contemporary conflict is not primarily determined by the skillful manipulation of violence in the many military battles that take place after a conflict is recognized to have begun. Rather, control of the situation is the product of connecting and weighting the various elements of national and international power within the context of strategic appraisals, strategic vision, strategic objectives, and strategic clarity. Thus, ad hoc, tactical, and operational-level recommendations will be of little help in dealing with contemporary irregular conflict until fundamental strategic changes in the U.S. interagency organizational architecture are implemented that will ensure effective institutional-national and transnational unity of effort and until strategic leaders understand and can deal with unconventional irregular conflict more comprehensively.

Organizational Mechanisms for Unity of Effort

As the currently amorphous U.S. interagency community transitions to deal more effectively with the realities and requirements of the twenty-first century, it must respond to responsible recommendations that go beyond the present Goldwater-Nichols legislation, which mandated a more cohesive military unity of effort. In essence, the argument is that the entire civil-military interagency community must come together to provide the nation with the capability to better utilize all the instruments of hard and soft power in the contemporary global security arena.

Such unity of effort recommendations may be found, for example, in the Phase 1, 2, and 3 reports of the Center for Strategic International Studies (CSIS). These comprehensive reports are entitled "Beyond Goldwater-Nichols: Defense Reform for a New Strategic Era," "Beyond Goldwater-

Nichols: U.S. Government and Defense Reform for a New Strategic Era," and "The Future of the National Guard and Reserves."[107] Additionally, James R. Locher III and his associates at the Project on National Security Reform are making recommendations on reforming the interagency community that are similar to those passed by the U.S. Congress in the Goldwater-Nichols Department of Defense Reorganization Act.[108] The recommendations of these organizations focus on the bases from which the U.S. interagency community might develop a more effective organizational capability to work synergistically over the long term in complex, irregular, and politically ambiguous contemporary conflict situations.

The primary intent of recommended new legislation would be to promulgate an executive-level management structure that can and will ensure continuous cooperative planning and implementing of policy among and between the primary U.S. internal players. That structure must also be capable of continuous, cooperative planning and execution of policy among and between primary external actors (such as primary external allies, other coalition partners, international organizations, and nongovernmental organizations). In these terms, structural mechanisms must be developed whereby U.S. civil-military planning and implementing processes can be integrated with coalition/partner governments and armed forces, nongovernmental agencies, and international organizations.

That same structure must also ensure that all political-economic-informational-military actions at the operational and tactical levels directly contribute to the achievement of a mutually agreed-upon, strategic, political end state. This requirement implies a need to develop an effective end-state planning mechanism, allowing the interagency leadership to

- Think logically, in synchronized small phases, about the conditions they seek to create;
- Synchronize the utilization of appropriate national and international hard and soft civil-military instruments of power for each phase of a given effort; and
- Ensure that every civil-military effort contributes directly to the achievement of the ultimate political objective (end-state).

At a base level, unity of effort requires educational as well as organizational solutions. Even with an adequate planning and organizational structure, ambiguity, confusion, and tensions are likely to emerge. Unity of effort ultimately entails the type of professional civilian and military educational and leadership development that leads to effective diplomacy, enabling collegial and cooperative work.[109]

The Development of Civilian and Military Strategic Leaders

Because of acknowledged political and organizational difficulties at the interagency level, leaders must be developed who can generate strategic clarity and make it work. As with other members of the interagency community who act as instruments of U.S. national power, the expanding roles and missions of the armed forces will require that new doctrine, organization, equipment, and training be developed to confront the challenges of irregular contemporary conflict. The armed forces must also respond to responsible recommendations that go beyond present-day conventional warfare.

Examples of such recommendations, although specific to the U.S. Army, may be found in "TF Irregular Challenge CSA Outbrief" and "TF Irregular Challenge DAS Decision Brief on Interagency Cadre Initiative," presented by the Strategic Studies Institute of the U.S. Army War College in 2005 and 2006.[110] The recommendations in these documents center on the cultural mindset required to transition from the kinetic fight to non-kinetic conflict. The recommended strategic-leader development process will encourage mental agility, enterprise management, governance, and cross-cultural savvy. This will help officers to operate more successfully with representatives of U.S. agencies / organizations other than their own, non-U.S. civilian and military agencies and organizations, international organizations, nongovernmental organizations, and local and global media.[111]

As a prerequisite to any possible legislation mandating a more unified whole-of-government effort to deal with the challenges of irregular conflict, there are at least four doctrinal, educational, and cultural imperatives that the U.S. Army should consider and act on.

1. The study of the fundamental nature of conflict has always been the philosophical cornerstone for understanding conventional conflict. It is no less relevant to asymmetric irregular conflict. Thus, the army should take the lead in promulgating twenty-first-century concepts, definitions, and doctrine for key terms such as "enemy," "war," "victory," and "power."
2. Nontraditional interests centering on national and international stability need to be reexamined and redefined. At the same time, the application of all the instruments of national and international power—including the full integration of legitimate civil and military coalition partners—to achieve political ends has to be rethought and redefined.
3. Efforts that enhance interagency as well as international cultural awareness—such as civilian and military exchange programs, language training programs, culture-orientation programs, and combined (multinational/multilateral) civilian and military exercises—must be revitalized and expanded.
4. Strategic leaders at all levels must understand the strategic and political-psychological implications of operational and tactical actions in contemporary conflict. In these terms, leaders must understand how force can be employed to achieve political ends and the ways in which political considerations affect the use of force. Additionally, strategic leaders must understand the challenges of ambiguity so that they may be better prepared to deal with these challenges.[112]

Additionally—but first—expanding U.S. Army roles, missions, force structure, and doctrine and developing new forms of indirect confrontation against irregular asymmetric 4GW forces will require new initiatives from the Executive Office of the Headquarters, U.S. Army, and G-3/5/7; increased interagency engagement in general; and robust involvement with the Department of State Office of the Coordinator for Reconstruction and Stability Operations (S/CRS).[113]

These recommendations are nothing radical. They are simply the logical extensions of basic security strategy and national and international asset management. By accepting these realities and making the necessary cognitive and organizational adjustments, the United States can help to replace confrontation with cooperation and harvest the hope and fulfill the promise offered by a new multidimensional paradigm for dealing with asymmetric irregular conflict.

EXTERNAL RESPONSES TO THE BOLIVARIAN PROGRAM FOR THE LIBERATION OF LATIN AMERICA

There is one school of thought in Latin America—expressed privately, if not publicly—that firmly supports Hugo Chavez and his supranational Bolivarian dream even as the leadership of the United States has tended to ignore the larger problem of responsible governance and concentrated on the war on drugs. Although the United States has demonstrated concern with the diminishing of democracy in Venezuela, that concern has not been translated into a viable and proactive program. Ideally, that program would deal with the failure of regional governments to combat political incompetence and corruption and to generate the security and well-being that they are "democratically elected" to provide their peoples. Other countries in the Americas that might be affected by the destabilizing consequences of Bolivarian attacks against their regime legitimacy have not wanted to deal with the problem. Thus, there will apparently be no clearly defined threat in the hemisphere until large numbers of uniformed troops of one sovereign state invade the sovereign territory of another.

KEY POINTS AND LESSONS

- Although seemingly overambitious, Hugo Chavez's concept of a regional superinsurgency appears to be in accord with Qiao and Wang's notion of a supranational combination of means for conducting contemporary asymmetrical unrestricted war. This notion is thought to be quietly opening a new era in which problems will be resolved and objectives achieved by using supranational means on a stage larger than that of a single country.

- Chavez's 4GW superinsurgency model is complex, ambiguous, and hard to understand in its totality because it combines national, international, and nonstate political, economic, diplomatic, cultural, and psychological dimensions, in addition to land, sea, air, space, and electronic dimensions. The consequent interactions among all these factors have limited the dominance of the military dimension in asymmetric war.
- Hard-learned lessons from past and present conflicts demonstrate one common phenomenon: the winner is the political actor that best combines all the instruments of power associated with each of the supranational dimensions.
- The Chavez 4GW model stresses that the human factor (not technology) is the decisive element, regardless of whatever dimension or combination of dimensions are operating in a given conflict situation.
- The threat, in this context, is not an enemy military force or the debilitating instability generated by an asymmetric aggressor. Rather, at base, the threat is the inability or unwillingness of a government to take responsible and legitimate measures to provide security and well-being for its peoples. That governmental inability is what gives an oppositionist aggressor the justification for existence and action.
- 4GW is the only type of war that a modern world power has ever lost. That the world's only superpower does not have a unified strategy and interagency command structure to deal with such a war boggles the mind.

What Hugo Chavez is doing in Venezuela and Latin America is being watched carefully by militant reformers, disillusioned revolutionaries, and sidelined Marxist-Leninist functionaries all over the world. He is developing a multidimensional insurgency model that puts the lie to Che Guevara's foco (military) shortcut approach to revolutionary power. It is too early to come to any definitive conclusions regarding the planning and conduct of the Chavez model, but in its concept it exemplifies the wisdom of Sun Tzu: "In war, do not advance relying on sheer military power."[114]

CHAPTER 3

A Multidimensional Paradigm for Political-Terrorist War

Al Qaeda's Approach to Asymmetric Warfare

There is no body of international relations literature that effectively addresses nonstate irregular (insurgency) conflict at the global level. Rather, insights must be drawn from three different sets of literature that range from the broadest grand-strategy level to a more specific tactical level: hegemonic stability / power transition; traditional terrorism; and revolutionary / asymmetric / insurgent / guerrilla / irregular warfare.[1] All three of these sets of international relations scholarship focus primarily on the nation-state, and conflict is defined generally in military terms. The one area of divergence in this dialogue is that the terrorism and revolution scholars recognize that nonstate actors can sometimes play more than bit parts in the global security arena. Nevertheless, the mainstream international relations literature articulates that nonstate actors are, at base, local law enforcement problems and do not require sustained national security policy attention.[2]

Al Qaeda is somewhat of an anomaly because it does not fit completely into any one set of the literatures noted above. Were Al Qaeda a rival state power, it could easily fit into the hegemonic stability / power transition theories. Were it a terrorist organization mostly confined to seeking limited goals, it could easily fit into the traditional terrorism literature. Were it a revolutionary organization seeking the overthrow of a nation-state through sequential warfare, with or without the use of terror tactics, it could fall within the traditional revolutionary warfare literature. But Al Qaeda's global reach, combined with its strategic ability, elevates it onto a different plane. That is, Al Qaeda is a hegemonic, terrorist insurgency.[3]

The violent attacks executed by Osama bin Laden's Al Qaeda ("the base") on the Twin Towers in New York City and the Pentagon in Washington, D.C., on September 11, 2001, reminded Americans of realities long understood in Europe, the Middle East, Asia, and Latin America. Those realities remind one that (1) revolutionary nonstate organizations can elevate asymmetric insurgent warfare into the global security arena—and Al Qaeda is engaged in hegemonic warfare as if it were a nation-state attempting to overthrow another; (2) terrorism, rather than conventional weaponry, is a very practical, calculated, and cynical tactic and strategy for the weak to use against the strong; (3) Al Qaeda has institutionalized political-psychological innovations with the ruthless application of power as a substitute for conventional war; and (4) Al Qaeda is not a unique or totally isolated case—armed nonstate groups all over the world are threatening the stability and existence of governments, transnational corporations, and the entire world order.[4]

In this security environment, war, the power to make war, and the power to destroy or radically change nation-states—and even the international system—is now within the reach of rogue states, substate and transnational political actors, insurgents, illegal drug traffickers, organized criminals, warlords, militant reformers, ethnic cleansers, and a thousand other "snakes with a cause."[5] The intent of all these "destabilizers" is to impose self-determined desires for change on selected societies, nation-states, and other perceived symbols of power in the global community. Some militant fundamentalist reformers, including the leaders of Al Qaeda, would reject many aspects of modernity and revert back to the questionable glories of the seventh century. As a consequence, the United States and the rest of the international community now confront a succession of failing and failed states, destabilized by contemporary conflict. There is little choice but to rethink contemporary and future unconventional conflict in light of the salient example of Al Qaeda's asymmetric global challenge.[6]

CONTEXT

An explanation of Al Qaeda's ascension to the status of a global insurgent must begin with three contextual realities. First, the basic political-historical background of the movement is key to understanding the contemporary situation and the use of extreme terrorist strategies. Second, as a corollary, a history of the law (*shiria,* or sharia) further elaborates the rationale for the use of terrorist strategies. Third, the theoretical conflict context within which Osama bin Laden operates is important and instructive. These political-military realities begin the process of explaining the "who, what, why, how, so what?" questions of Al Qaeda's challenge to the Western world.

Political-Historical Background

The Muslim peoples, like everyone else in the world, are shaped by their history, but unlike many Westerners, they are more keenly aware of it. Their perception of history is nourished from the pulpit, by the schools, and by the media; although it may sometimes be slanted and inaccurate, it is always vivid and powerfully resonant. A major difference between the Western and Muslim understandings of their respective histories is that in the Western world, since 1648 and the Peace of Westphalia, the basic unit of human organization is the nation-state. The nation may be subdivided in various ways, one of which is by religion. In contrast, Muslims tend to see the reverse situation: they see their religion subdivided into nations. According to Bernard Lewis, this is because most of the nation-states that now make up the contemporary Middle and Far East are relatively new and artificial creations. They preserve the state-building and border demarcations of their former imperial masters—as examples, Britain and France in the Middle East and Holland in the Far East (Indonesia). Islamic commentators almost always refer to their opponents not in territorial or ethnic terms but as infidels (*kafir*). They do not refer to those on their own side by nationality, as Arab or Turkish; instead, they identify themselves as Muslims.[7]

During the medieval period of European history, the most advanced civilization in the world was that of Islam. During that time, one of the basic tasks of Muslims was *jihad* ("to strive in the path of God").[8] That task has been interpreted to mean armed struggle for the defense or advancement of Muslim power. In that connection, the world was divided into two houses: the House of Islam and the House of War. The House of Islam was ruled by Muslim law and government. The rest of the world, the House of War, was ruled by infidels. Accordingly, there was to be a perpetual state of war until the entire world either embraced Islam or submitted to the rule of the Muslim state. Nevertheless, there were some infidels who were more threatening to Islam than others—Christians were considered to be the primary rivals in the struggle for world domination. For the early Muslims, the leader of Christendom (the Christian equivalent of the Muslim caliph) was the Byzantine emperor in Constantinople. Later, his place was taken by the Holy Roman Emperor in Vienna and, still later, by the new rulers of the West. Each of these Western (Christian) leaders, in his time, was the principal adversary of jihad.[9]

Under the medieval caliphate, and again under the Persian and Turkish dynasties, the Islamic empire was arguably the richest, most powerful, most creative, and most enlightened region in the world. Christendom was on the defensive during much of the Middle Ages, but in the fifteenth century, the situation began to change. First, the Tartars were expelled from Russia and the Moors from Spain. Then, in 1683, the Turks were defeated at Vienna and began a headlong retreat back to Constantinople. Defeat followed defeat, and Christian European forces expanded their empires into Africa and around Africa into South and Southeast Asia—often at the expense of the Muslims. Even small European powers such as Holland and Portugal were able to build great trading empires in the East. This unaccustomed adversity gave rise to a debate in Islam that has been ongoing ever since, centered on the questions "Why had the once victorious Islamic armies been defeated by the despised Christians?" and "How can we restore the previous situation?"[10]

By the early twentieth century, almost all of the Muslim world had been incorporated into the empires of Britain, France, Russia, and Holland. To be sure, there were a few exceptions, such as Afghanistan, Iran, and Turkey, but Britain and France—and later the United States—effectively dominated the Middle East. In the Second World War, Muslims tended to look to Germany (the enemy of their enemies) as an ally. In the cold war, the Muslims turned to the Soviet Union (again, the enemy of their enemies). Then, with the collapse of the Soviet Union, the United States was the only remaining superpower. In the absence of an ally that was the enemy of their enemies, Middle Easterners found themselves obliged to mobilize their own forces of resistance. "Al Qaeda—its leaders, its sponsors, its financiers—[became] one such force."[11]

Today, almost the entire Muslim world is affected by poverty and repression, both of which are attributed to the United States: American economic dominance and exploitation, thinly disguised as globalization, is blamed for Muslim poverty; and American support for Muslim rulers who advance U.S. interests is considered to be the root cause of poverty and repression. The resulting anger and hostility over all Islamic ills are directed against those compromised rulers and against those infidels seen as keeping the rulers in power. Closely related to those problems is the problem of modernization. Some Muslim fundamentalists argue that the primary struggle is not against the United States and the West per se but against those at home who have imported and imposed infidel ways on Muslim peoples. In any event, the principal task of Muslims is to depose these rulers and facilitate the return to a purely Islamic way of life.[12]

Within this political-historical context, Osama bin Laden and Al Qaeda must be seen as complying with the Islamic obligation to "strive in the path of God" (jihad). Thus, for bin Laden, 9/11 (2001) marks the resumption of the war for religious dominance against the House of War that began the seventh century. Certainly, in this situation, there can be no scruples. There is no doubt that the creation of Al Qaeda and the subsequent declaration of war by Osama bin Laden marked the beginning of new and ominous phases in Islamic history and in the conduct of war.[13] Conventional war has been tried—and it has failed, time after time. The time has come to try something new.

The Legal-Historical Corollary

A significant aspect of the need for change in the approach to contemporary conflict arises from what David Forte calls "Islam's Trajectory." According to Forte, the history of the law (shiria), the empire, and the tribe have deflected the original moderate teachings of the Prophet

Muhammad. Thus, there is now a relatively sound legal basis for killing apostates.[14] An apostate is anyone who "wages war on Islam." This concept evolved as a result of killing rebels during the period of the empire and was subsequently extended to killing outlaws and, later, to killing nonbelievers (apostates). The linkage between rebellion and apostasy is that treason (of any kind) and apostasy were synonymous. As a result, no connection with rebellion is required for the death penalty to be imposed. All that is needed now is some evidence of disbelief, which constitutes "waging war on Islam."[15] Osama bin Laden has accepted those teachings. He has endorsed *fatwas* (juridical statements regarding the law), such as "International Islamic Front for Jihad on the Jews and Crusaders," to the effect that Muslims should kill all Americans anywhere in the world.[16]

Moreover, jurists, in the legal processes of extending apostasy from an act of treason to an act of unbelief, allowed personal vengeance to return to Muslim society. The Prophet Muhammad had decreed that there would be no personal vengeance between or within tribes; no retaliation would be allowed until the guilt of the malefactor was proven to an impartial third party.[17] This is a fundamental legal principle in any ordered society. Nevertheless, in the evolution of Islamic law, any kind of criminal act (apostasy) may become an offense against the honor of the tribe or family of the victim. Thus, through tradition and the law, intolerance regarding any personal, group, or governmental deviance from accepted behavior allows the kind of massacres against apostates that have taken place from early Islamic history to the 9/11 (2001) mass murder in New York City, to the subsequent indiscriminate killings in Madrid and London (2004 and 2005, respectively) and elsewhere around the world to the present.[18] To be sure, there are those in the Muslim community who do not hold these extreme views. But Al Qaeda does hold these views, and it is currently the best organized and most successful of any contemporary revolutionary movement in Islam.

The Supratier Combination Approach to Contemporary Conflict

The global security environment in which Al Qaeda operates is described by some as "radical fundamentalist Islamic guerrilla warfare," or terrorism, or fourth-generation war.[19] Regardless of what it is called, the U.S.

Army's Robert M. Cassidy, an able military strategist, aptly describes Al Qaeda as a "mutating and ideologically driven global insurgency engendered by a stateless, adaptive, complex, and polycephalous host."[20] Moreover, Al Qaeda's approach to conflict is the kind that the United States and the West are most likely to confront in the foreseeable future.[21] That approach stems from an Eastern tradition of conflict that relies on indirectness, perfidy, and protraction. Inherently, it is more irregular, unorthodox, and asymmetric than the Western military tradition of maneuver and attrition.[22]

Two Chinese colonels, Qiao Liang and Wang Xangsui, have explained that any number of completely different scenarios, actions, and protagonists can be put together into hundreds of different "Cocktail Mixtures" (combinations) by a "Great Master" of warfare. The only constraint is the master's imagination.[23] One can readily see Al Qaeda's adaptation to that Chinese mixture. The basic components of the mix constitute a "supratier combination" of efforts in which there is no territory that cannot be bypassed or used; no national boundaries or laws that cannot be ignored or used; no method (means) that cannot be disregarded or used; no battlefield (dimension of conflict) that cannot be ignored or used; and no nation, transnational or nonstate actor, or international organization that cannot be ignored or used in some combination.[24]

Levels of Conflict and the Supratier Combination

The first level of conflict is the supranational combination, the second is the supradomain combination, and the third is the suprameans combination. Altogether, the whole is greater than the sum. Regardless of whether a war took place three thousand years ago or last year, the evidence indicates that all victories display one common denominator—the winner is the power or the power bloc that best combined the three levels of conflict.[25]

The Supranational Combination

Resolving conflicts or conducting warfare is not accomplished with national power alone. At the grand-strategy level, even a superpower can benefit from as much of a combination as can be generated of other nations' power, transnational and nonstate actors' power, and international organizations' power. The intent is to organize a worldwide system of power that is a great force multiplier and facilitator in the global arena. This concept works on two levels: offensive and defensive. At the positive or offensive level, one can develop power beyond one's own capabilities for maximum effect against an adversary. At the negative or defensive level, a protagonist can take measures to deprive the enemy of as much supranational support as possible, thereby gaining a relative advantage.[26] A positive-level example would be the combination of powers that the first President Bush put together and General Norman Schwarzkopf used so effectively in the 1991 Persian Gulf War. A negative-level example would be Al Qaeda's taking Spain out of the second President Bush's "coalition of the willing" in the current Iraq War.[27]

The Supradomain Combination

At this next strategic level, the supradomain combination broadens and strengthens a protagonist's power base by combining "battlefields." Each domain (factor or dimension) is a battlefield in its own right: military, political, economic, informational, cultural, and technological, in addition to land, sea, air, space, and electronic dimensions of conflict. Each dimension or its subparts—for example, economic war may be subdivided into trade war, financial war, and sanctions war—can be combined with as many others as a protagonist's organization can deal with. That combining of domains or subdomains provides considerably greater strength (power) than one or two operating by themselves. And, of course, this concept can and must be applied in terms of the supracombination of other actors' capabilities. The interaction among many dimensions (domains) of conflict prevents the military, technological, or any other factor from serving as the automatic dominant factor in any given war situation. This gives new and greater meaning to the idea of a nation-state using *all* available instruments of national and international power to protect, maintain, or achieve its vital interests. This requires the understanding of warfare as a whole and the need to develop organization and doctrine to enable a comprehensive unity of effort.[28]

The Suprameans Combination

Suprameans involves the combination of all available methods of conducting conflict, involving military and nonmilitary, lethal and nonlethal, and direct and indirect methods. As only a few examples, combinations of military, transmilitary, and nonmilitary warfare would include the following:

1. Conventional war / network war / sanctions war
2. Guerrilla war / drug war / media war
3. Biochemical war / intelligence war / resources war
4. Terrorist war / financial war / ideological war, and
5. Atomic war / diplomatic war / trade war

Regardless of what combination of participants, forms, or efforts a given conflict may take, the battlefield is everywhere and involves everyone. Self-interest is the only constant. In pursuit of the goal of achieving one's self-interests, any of the above types of operations can be combined with others to form completely new methods of conflict. There are no means that cannot be combined with others. The only limitation would be one's imagination.[29]

Conclusions: Unrestricted War

"Even the last refuge of the human race—the inner world of the heart—cannot avoid the attacks of [adroit] psychological war."[30] This "inner world of the heart" is susceptible to the planning, coordinating, and implementing of supranational, supradomain, and suprameans combinations at home and around the world, whether by a superorganization created by the United States in pursuit of our own self-interests or by opponents that would see the current world order replaced by a caliphate. Moreover, the members of that superorganization must not only be expert in their functional fields (trade war, cyber war, and psychological war) but must also be knowledgeable about and sensitive to the specific cultures they address. The planning for and implementing of supratier combinations by such a superorganization require continuous innovation, as the successful protagonist in any conflict must seek to always go beyond limits. This is why Qiao and Wang call this kind of war "unrestricted war."[31]

The notion of supratier combinations of unrestricted war cannot be considered to be too ambiguous, too complex, or too hard to deal with. All of that may be true, but to admit that and do nothing would be to admit defeat. In turn, such a response would likely submit one's posterity to unconscionable consequences. To emphasize the odious consequences of an all-too-probable "cocktail mixture" of asymmetric warfare that might be prepared for a stronger adversary, I offer Qiao and Wang's scenario:

> If the attacking side secretly musters large amounts of capital without the enemy nation being aware of this, and launches a sneak attack against his financial markets, then after causing a financial crisis, buries a computer virus and hacker detachment in the opponent's computer system in advance, while at the same time carrying out a network attack against the enemy so that the civilian electricity network, traffic dispatching network, financial transaction network, telephone communications network, and mass media network are completely paralyzed, this will cause the enemy nation to fall into social panic, street riots, and a political crisis. There is finally the forceful bearing down by the army and military means are utilized in gradual stages until the enemy is forced to sign a dishonorable peace treaty.[32]

This type of warfare is not a test of expertise in creating instability, conducting illegal violence, or achieving commercial, ideological, or moral satisfaction. Ultimately, it is an exercise in survival. Failure in unrestricted supratier combination warfare is not an option.[33]

AL QAEDA: "THE BASE" ORGANIZATION

If the appropriate magic could be conjured and one could look down through the familiar artificial lines and colors of a current world map into the twenty-first-century strategic reality, one could see a complex new global security environment. That milieu would contain several types of ambiguous and uncomfortable wars—and their aftermath. A deeper look into that picture would provide several snapshots that display the Al Qaeda concept of leadership and organization designed to successfully conduct contemporary unrestricted asymmetrical war.

The Leader and His Vision

Osama bin Laden was and is the main leader of Al Qaeda ("The Base") from its beginnings in the last months of the Soviet occupation of Afghanistan, about mid-1988. He played the lead role in the formation of that base organization, with the idea of maintaining the Islamist momentum gained from the defeat of the Russian army. As a consequence, Al Qaeda was created for long-term durability, the institutionalization of the organizational mechanisms developed in the war against the Soviet Union, and the further development of the organization to support the expansion of the Islamic revolution around the world.[34] Accordingly, the main job of the leader was and is to provide the vision, unity of effort, and direction for the accomplishment of these purposes.[35]

In this connection, bin Laden represents a militant, revolutionary, and energetic commitment to a long-term approach to bringing about a return to Islamic governance, social purpose, and tradition. He has further identified the primary objective of the movement as power.[36] Power is absolutely necessary for implementation of the political, economic, and social changes explicit and implicit in the idea of a return to Islamic governance of Muslim peoples and the resurrection of an Islamic caliphate.[37] Power is generated by an intelligent, well-educated, well-motivated, and disciplined organization that can plan and implement an effective program for gaining control of societies and states. Power is maintained and enhanced as the organization acts as a virtual state-within-a-state and replaces the artificial and illegitimate (apostate) governments that impose their rule on contemporary Muslim societies.[38] Thus, Al Qaeda members—from those in the highest positions to new recruits—have had to pledge their lives for the achievement of this vision. And, as in the time of the empire, they all must pledge their allegiance to the leader (caliph).[39]

The Organization

Osama bin Laden's first and continuing concern must center on organization. The preparatory activities to begin to achieve his long-term vision are classical Leninist and Maoist. He established a dedicated cadre, a political party–type infrastructure, a guerrilla army, and a support mechanism for the entire organization.[40] Organizational vitality, breadth, and depth also provide bases for local, regional, and global effectiveness. Thus, the organization, not operations, is considered key to Al Qaeda success.

Generally, Al Qaeda appears to be structured much like a classical Leninist-Maoist movement along rigid, close-knit, and secretive lines, in a hierarchical pyramid structure. This multilevel organization indicates a substantial corporate enterprise, designed especially for conducting large- and small-scale business operations and terrorist activities all around the globe. As a result, this organization looks much like transnational gang organizations in the Americas that can quickly and flexibly respond to any kind of changing situation. Thus, it is probably more helpful to look at Al Qaeda in terms of concentric circles rather than the traditional pyramid.[41]

The inner circle of the Al Qaeda organization comprises a small council (*shura*) of elders, along with several hundred carefully selected and talented members who operate the functional structures considered to be essential to long-term effectiveness and durability—regardless of who serves as the leader. There are at lease six of these functional organizations within the base organization: military, funding, procurement, manpower and logistics, training and personnel services, and communications and propaganda.[42] This inner circle provides strategic and operational-level direction and support to its horizontal network of compartmentalized cells and allied associations (groups or networks). This structure also allows relatively rapid shifting of operational control horizontally rather than through a vertical chain of command; thus, this organization can respond to an unexpected problem or to a promising opportunity in a more timely manner.[43]

The second ring consists of more than a thousand "holy warriors" who are veterans of the early Afghani campaigns against the Russians. They are proven and trustworthy and provide leadership and expertise to the worldwide multidimensional network. The third ring consists of thousands of Islamic militants. These individuals make up a loose alliance of political parties and groups, as well as transnational criminal, insurgent, and terrorist organizations that can be called on at virtually any time for aid, sanctuary, and personnel. The outer ring of this organization consists of more-amorphous groups of Muslims, in ninety countries around the world, who support Osama bin Laden's view of the West as the primary enemy of Islam.[44]

As might be assumed, active support for Al Qaeda comes from a broad range of social classes, professions, and other Muslim groups. Michael Scheuer asserts that the next generation of membership will be larger, more professional and less operationally visible, and more adept at using the communications and military tools of modernity.[45] One example of the quality and talent of the people who are working in bin Laden's contemporary base structure is his world-class media organization. This apparatus is already very sophisticated, flexible, and omnipresent in nearly every country in the world. Al Qaeda's media people produce daily combat reports, videos of attacks on enemy targets, interviews with various Al Qaeda and other Islamic leaders, and a steady flow of news bulletins to feed 24/7 satellite television networks around the globe. Al Qaeda media are telling the Muslim world its version of the war in Iraq—and elsewhere—professionally, reliably, and in real time.[46] If Scheuer is right, the next generation can only be more sophisticated and formidable than the present one, and this will only enhance Al Qaeda's position as a global revolutionary power.

The Al Qaeda Program for Gaining Power

A deeper look into our magical map and into the reality of contemporary asymmetric battlefields and ambiguous internal wars reveals a number of fuzzy nationalisms that cannot be shown on two-dimensional space. Nationalist discontent, often accompanied by religious militancy, appears to be growing and dividing in an amoeba-like manner. This discontent becomes malignant as corrupt, incompetent, insensitive, misguided, and weak governments fail to provide political, economic, and social justice and basic personal security for their peoples. In turn, these injustices fuel regional and global conflict and related terrorist-type activities. One example that can be seen clearly is that groups similar to Al Qaeda—from street gangs to other revolutionary movements to hegemonic nation-states—are looking for new and more-effective models within the fourth-generation war construct to help them achieve their self-anointed objectives. The Al Qaeda program for attaining power is one such model that shows great promise.

Al Qaeda envisages what Osama bin Laden calls a "defensive jihad" that calls for three different types of war—military, economic, and cultural-moral—divided into four stages and with well-defined strategic-, operational-, and tactical-level objectives.[47] This concept allows military, political, and other facets of the Al Qaeda insurgency to be conducted in tandem. The different types of war and their associated stages are sometimes overlapping and may be altered. Also, additional stages may be assumed as various milestones are met or not met. Moreover, objectives, and the types of battlefields chosen to achieve these objectives, may be adjusted as a given situation dictates. Flexibility in planning and implementation of the program to achieve power is, then, the operative consideration when examining this Al Qaeda model.[48]

The dominating characteristic of a given war is defined as either military, economic, or cultural-moral. Within the context of "combinations" or "collective activity," it is important to understand that there is a difference between the "dominant" sphere and the "whole." There is a dynamic relationship between a dominant type of war (for example, military, economic, or moral) and the supporting elements that make up the whole. As an example, military war is always supported by media (information) war and a combination of other types of war such as economic war, cyber-network war, or diplomatic war.[49] At base, the intent of every type of war—with its dynamic combinations of multidimensional efforts—is to directly support one or more of the five main political objectives in the Al Qaeda endgame: (1) to drive the United States from the Middle East; (2) to open the path to destroy both Israel and the apostate Arab regimes in the area; (3) to preserve energy resources for Islamic benefit; (4) to enhance Muslim unity; and (5) to install sharia rule throughout the region—one place at a time.[50]

Al Qaeda's program for gaining power is further divided into four general multiphased stages. The first stage of Islamic conflict against the

House of War is to "inspire Muslims all around the globe." This is a classic first organizational stage in which bin Laden concentrates on doctrine and leadership development and on expanding his base organization's relationships with potential supporters—Muslim and non-Muslim—throughout the world. With this comprehensive foundational effort, Al Qaeda does not have to depend on any one or two or three sources of logistical, financial, manpower, sanctuary, or political support. Rather, Al Qaeda support is diversified to the point at which an enemy is unable to shut it down.[51]

The second stage of Islamic war involves the creation of corporate-type "franchise" organizations. This is a logical organizational step directed at generating reliable infrastructure and alliances out of first-stage support. Additionally, these franchise organizations contribute toward unification of efforts "under the banner of monotheism."[52] These organizations can, when ready, open new fronts (stages of war) virtually anywhere that Al Qaeda considers useful within its grand strategy.

The third stage is overtly more active and military / terrorist-oriented. This stage of war might be called "moving into the offensive." At this point, Al Qaeda and its allied and supporting organizations can begin to attack the symbols of power in enemy states and the global community. The kinds of attacks would range from (1) hanging dogs and cats from lamp posts as warnings to apostate functionaries and supporters of an illegitimate state or multinational corporation to (2) bombing buildings, railroad stations, and other symbols of so-called illegitimate national, regional, and global power. The objectives of this kind of terrorist violence are, first, to begin to destroy or impair communications between a government and its population and, second, to eventually break the bonds between a government and its population and to subsequently break the bonds between a government, its security organizations, and the people. Ultimately, this action could lead to the destruction of governmental authority and the creation of a political vacuum that would allow Al Qaeda and its allied organizations to become the de facto authority in areas uncontrolled or abandoned by the targeted state.[53]

The fourth stage of Islamic war is the gradual widening of the global battlefield to the point at which Al Qaeda becomes less relevant and the Islamic caliphate begins to take control of the general struggle against the

House of War. This may mistakenly be considered to be the decisive and final stage of the Al Qaeda revolution. However, this stage of conflict will not be the result of any one spectacular action. It is supposed to be a gradual process that will allow a small—but direct—military / terrorist assault to bring about the desired end state. Another aspect that must be factored in is that the caliphate will expand by one piece of territory or country at a time—over time. Thus, Stage One operations will be beginning at geographical points A and B, even while Stage Two efforts are ongoing at points C and D, Stage Three efforts are being undertaken at points E and F, and Stage Four processes can be simultaneously ongoing at points G and H, and so forth, at any given time and place in the struggle between the House of Islam and the House of War.[54]

Where Al Qaeda Leads: Strategic, Operational, and Tactical Implications

At the strategic level, then, Al Qaeda will be conducting combinations of various wars and using combinations of various battlefields and methods throughout the global community. Nevertheless, it will continue to focus its primary attack on the legitimacy of apostate governments—or any possible rival—to govern or control the Islamic peoples. Aside from various shows of force, there are not likely to be direct confrontations with enemy security forces on any large or lengthy scale. At the same time, Al Qaeda will continue working toward broader support in the Islamic world and in any state that pledges not to attack Muslims or intervene in their affairs. In short, Al Qaeda will do what it can to move closer and closer to the achievement of the five objectives that define its political end state.[55]

At the operational level, Al Qaeda will concentrate its efforts in two areas: changing the antagonistic policies of the United States and its allies; and eroding public support from apostate governments and stripping away allies from the United States. The intent is to increasingly isolate the United States and constrict its actions within the global security arena. Tactically, Al Qaeda will continue to use the ruthless application of terrorist violence along with a strong media campaign to further the movement down the path toward the destruction of the American position in the Middle East and to destroy the apostate regimes in the region. Al Qaeda can also continue to put effort and resources into developing its relationships with kindred and supportive groups in other parts of the world.[56]

Then, as these strategic, operational, and tactical activities come to fruition in various parts of the globe, Al Qaeda can open additional stages or campaigns somewhere else, against another member or part of the House of War. Ironically, we see a theoretical contradiction developing here. Despite calls for peace and truces, it is doctrinally impossible to achieve peace or permanent truces without the House of Islam first subduing the House of War. Over time, there will always be another apostate to deal with. There always has been—even going back to the height of the empire. As a consequence, in the clash between the Islamic world and the West, a long war is virtually guaranteed. Indeed, the outlook for the future is bleak.

AL QAEDA: A CLOSER LOOK

Looking further down through our magic map, we can discern numerous additional activities and reasons for those actions in the struggle for power that dominates life throughout much of the world today. The first thing we see is some sort of reason governing Al Qaeda terrorism. In our previous view of contemporary asymmetric battlefields, there did not seem to be any particular strategic reasoning behind those events. But there is. We can see in the Spanish case, for example, that acts of ruthless violence have specific purposes. The second thing we observe is what is happening with the first and second stages of the development of the amoeba-like Al Qaeda organisms. A quick look at Europe shows slow but perceptible organizational movement toward the ability to generate third-stage offensive actions. Then, with another adjustment of focus into the context of Al Qaeda activity, we can see some subtle actions that govern its basic ends-ways-and-means strategy. Those governing rules can determine the outcome of a given activity.

The Terrorist Action in Spain, March 2004

On March 11, 2004, ten rucksacks packed with explosives were detonated in Madrid, Spain. That seemingly random act killed 191 innocent and unsuspecting people and injured over 1,800 more. That terrorist act was considered to be the most deadly in Western Europe since the 1988 bombing of Pan American Flight 103 over Lockerbie, Scotland, which killed 270 people. The 1,470-page official summary of the investigation of the Madrid bombings provided very little information. It indicated that 29 individuals were involved in that attack: 6 were charged with mass murder, and the remaining 23 were indicted on charges that ranged from collaborating with a terrorist organization to trafficking in explosives. The 29 men accused of these crimes included 15 Moroccans, 4 Arabs, a Syrian with Spanish citizenship, and 9 Spaniards. The report also indicated that the 29 accused individuals were members of a radical group active in North Africa and that Al Qaeda exercised only a kind of guiding influence (for example, these bombers had learned their bomb-making skills not from Al Qaeda but from the Internet).[57]

Subsequent information regarding the March 2004 bombings in Madrid indicated more than a casual relationship with Al Qaeda, however. Four of the bombers were Al Qaeda "veterans" who provided leadership and expertise for the operation. Specific funding came from drugs-for-weapons exchanges. Most of these men involved in the planning and implementation of the attack had been involved in criminal activities such as jewel and precious metals theft, counterfeiting, and credit card fraud. Reportedly, these criminal efforts were interrupted to allow the twenty-nine accused men to take on the bombing mission. The purpose of the criminal activities had been simply to help raise funds to send Spanish recruits to help Al Qaeda in Iraq.[58] This kind of information leads to conclusions to the effect that (1) the organization that actually planned and executed the Madrid bombings was acting as a part of Al Qaeda's first or second stage of contemporary war, in which that "base organization" was expanding its relationships with supporters; (2) that the Al Qaeda veterans who provided leadership and expertise came out of the second level (ring) of the organization; and (3) that prior to the planning and implementation of the bombing, the twenty-five nonveteran members of the bombing group had been acting very much like second- or third-generation gangs in Central and South America and the Caribbean.[59]

While this information was not particularly alarming, the results achieved by the small twenty-nine-member cadre that was directly responsible for the March 2004 bombings in Madrid were significant and far-reaching. First, the sheer magnitude and shock of the attack changed Spanish public opinion and the outcome of the parliamentary elections that were held just three days later. In those elections, the relatively conservative, pro-U.S. government of Prime Minister Jose Maria Aznar was surprisingly and decisively defeated. That defeat came at the hands of the anti-U.S. / anti–Iraq War leader of the socialists, Jose Luis Rodriguez Zapatero. Prior to those elections, the Spanish government had been a strong supporter of both the United States and U.S. policy regarding the global war on terror (GWOT) and the Iraq War. Shortly after the elections, Spain's 1,300 troops were withdrawn from Iraq, and Spain ceased to be a strong U.S. ally.[60]

Second, the Madrid attack sent several messages to the Spanish people, the rest of the Western world, and Muslim communities around the world. The various messages went something like this: it is going to be very expensive to continue to support the United States in its GWOT and in Iraq; any country not cooperating fully with Al Qaeda will be a target; look what we can do with a minimum of manpower and expense; we are capable of moving into Stage Three (offensive) operations in Europe and elsewhere, should we desire to do so; and we have stood up against the United States and one of its allies—and succeeded.[61]

Additionally, Al Qaeda demonstrated that it had skillfully applied fourth-generation war techniques to modern asymmetric war and had done so with impunity. The effort was deliberately executed in a way that made virtually any kind of Western or U.S. response impossible. The worst thing that has happened is that only one person has been convicted in connection with the Madrid attack—he pleaded guilty to illegally transporting explosives. As a result, that very positive publicity throughout the Muslim world was expected to generate new sources of funding, new places for training and sanctuary, new recruits to the Al Qaeda ranks, and additional legitimacy. The response to this murderous attack was also an illustration of the fact that Spain and most of the rest of Europe considered terrorism and other activities associated with Al Qaeda or any other nonstate actor—including gangs—as simple law enforcement problems. In Western Europe, there were few, if any, indications that Al Qaeda's ruthless application of terror was taken as any kind of serious national security problem.[62]

Subsequent Activities in Western Europe

The long, but almost irrelevant, official summary of the Madrid bombings left more than a few people wondering why and how "a massacre of that size [could be] carried out by just a few delinquents."[63] The answers to those questions did not begin to become clear until after the attacks in London, England, on July 7, 2005. The British and, later, other similar investigations of terrorist attacks in Western Europe provided several frustrating and sobering findings. Among these is the discovery that Al Qaeda was no longer using jihadi veterans to play major roles in the London and subsequent terrorist acts. Rather, by 2005, Al Qaeda was able to use "homegrown" radicalized adolescents to conduct suicidal acts. At the same time, it became known that the British suicide bombers in every case had crystal-clear intent to cause fatalities on a large scale. And it became apparent that the local terrorist expertise was developed through Al Qaeda channels and assets. As one example, two of the four British bombers involved in the July 7, 2005, attacks had previously traveled to Pakistan and had received military and explosives training there. Lastly, it became clear that there were several active Al Qaeda cells operating all over Europe.[64]

SPAIN

After the March 2004 bombings in Madrid, police began finding large numbers of Islamic militants in the major cities of the country. The main activities of those "militants" (no longer "delinquents") appeared to center on recruiting fighters to join the Iraqi insurgency. These militants were also found to be engaged in other supporting operations for the jihad in Iraq, in terms of money, equipment, and arms. Police also claim to have foiled at least four additional attacks that were allegedly directed at internal Spanish infrastructure. An important detail is that the large majority of the Islamic militants apprehended in Spain since 2004 have been North African—mainly Moroccan—immigrants. As a consequence, the radicalization of Muslims living in Spain constitutes an enormous social, as well as terrorist, challenge for now and the future.[65]

Britain

In the United Kingdom—as well as France and Italy—we see patterns similar to those in Spain and an escalation of Al Qaeda terrorist activity. In a rare public statement, the director-general of the British security service, known as MI5, recently made it clear that "[t]here is a steady increase in the terrorist threat to the UK"; that "Al Qaeda–related terrorism is real, here, deadly, and enduring"; that "[s]ome 200 groupings or networks, totaling more than 1,600 identified individuals, are actively engaged in plotting and facilitating terrorist acts here or overseas"; and, again, that plots in the UK "often have links back to Al Qaeda in Pakistan."[66]

France

The French security services have found that there is an ongoing "triangular trade" that consists of weapons, stolen goods, and narcotics. Three, four, or more Al Qaeda affiliates, including the Algerian-based GSCP (Selafist Group for Call and Combat), are beginning to engage in jihad against France and other countries in Europe. GSCP is particularly important because it has already established its credentials for attacking military targets and its training of recruits for action in Iraq. Nevertheless, Al Qaeda's main efforts at present in France are thought to continue to center on the triangular trafficking to fund and support jihadi operations in Iraq and elsewhere in the Middle East. Additionally, because of France's large immigrant Muslim population, that country is considered to be a prime source of recruits for all Al Qaeda operations. And because of France's geographical location—along with Spain—that country is also used as a convenient trans-shipment point for funneling recruits and material support to Al Qaeda affiliates in North Africa and the Middle East.[67]

Italy

Italy is clearly another Al Qaeda base of operations in Europe from which Al Qaeda targets objectives not only in Italy but also in other countries in Europe and elsewhere. As examples, in September 2005, Italian police detained Algerians who were alleged to be planning an attack on the Spanish National Court in Madrid. And in November 2005, several North Africans were arrested who were allegedly planning a new series of attacks in the United States. Reportedly, they were targeting ships, stadiums, and railway stations in an attempt to surpass the 9/11 (2001) attacks on New York City and Washington, D.C. And again—as in Britain, France, and Spain—those suspected terrorists were first-generation immigrants with significant military/terrorist training and experience. The return of jihadis to Italy and elsewhere in Europe from their sojourns in Afghanistan, Iraq, the Middle East, and North Africa is causing some concern. The logic of the situation argues that Europe is no longer only a logistical and personnel support base for Al Qaeda. Italy (and perhaps other countries in Europe) is now thought to be a "forward terrorist planning center." Unfortunately, not many of the above allegations have been proven in courts of law—indeed, adequate legal evidence is difficult to obtain. As a result, suspected militants are generally convicted on minor charges (such as transporting illegal explosives) or for drug-related crimes.[68]

The Impact of Terrorist Actions in Europe

In sum, at least since early 2004, some European countries have become support centers for Al Qaeda–associated terrorists. The assumption there, among those responsible for countering terrorist activities, is that these militants "have come here because the penalties have been light."[69] Thus, these countries continue to provide safe havens, false documentation, financing, weapons and equipment, and recruits for Al Qaeda operations. The support organizations comprise both radicalized native-born individuals and immigrants who have been trained and gained experience in Al Qaeda–associated facilities and conflicts ranging from North Africa through Iraq and to Asia (Afghanistan and Pakistan). Now, European countries also appear to be more than support centers for international criminal and terrorist activity. There is evidence that these countries are hosts to a rapidly expanding and homegrown terrorist threat. Nevertheless, generally, the European response is not so much to a terrorist threat as to a serious social and law enforcement problem.[70]

Consequences at the National Security Level

In addition to increasing the operations tempo of law enforcement problems in various European countries, Al Qaeda actions have resulted in significant consequences at the national security level. As examples, after Spain took itself out of the United States–led alliance in the Iraq War,

> British Prime Minister Tony Blair was compelled to appease his opposition by announcing that he would step down from the premiership before he had intended. His own Labor Party's anger—backed by many public opinion polls—stemmed from Blair's strong support for the U.S. war on terrorism.
>
> French sources indicated, in mid-October 2006, that President Jacques Chirac's government was formulating plans to withdraw its forces from Afghanistan in 2007. This was done in the face of rising violence in Afghanistan and public condemnation of the Iraq War.
>
> Italian Prime Minister Silvio Berlusconi's conservative, pro–United States government was defeated by a narrow margin in the summer of 2006. Because of mounting opposition to Italian support for the U.S.-led war in Iraq, the new government is expected to reduce the number of Italian troops in that conflict.

These political changes did not come about by accident. Al Qaeda's media organization worked hard to generate the changes in public opinion and governmental policies in these European countries. Of course, none of the changes noted above falls within the traditional definition of "diplomatic successes," and none of those changes can be credited as "war winners" for Al Qaeda. Nevertheless, each of those changes clearly advances the objectives of political war that bin Laden has set forth: erode popular support for the war on terrorism among the populations of American allies and gradually isolate the United States from its allies.[71]

THE GOVERNING RULES THAT MAKE WAR POLITICALLY EFFECTIVE

Asymmetric insurgency wars will likely have different names, different motives, and different levels of violence that will be a new part of the old problem. Nevertheless, whether they are called "teapot wars," "camouflaged wars," "unrestricted wars," or something else, present and future insurgency wars can be identified by the lowest-common-denominator motive.[72] As a corollary, whether they are considered to be "spiritual" insurgencies, "ideological" insurgencies, "commercial" insurgencies, or anything else, these wars are the organized application of coercion or threatened coercion intended to resist, oppose, or overthrow an existing government and to bring about political change.[73] To make this definition more meaningful, Guillen states that "[a] popular victory would exchange the existing order of [social] classes, private property, social relations, internal and external politics, and a capitalist [economic] regime for a socialist society. Consequently, revolutionary war is total war. . . . [It is] a struggle without clemency that exacts the highest political tension."[74]

Yet every asymmetric insurgency war will be unique. It will reflect the history, geography, and culture of the society in which it takes place. But despite its ambiguity, complexity, and uniqueness, there will be analytical commonalities—strategic-level principles (rules)—that are relevant. Qiao and Wang argue very practically that these rules, when applied to the universally common ends-ways-and-means strategy, generate value added to power and are the essential ingredients for making war politically effective.[75] We have seen these rules at work in the past and in the present. Again, Qiao and Wang make the point: "If too many accidents demonstrate the same phenomenon, can you still calmly view them as accidents? No, at this moment, you have to admit that there is a rule here."[76]

Al Qaeda has transformed itself from a relatively ordinary violent nonstate actor into a hegemonic power that is capable of challenging both the United States and the existing international order. This has been accomplished in large part because Al Qaeda has adopted some specific "rules of victory"[77] to its basic strategy and also adjusted that strategy to exploit American weaknesses and vulnerabilities. These rules (the SWORD model) have been validated through both qualitative and quantitative analysis; they identify seven dimensions (factors) that are critical to long-term success. Using Kim Fishel's terms, not Al Qaeda's, they are (1) legitimacy, (2) unity of effort, (3) efforts against counterterrorist actions, (4) efforts against support actions, (5) external support to Al Qaeda, (6) actions against subversion, and (7) efforts to weaken enemy military actions.[78] Once Osama bin Laden's strategists grasped the essence of these factors and applied them to Al Qaeda strategy, that organization elevated insurgency onto the global level. In these terms,

1. Moral legitimacy remains the most important principle of the post–World War II era. It can be seen in three different contexts. First, in Al Qaeda's communiqués and declarations, it invariably attempts to rely on de jure legitimacy in an attempt to acquire universal de facto legitimacy among Muslims. This de jure legitimacy is grounded in the law (shiria) and in the Koran. Second, Al Qaeda is constantly attacking the legitimacy of apostate Muslim governments. This is an attempt to acquire de facto legitimacy for its terrorist and other actions, based on Muslim global nationalism. In this instance, Al Qaeda attempts to delegitimize a targeted county by focusing on the apostate nature of its government and placing the blame for perceived injustices on the United States, other Western countries, and the global system. Third, Al Qaeda is attempting to create a "new" legitimacy within the base of its supporters who argue that inflicting damage, casualties, and even mass destruction on its enemies is the only path to victory. This use of legitimacy turns the original concept upside-down and is recognizable as the legitimacy that "comes from the barrel of a gun."[79]
2. Unity of effort is derived from Al Qaeda's leadership structure, which provides strategic direction and operational and tactical support to its vertical and horizontal network of compartmentalized cells and affiliate organizations. This kind of unity gives

Al Qaeda a global presence while at the same time allowing it to shift control of operations from the vertical to the horizontal as necessity dictates. Unity will be further enhanced and institutionalized as "true Islamic" states are created in the Middle East and elsewhere.[80]

3. Efforts against counterterrorist actions range from financial and Internet war, to the creation of an Islamic front (the fourth stage of war) that can use weapons of mass destruction (WMD), to keeping enemies off balance as a result of direct attacks on enemy targets such as the USS *Cole,* embassies, and train stations. On the other side of that same proverbial coin, Al Qaeda actions against counterterrorist actions include building morale and a certain legitimacy in Muslim communities through the publicity of its own terrorism. As one example, Colonel Hammes cites a poem that Osama bin Laden wrote after the attack on the *Cole*:

   A destroyer, even the brave might fear,
   She inspires horror in the harbour and the open seas,
   She goes into the waves flanked by arrogance, haughtiness
   And fake might,
   To her doom she progresses slowly, clothed in a huge illusion,
   Awaiting her is a dinghy, bobbing in the waves.[81]

4. Al Qaeda efforts against support actions of the intervening power (U.S.) begin with blaming the United States and/or the global system as the root cause of the problems of the Muslim world. From there, that effort progresses to other attempts to weaken the resolve of U.S. allies and to isolating the U.S. government from its internal popular support and from its external popular and governmental support. Clearly, this dimension of contemporary war is closely related to efforts against counterterrorist actions, but for analytical purposes, counterterrorist actions must be differentiated from actions against external and internal support to the enemy.[82]
5. External support to Al Qaeda is as important to Al Qaeda as external support is to an enemy. That support, in either case, is a force multiplier and can mean the difference between success or

failure: thus, the importance of Stage One and Stage Two war efforts to build, maintain, and expand a global support network. That network can provide everything from funding to sanctuary to personnel to legitimacy. Al Qaeda's worldwide financial and media networks are key to these endeavors—and to becoming a global revolutionary power. In this connection, as Al Qaeda develops its global support base, it can extend its reach and strike out at its enemies in numerous places in various parts of the world, without much fear of retribution.[83]

6. Actions against subversion include three different but important elements: intelligence, psychological operations, and population and resource control. The concept that these controlling elements must be organized and set into place as early as possible—even before a conflict is recognized to have begun—is fundamental. Together, intelligence, psychological operations, and population controls must be designed to quickly locate, isolate, and neutralize the enemy. War against subversion, thus, means attacking the enemy leadership politically and psychologically. In turn, that means weakening direction and control, fragmenting the organizational infrastructure, and ultimately destroying the effectiveness of the entire organization by breaking the bonds to the social system that sustains it. Al Qaeda's involvement in, and observation of, conflict around the world—including the way the United States acts in those conflicts—is a primary factor in Al Qaeda's ability to successfully challenge U.S. government leadership *and* popular political-social support for that leadership. In sum, intelligence is the vehicle that enables both psychological operations and population and resource control in enemy countries.[84]
7. Efforts to weaken enemy military actions take us to the "shooting" part of contemporary multidimensional war. In that context, the appropriate use of military or other related physical force is still a key factor in determining success or failure in asymmetric war. Al Qaeda has chosen the strategy and tactics of terrorism with the underlying legitimizing concept of jihad as its primary vehicle (method) for forcing the achievement of its

strategic, operational, and tactical objectives. Al Qaeda has also chosen psychological media (information) operations as the primary supporting method for achieving its desired end state. The combination of the concerted quest for ultimate destructive power (WMD) and the ability to generate control of popular resolve distinguishes Al Qaeda as a global hegemon.[85]

CONFRONTING AL QAEDA

The problem of understanding Al Qaeda as a global power is exacerbated by the fact that it is not a traditional peer-level competitor state. It is a nonstate revolutionary-terrorist actor. This may help explain why the United States and other countries have treated Al Qaeda as more of a law enforcement problem than an enemy in a total war that threatens the national security and sovereignty of targeted states. An important first step in confronting an actor who has declared hegemonic war—and maintains an increasing commitment to destroy the United States and the global system—is understanding the actor and the reality of the threat he generates. To do so requires an understanding of both what that actor (enemy) is doing and why and how he is doing it. Thus, it is also important to understand those factors that lead to success or failure in contemporary asymmetric insurgency war and to understand how these factors are being adapted to elevate insurgency into the global security arena. If the United States and its allies can recognize the Al Qaeda challenge as an authentic national and international security issue, they can be better prepared to fight and defeat that enemy. At the same time, they can be prepared to direct progress toward social justice, democracy, stability, and sustainable peace. Otherwise, the Al Qaeda challenge to the West can easily be perceived as simply "the antithesis of the United Nations project" or "perpetual war" and what others are calling the "Long War."[86]

KEY POINTS AND LESSONS

- Al Qaeda has demonstrated that a nonstate actor can effectively challenge a traditional nation-state—and indeed symbols of power in the global system—without conventional weaponry and manpower.

- Al Qaeda understands that success can be achieved as a result of the careful application of a complex multidimensional paradigm that begins with political-psychological war innovations, combined with the ruthless application of terror.
- That paradigm is enhanced by the addition of economic, cultural, informational, and other components that give a relative advantage to Al Qaeda over an opponent that uses a unidimensional military approach to conflict.
- These various dimensions of contemporary conflict are further combined with military and nonmilitary, lethal and nonlethal, and direct and indirect methods of attacking an enemy. Together, these combinations generate a powerful asymmetrical substitute for conventional war.
- The most important and effective component of the Al Qaeda paradigm is the indirect, nonmilitary, and nonlethal political-psychological-cultural-moral attack on the legitimacy of a targeted government and its allies.

Since the end of World War II, the United States and other Western powers have been engaged—directly or indirectly—in hundreds of long-term, asymmetric irregular insurgency wars. It is surprising and dismaying that these countries do not yet understand some of the most fundamental principles that Sun Tzu's translator, Samuel B. Griffith, reminds us Sun Tzu taught 2,500 years ago. In short, "war is to be preceded by measures designed to make it easy to win. The master conqueror frustrated his enemy's plans and broke up his alliances. He created cleavages between sovereign and minister, superiors and inferiors, commanders and subordinates. His spies and agents were active everywhere, gathering information, sowing dissension, and nurturing subversion. The enemy was isolated and demoralized; his will to resist broken. Thus without battle his army was conquered, his cities taken and his state overthrown. . . . [But the] indispensable preliminary to battle is to attack the mind of the enemy."[87]

CHAPTER 4

Sovereignty under Siege

Gangs and Other Criminal Organizations in Central America and Mexico

Another kind of war within the context of a "clash of civilizations" is being waged in various parts of the Americas, Africa, Asia, Europe, the Middle East, and everywhere else around the world today.[1] Some of the main protagonists are those who have come to be designated as first-, second-, and third-generation street gangs, as well as the more traditional transnational criminal organizations (TCOs), such as Mafia families, illegal drug traffickers, warlords, terrorists, insurgents, and so forth. In this different ("new") kind of war, TCOs are not sending conventional military units across national borders or building an industrial capability in an attempt to "filch some province" from some country.[2] These nonstate actors are more interested in commercial profit and controlling territory (turf) to allow maximum freedom of movement and action. In addition to drug smuggling, these criminal organizations are known to have expanded their activities to—among others—smuggling people, body parts, weapons, and cars, along with associated intimidation, murder, kidnapping and robbery, money laundering, home and community invasion, and other lucrative societal destabilization activities. That freedom of action within countries and across national frontiers ensures commercial market share and revenues, as well as secure bases for market expansion. The corrosive effects of the associated criminal violence and gratuitous cruelty of that freedom of movement also generate a different kind of clash of civilizations. It is not a clash of Western and Eastern cultures; rather, it is a clash of values between liberal democracy and criminal anarchy.[3]

What makes all of this into a new type of war is that the national security and sovereignty of affected countries are being impinged upon every day, and the illicit commercial motives of TCOs are becoming an ominous political agenda.[4] Rather than trying to depose a government in a major stroke (*golpe* or *coup*) or a prolonged revolutionary war, as some insurgents have done, gangs and other TCOs more subtly take control of turf one street or neighborhood at a time (*coup d' street*) or one individual, business, or government office at a time. Thus, whether a gang or another TCO is specifically a criminal- or insurgent-type organization is irrelevant. The putative objective of all these illegal entities—the common denominator that directly links gangs, other TCOs, and insurgents—is to control people, territory, and government to ensure their own specific ends. That is a good definition of insurgency: a serious political agenda and a clash of controlling values.[5]

Although these various organizations may differ in terms of motives and modes of operation, each type of nonstate actor must eventually seize political power to guarantee the freedom of action, as well as the desired ideological or commercial enrichment environments. Additionally, the protean nature of the gang phenomenon, organized crime, and contemporary insurgency does not accommodate complete conformity to any prescribed typology. Thus, I maintain the position that I took in 2005—that is, the common denominator that defines gangs and TCOs as mutations of insurgents is the irrevocable need to depose or control an incumbent government. As a consequence, the "duck analogy" applies: when second- and third-generation gangs and other TCOs look like ducks, walk like ducks, and talk like ducks—although they may be a peculiar breed, they are, nevertheless, ducks![6]

The gang phenomenon poses a serious threat in the global security arena. The cases of the gang phenomenon in Central America in general—and in El Salvador and Mexico, specifically—demonstrate how differing types of criminal gang activities contribute to the instabilities that lead to the erosion of nation-state sovereignty and the processes of state failure and also serve as an illustrative example of the struggle between democratic and criminal values. This examination of cases permits certain broad recommendations for countering the threat that gangs pose to global security. All this is designed to lead civilian and military leaders to the broad strategic vision necessary to begin to solve the next big set of gang-related security problems and the associated authoritative allocation of values in the twenty-first century.[7]

CONTEXT: GANGS AS NONSTATE THREATS IN THE GLOBAL SECURITY ARENA

The evolution of street gangs from small, turf-oriented, petty-cash entities to larger, internationalized, commercial-political organizations is often slow and generally ad hoc—depending on leadership and the desire and ability to exploit opportunity. Thus, the development of gang violence from the level of "protection," gangsterism, and brigandage, to drug trafficking, smuggling of people, body parts, armament, and other lucrative "items" associated with global criminal activity, to taking political control of ungoverned territory and/or areas governed by corrupt politicians and functionaries can be uneven and incomplete. That is, most gangs never move beyond protectionism and gangsterism. Other gangs, however, act as mercenaries for larger and better-organized criminal organizations. And as other gangs expand their activities to compete with, or support, long-established TCOs, they expand their geographical and commercial parameters. Then, as gangs operate and evolve, they generate more and more violence and instability over wider and wider sections of the political map and generate subnational, national, and regional instability and insecurity. Finally, as gangs evolve through these developmental and functional shifts, three generations emerge to analytically clarify the gang phenomenon.

Three Generations of Gangs: Organization, Motives, and Level of Violence

First-Generation Gangs

An analysis of urban street gangs shows that some of these criminal entities have evolved through three generations of development. The first-generation—or traditional street gangs—are primarily turf oriented.

They have loose and unsophisticated leadership that focuses on turf protection to gain petty cash and on gang loyalty within their immediate environs (such as designated city blocks or neighborhoods). When first-generation street gangs engage in criminal enterprise, it is largely opportunistic and individual in scope and tends to be localized and operating at the lower end of extreme societal violence—gangsterism and brigandage. Most gangs stay firmly within this first generation of development, but more than a few have evolved into the second generation.[8]

Second-Generation Gangs

This generation of street gangs is organized for business and commercial gain. These gangs have a more centralized leadership that tends to focus on drug trafficking and market protection. At the same time, they operate in a broader spatial or geographic area, which may include neighboring cities and countries. Second-generation gangs, like other, more-sophisticated criminal enterprises, use the level of violence necessary to protect their markets and control their competition. They also use violence as political interference to negate enforcement efforts directed against them by police and other national and local security organizations. And as they seek to control or incapacitate state security institutions, they often begin to dominate vulnerable community life within large areas of the nation-state. In this environment, second-generation gangs almost have to link with and provide services to TCOs. As these gangs develop broader, market-focused, and sometimes overtly political agendas to improve their market share and revenues, they may overtly challenge state security and sovereignty. If and when they do, second-generation gangs become much more than annoying law enforcement problems.[9] This point was made over three years ago in the following statement by former El Salvadoran vice-minister of justice Silvia Aguilar: "Domestic crime and its associated destabilization are now Latin America's most serious security threat."[10]

Third-Generation Gangs

More often than not, some elements of some gangs continue first- and second-generation activities while other elements expand their geographical bounds as well as their commercial and political objectives. As they evolve, they develop into more-seasoned groups with broader drug-related markets and also increase their level of sophistication, with ambitious economic and political agendas. As a result, third-generation gangs inevitably begin to control ungoverned territory within a nation-state and / or begin to acquire political power in poorly governed space.[11] This political action is intended to provide security and freedom of movement for gang activities. As a consequence, the third-generation gang and its leadership challenge the legitimate state monopoly on the exercise of political control (authoritative allocation of values) and the use of violence within a given geographical area. The gang leader, then, acts much like a warlord or a drug baron.[12] That status, clearly and unequivocally, takes the gang into intrastate war or nonstate war. Here, gang objectives include (1) controlling or deposing and replacing an incumbent government; (2) controlling parts of a targeted country or subregions within a country and thereby creating autonomous enclaves, which are sometimes called criminal free-states or parastates; and (3) radically changing (through the preceding objectives) the authoritative allocation of values (governance) in a targeted society to those of criminal leaders.[13]

Orientation and Objectives

First-generation gangs are traditional street gangs with a turf orientation. When they engage in criminal enterprise, it is largely opportunistic and local in scope. Second-generation gangs are engaged in business. They are entrepreneurial and drug centered and tend to pursue implicit political objectives. Third-generation gangs are primarily mercenary in orientation, and many of them have sought to further explicit political and social objectives. As such, third-generation gangs find themselves at the intersection between crime and war—and politics, where there is only one rule: that is, there are no rules (criminal anarchy).[14]

The Challenge and the Threat

A government's failure to extend a legitimate sovereign presence throughout its national territory—Mexico is only one example—leaves a vacuum in which gangs, drug cartels, leftist insurgents, the political and narco-right, and the government itself may all compete for power. In that regard, ample evidence clearly demonstrates that Central American, Caribbean, and South American governments' authority and presence have diminished over large geographical portions of those regions.[15] However, contrary to popular perceptions, such areas are not "lawless" or "ungoverned." These territories are governed by the gangs, insurgents, warlords, and/or drug barons, who operate where there is an absence or only partial presence of state institutions. In this sense, gangs' activities are not simply criminal and commercial in nature. For their own preservation and expansion, the second- and third-generation gangs—and sometimes even first-generation gangs—have little choice but to challenge the state either indirectly or directly. This unconventional type of conflict pits nonstate actors (gangs, warlords, drug barons, and/or insurgents) directly against nation-states and requires a relatively effective "defense" capability.[16]

Tom Bruneau has paraphrased five operational-level national security challenges associated with the transnational gang phenomenon:

1. They strain government capacity by overwhelming police and legal systems through sheer audacity, violence, and numbers.
2. They challenge the legitimacy of the state, particularly in regions where the culture of democracy is challenged by corruption and reinforced by the inability of political systems to function well enough to provide public goods and services.
3. They act as surrogate or alternate governments in so-called ungoverned areas.
4. They dominate the informal economic sector. They establish small businesses and use violence and coercion, as well as co-optation of government authorities, to unfairly compete with legitimate businesses.
5. They infiltrate police and nongovernmental organizations to further their goals and in doing so demonstrate latent political aims.[17]

The gang challenge to national security, stability, and sovereignty in combination with the attempt either to control or to depose governments take us to the strategic-level threat. In this context, remember that crime, violence, and instability are only symptoms of the threat: the ultimate threat is that of either state failure or the violent imposition of a radical socioeconomic-political restructuring of the state and its governance in accordance with criminal values. In either case, gangs contribute to the evolutionary state failure process, which is a process by which the state loses the capacity and / or the will to perform its fundamental governance and security functions. Over time, the weaknesses inherent in its inability to perform the business of the state are likely to lead to the eventual erosion of its authority and legitimacy. In the end, the state cannot control its national territory or the people in it.[18]

But just because a state fails does not mean that it will simply go away. (Haiti comes immediately to mind.) In fact, failing and failed states tend to linger and go from bad to worse. The lack of responsible governance and personal security generate greater poverty, violence, and instability—and a downward spiral in terms of development. It is a zero-sum game in which the gangs, and the other TCOs involved, are the winners and the rest of the society is the loser. Additionally, the longer failing and failed states persist, the more they and their spillover effects endanger regional and global peace and security. Failing and failed states become dysfunctional states, rogue states, criminal states, narco-states, new "people's democratic republics," or draconian states (such as military dictatorships), or they are reconfigured into entirely new entities.[19] But these various possibilities do not delineate the end of the state failure problem. Sooner or later, the global community must pay the indirect social, economic, and political costs of state failure. At the same time, the global community will increasingly be expected to provide the military and financial leverage to ensure peace, security, and stability in an increasing number of postconflict and stability situations. The consistency of these lessons derived from relatively recent experience—from Asia's Golden Triangle to the Middle East, to Mexico, and from Central America to Haiti and the rest of the Caribbean Basin, and to the White Triangle coca-producing countries of South America's Andean region—inspires confidence that these lessons and the associated threat are valid.[20]

THE GANG PHENOMENON IN CENTRAL AMERICA, EL SALVADOR, AND MEXICO

In this global security environment, governments, military and police forces, and other agencies responsible for various aspects of national security have little choice but to rethink security as it applies to "new" unconventional threats that many political and military leaders have tended to ignore or wish away. Probably the most significant unconventional threats facing leaders today are those generated by the gang phenomenon. The case of the Mara Salvatrucha (MS-13) and Eighteenth Street (M-18) gangs spreading from the United States across Central America and Mexico and into Europe illustrates the real impact of second- and third-generation gangs functioning as networks with extensive transnational linkages.[21] Examples of the gang phenomenon in Central America, El Salvador, and Mexico serve to delineate their strategic architecture in a way that can be applied more globally. That architecture focuses on motives and vision, organization and leadership, programs of action, and results.

The Basics of the Situation in Central America

The consensus among those who study this phenomenon is that many transnational gangs in Central America originated in Los Angeles, California, during the early 1990s. They were formed by young immigrants whose parents had come to the United States to avoid the ongoing instability and violence in Central America during the 1980s. Once in the United States, many of the young immigrants were exposed to and became involved with gangs in the rough neighborhoods where they grew up. The gangs began moving into all five Central American republics in the 1990s, primarily because convicted felons were being sent from prisons in the United States back to the countries of their parents' origins. These gangs include the famed Mara Salvatrucha (MS-13), Mara-18, other smaller gangs in El Salvador, and an estimated 63,700 kindred spirits in Guatemala, Honduras, and Nicaragua.[22] It is noteworthy that the word *mara* is a slang term for "gang" and is derived from the name of a type of ant known for its ferocity. Literally, *trucha* means "trout" and is also a slang term for "shrewd Salvadoran." Thus, "Mara Salvatrucha" means "a gang of shrewd Salvadorans." Additionally, Mara-18 is the designation for the Eighteenth Street Gang.

What the Maras Do

Even though gangs in each country have some unique characteristics and can be bitter rivals for control of neighborhoods and other disputed territory, or "turf," their origins, motives, and patterns of action are similar. These similarities begin with the various Central American gangs and their activities being intricately linked across international borders. Virtually all of them have flourished under the protection and mercenary income provided by larger and older TCO networks. The basis for those alliances is the illegal drug trade, which is credited with the transshipment of 60 to 90 percent of the cocaine that enters the United States. In addition to trafficking in drugs, as noted above, Central American gangs are engaged in trafficking in human beings and weapons and are responsible for kidnappings, robberies, extortion, assassinations, and myriad other illicit high-profit-generating activities.[23] On another level of activity, gangs and other TCOs are engaged in intimidating and killing journalists, schoolteachers, and candidates for political office who are not sympathetic to their causes.[24]

The root causes of gang activity in Central American countries and Mexico are similar: gang members growing up in marginal areas with minimal access to basic social services; high levels of youth unemployment, compounded by insufficient access to educational and other public benefits; overwhelmed, ineffective, and often corrupt police and justice systems; easy access to weapons; dysfunctional families; and high levels of intrafamilial and intracommunity violence. Remember, though, that poverty, injustice, and misery are not what willfully kill, maim, and destroy; individual men and women (and, sometimes, boys and girls) choose to implement all kinds of horrible and coercive "intimidations" and "instabilities" in their personal search for status and well-being.[25]

Thanks to the activities of disaffected youth gangs, overall crime rates have increased dramatically throughout the Central American region. Honduras has a murder rate of 154 per 100,000 population—double that of Colombia, even though that country is fighting three different insurgencies as well as its various drug cartels. In El Salvador, the homicide rate is about 40 per 100,000 inhabitants; Guatemala's murder rate rose 40 percent from 2001 to 2004 and is now approximately 50 per 100,000. The murder rate in Mexico is estimated to be about 14 per 100,000. The Mexican figure is low by Central American standards but is considered "epidemic" by the World Health Organization (WHO). Additionally, as if these statistics were not grim enough, Mexico has the highest incidence of kidnapping in the entire world—with an estimated 3,000 kidnappings in 2004.[26]

THE GENERAL RESULTS OF GANG ACTIVITY IN CENTRAL AMERICA

The impact of gang violence on regional economies is significant. The Inter-American Development Bank (IDB) estimates the cost of violence throughout all of Latin America to be 14.2 percent of gross domestic product (GDP).[27] Despite the fact that the data required to calculate these costs are admittedly vague and inconsistent, the governments of all five Central American countries and Mexico have expressed serious concerns. For example, Belize, Guatemala, and Mexico have signed a multilateral agreement committing their governments to combating narco-terrorism and criminal gangs.[28] In the meantime, El Salvador and Honduras unilaterally continue to pursue hardline antigang policies that include stronger law enforcement efforts and longer prison sentences.

Clearly, Central American gangs, their activities, and the impacts of these activities are linked across borders. An instability threat is definitely spilling out of the region into neighboring countries. Although this is a regional problem that requires regional solutions, analytical clarity is best served through a single example, a brief examination of the two major gangs in El Salvador.

The Basics of the Situation in El Salvador

As noted above, the roots of the maras' presence in El Salvador can be traced to Southern California in the 1980s and 1990s. In the aftermath of the 1992 Los Angeles riots, police determined that local gangs—including a little-known group of Salvadoran immigrant youths known as the Mara Salvatrucha—had carried out most of the looting and violence. In response, California passed strict antigang laws. Then, with the subsequent "three strikes and you're out" legislation of 1994, the prison population in that state increased dramatically. Additionally, in 1996, the U.S.

Congress passed a "get tough" approach to immigration law. As a result of these successive pieces of legislation, thousands of convicted felons have been deported to El Salvador over the past several years. Significantly, until very recently, the Immigration and Naturalization Service's rules prohibited U.S. officials from informing El Salvadoran officials of the deportees' backgrounds.[29]

The results were disastrous for El Salvador. The deportees (also called "returnees"), many of whom had never lived in El Salvador, arrived with their outlandish tattoos, their "Spanglish" language, and their arrogant attitudes. They quickly introduced the California gang culture, illegal drugs with the related "crack dens" and "crack babies," extortions, car-theft rings, burglaries, and contract killings. At first, Salvadoran officials had no idea what was happening—and when they began to understand the depth and seriousness of the problems brought by the gangs, they did not have the knowledge, experience, organization, or resources to deal with them. Given its momentum, the gang problem in El Salvador is thought to have escalated faster than in any other Central American country, and that country now "is captive to the growing influence and violence of gangs."[30]

Organization

The two main gangs, MS-13 and MS-18, boast 10,000 to 20,000 members. The Salvadoran National Council on Public Security calculates 39,000 members: 22,000 in MS-13, 12,000 in MS-18, and another 5,000 in other gangs.[31] However, regardless of the lack of precise figures, both of those estimates are foreboding numbers in a country with a population of only 6.5 million. Like the estimated membership numbers, gang organization is not perfectly clear. Nevertheless, there appears to be a hierarchical pyramid structure that is common among Central American, Caribbean, and South American gangs.

At the top of the pyramid are the international bosses. Then, a second layer of international/transnational gang leadership exists. These second-level individuals oversee well-connected cells that are engaged primarily in trafficking global arms, drugs, and human beings. At the third level, gang cell members are involved in lower-level national versus international trafficking of all kinds. Despite their national orientation, third-level members are in touch with upper-level as well as second-level members. This third level of gang membership contains centralized command-and-control elements that manage operational planning, finances, and strategy and provide some administrative support to the higher and lower echelons. Thus, they may be considered parts of a "hollow corporate model." Additionally, national third-level gang cell members may manage geographically distributed "project teams."[32]

The fourth level of the generalized gang pyramid comprises the "neighborhood" gang members. This is a series of decentralized cliques (*clickas*), or cells, that are responsible for specific neighborhoods or areas. Fourth-level individuals are not full-fledged MS-13 or MS-18 members. They make up three distinct levels at the lowest level of the gang pyramid—"sympathizers," "aspirants," and "nobodies," who do the drudge work in the *barrios* (neighborhoods / slums). They also act as mercenary "soldiers" for higher-level cells and project teams, or they may act as contracted mercenaries for other TCOs. As might be expected, this fourth-level group represents the largest segment of the total gang population; the ages of gang members at this level range from 8 to 18.[33]

Program of Action to Maximize Profits

The gangs' multilevel organization indicates a substantial enterprise, designed especially for conducting large-scale and small-scale business all the way from the transnational (global) level down to specific streets in specific barrios (neighborhoods). This type of organization is also designed for quick and effective decision making and implementation of decisions. In short, the first priority of the Salvadoran MS-13 and MS-18 gang organizations is operating a successful business, along with its promotion and protection. More specifically, this type of organization permits continuous, protean operations over time. It allows for diversification of activities, diffusion of risk, and flexibility, so that quick adjustments to correct mistakes or to exploit developing opportunities may be made. The organization also provides a coherent mechanism for enforcing discipline and safeguarding operations at all levels. Additionally, it provides a planning facility that can deliberately expand or contract drug, mercenary, and other illicit operations—and increase profits—as a situation might require.[34]

Regarding expansion of operations, the Salvadoran gangs are positioned to negotiate the establishment of their own trafficking corridors through Central America and Mexico. They are positioned to organize friendly or unfriendly takeovers of small cartels. They have also become sophisticated enough to begin to prohibit members from getting new tattoos and to severely discipline (execute) members who break rules related to the consumption of crack and cocaine. All of this indicates an evolution from first-generation well into second-generation gang status. Nevertheless, the current organization of MS-13 and MS-18 also reflects that these gangs maintain a first-generation focus on turf. The gang members at that level of evolutionary development operate under loose leadership; engage in a broad range of opportunistic, petty cash–type criminal activity; and are often involved in serious intergang rivalry.[35]

The second-generation part of the MS-13 and MS-18 organizations is interested in market protection and expansion and focuses its illegal activities on drugs as a business. Gang members at this level are also known to engage in mercenary activities with TCO partners. As the generalized pyramid organization suggests, the upper echelons are more cohesive, and leadership is more centralized. This second-generation group does not retain a specific turf orientation. Drug trafficking and mercenary activities become group rather than individual activities, and the gangs exploit both violence and technology to control their competition and absorb new markets. Thus, both generations of gang members currently exist within the overall organization. The turf part of the gang is more prevalent, but the "marketers" are more productive, wealthy, and powerful.[36] As MS-13 and MS-18 continue to evolve in their internationalization and sophistication, they are more and more likely to develop explicit political aims that truly threaten nation-states. This cautionary corollary takes us to the "Sullivan-Bunker Cocktail."

Results of Salvadoran Gang Activities

John Sullivan and Robert Bunker outline a pragmatic "cocktail mix" of nonmilitary methods by which a transnational nonstate actor, such as a second-generation gang, can challenge the de jure security and sovereignty of a given nation. This "Sullivan-Bunker Cocktail" has proved to be the case in no less than fifteen municipalities in El Salvador and in other political jurisdictions in neighboring Central American republics, Mexico, and Brazil.[37] Here is how it works:

> If the irregular attacker—criminal gangs, terrorists, insurgents, drug cartels, militant environmentalists, or a combination of the above—blends crime, terrorism, and war, he can extend his already significant influence. After embracing advanced technology weaponry, including weapons of mass destruction (including chemical and biological agents), radio frequency weapons, and advanced intelligence gathering technology, along with more common weapons systems, the attacker can transcend drug running, robbery, kidnapping, and murder and pose a significant challenge to the nation-state and its institutions.
>
> Then, using complicity, intimidation, corruption, and indifference, the irregular attacker can quietly and subtly co-opt individual politicians and bureaucrats and gain political control of a given geographical or political enclave. Such corruption and distortion can potentially lead to the emergence of a network of government protection of illicit activities, and the emergence of a virtual criminal state or political entity. A series of networked enclaves could, then, become a dominant political actor within a state or group of states. Thus, rather than violently competing directly with a nation-state, an irregular attacker can criminally co-opt and begin to seize control of the state indirectly.[38]

This cocktail is an example of a second-generation gang developing secure support bases through the application of coercive physical-psychological-political measures. In creating those secure support bases, gangs dominate local populations and erode the will of the system to resist their commercial enrichment efforts. This kind of mix of nontraditional activities is also a good example of the gang phenomenon expanding its role while staying under the threshold of serious state concern and counteraction. Even though there may be no explicit political agenda, control of territory (turf) and the people in it are keys to the achievement of minimal goals. In these terms, gangs must eventually take or control political power to guarantee the kind of environment they want.

As a consequence, the gang nonstate actor evolves from second-generation toward third-generation status and represents a triple threat to the authority and sovereignty of a government and those of its neighbors. First, murder, kidnapping, intimidation, corruption, and impunity from punishment undermine the ability of the state to perform its legitimizing security and public service functions. Second, by violently imposing their power over bureaucrats and elected officials of the state, gangs and their allies compromise the exercise of state authority and replace it with their own. Third, by taking control of portions of a given national territory and performing the tasks of government, the gang phenomenon can de facto transform itself into states-within-a-state.[39] Accordingly, these parastates or criminal free-states "fuel a bazaar of violence where warlords and martial entrepreneurs fuel the convergence of crime and war."[40] And the criminal leaders govern these areas as they wish.

Response to the Gangs

In 2003, El Salvador's Flores administration passed a hardline (*mano dura*) law aimed at making it easier to jail gang members involved in criminal activity. However, that legislation was not considered to be strong enough. As a result, in 2004, new legislation was passed approving the new president's antigang program, called Super Mano Dura ("super firm hand" or "super hard line"). This law provided stiffer penalties for gang membership—up to five years in jail for gang membership and up to nine years for gang leadership. President Saco's government reported that this "get tough" program reduced the number of murders that year by 14 percent. The following year, in 2005, new legislation tightened gun ownership laws and began a complementary effort of prevention and rehabilitation called Mano Amiga ("friendly hand").[41]

The hardline approach sent the message to the Salvadoran public that law enforcement is the only effective way to deal with the gang problem; thus, prevention and intervention programs have received much less attention and fewer resources than would be necessary to make them effective. Unanticipated second- and third-order consequences resulted in straining the capacities of the already overcrowded prison system. Moreover, the judicial and police systems became saturated; there were not enough properly trained personnel in those systems to manage the gang problem. At the end of 2005, 12,073 prisoners were held in twenty-four prison facilities with a combined design capacity of only 7,312. Unfortunately, the gang problem has worsened significantly, and the only things that Salvadoran leaders agree on are that prison provides a "graduate education" for gang members and that "something must be done."[42] In sum, neither the Salvadoran government nor the United States has officially raised the level of the gang threat to the level of a threat to national security.[43] Granted, since 2005, Salvadoran army troops have been deployed from time to time, to help the police patrol the streets.[44] Nevertheless, the Maras are still treated as merely a problem for law enforcement and the judicial system. In the meantime, the Maras have come to control larger and larger parts of "turf" within the El Salvadoran national territory and effectively exercise their own sovereignty over the people in it. The Central American Maras have also evolved into an international network that extends from El Salvador through Central America to Mexico, the United States, and Europe.[45]

The Basics of the Situation in Mexico

Authorities have no consistent or reliable data on the gang-TCO phenomenon in Mexico.[46] Nevertheless, the gang phenomenon in that country is acknowledged to be large and complex. In addition, the gang situation is known to be different in the north (along the U.S. border) than it is in the south (along the Guatemala-Belize borders). Second, the phenomenon is different in the areas between the northern and southern borders of Mexico. Third, it is known that, regardless of the accuracy of the data, there is a formidable gang presence throughout the country and—given the weaknesses of national institutions—considerable opportunity for criminality to prosper.[47] As a result, the rate of homicides along the northern and southern borders is considered epidemic, and Mexico has the highest incidence of kidnapping in the world. Finally, violent gang and TCO activity in Mexico clearly threatens the economic and political development of the country.[48]

More specifically, the Central American Maras have made significant inroads into Mexican territory and appear to be competing effectively with Mexican gangs. In the south—along the Belize-Guatemalan borders—MS-13 and MS-18 have gained control of illegal immigrant and drug trafficking moving north through Mexico to the United States. The Central American Maras are also known to be used effectively by the northern drug cartels as mercenaries. Between the northern and southern borders, there is reportedly an ad hoc mix of up to 15,000 members of Mexican gangs and Central American Maras operating in more than twenty states.[49]

The gangs operating on the northern border of Mexico are long-time, well-established, "generational" (Mexican grandfathers, sons, and grandsons) organizations with forty–fifty-year histories. There are, reportedly, 24 different gangs operating in the city of Nuevo Laredo and 320 active gangs operating within the city of Juárez—with 17,000 members. The best-known gangs in the north are the Azteca, Mexicles, and Zeta organizations, whose members tend to work as hired guns and drug runners for the Juárez and Gulf cartels. In addition to the Juárez and Gulf cartels, there are the Sinaloa and Tijuana cartels; then there is the "Mexican Federation," which is a questionable alliance of the "Big Four" (Gulf and Tijuana plus Sinaloa and Juárez) cartels. The federation is reportedly trying to negotiate an agreement (truce) regarding access to the lucrative transit routes that carry an estimated 90 percent of all cocaine consumed in the United States and also access to the newly developing domestic Mexican market. In the meantime, the various cartels and their gang allies are fighting each other over territory ("turf") in cyberspace.[50] To further complicate matters, there is the Mexican Mafia (EME). At one time, all gangs operating south of Bakersfield, California, and into northern Mexico had to pay homage to and take orders from EME. That is no longer a rigid requirement, however; MS-13 and MS-18 are known to have broken that agreement as early as 2005.[51]

This convoluted array of Mexican gangs—Central American Maras, Mexican cartels, and the EME—leaves an almost anarchical situation throughout all of the country. As each gang and TCO violently competes with the others and positions itself to maximize market share and freedom of movement and action, we see an operational environment characterized by the blurring of crime and war. In addition to generating outrageous violence and bloodshed, this environment is also creating small and large criminal free-enclaves in the cities and states of the Mexican nation-state. Moreover, the spillover transcends the sovereign borders of Mexico and its neighbors. This situation reminds one of the feudal medieval era. Violence and the fruits of violence—arbitrary political control—seem to be devolving to small, private nonstate actors. This is a serious challenge to existing law and order in Mexico and to the effective sovereignty of the other nation-states within and between which the TCOs move.[52]

Organization and Motives

Mexican gangs and other TCOs are not homogeneous. There is no typology that is applicable to every one. Power is migrating to small gangs and TCO nonstate actors who can organize into sprawling networks more readily than the traditionally hierarchical nation-state actors can accomplish. The loosely organized violent criminal entities operating in Mexico are among those evolving from the generalized pyramid structure into a flat internetted transnational organization.

In this context, gangs and their TCO allies in Mexico—as in other countries—are organizing in virtually the same way as any multinational Fortune 500 company. Thus, the phenomenon is a business organization striving to make money, expand its markets, and move as freely as possible in the political jurisdictions within and between which they work. The general organization employs its chief executive officers and boards of directors, council, system of internal justice, public affairs officers, negotiators, and franchised project managers to perform the requisite business tasks with superefficiency and thereby to maximize profit. And, of course, this company has a security division—somewhat more ruthless than those of a bona fide Fortune 500 corporation![53]

The equation that links illegal narcotics trafficking to insurgency and to gangs in Mexico—and elsewhere in the Western Hemisphere—turns on a combination of need, organizational infrastructure development, ability, and the availability of sophisticated communications and weaponry. For example, the drug cartels possess cash and lines of transportation and communication. Gangs, insurgents, and paramilitary organizations have followers, organization, discipline, and arms. Illegal drug traffickers consistently need these kinds of people to help protect their assets and project their power within and among nation-states. Gangs, insurgents and paramilitaries are in constant need of logistical and communications support—and money.[54]

The annual net profit from gang-TCO-related activities in Mexico is estimated to be in the billions of dollars, although the precise numbers are not what is important: the enormity of the amount of money involved *is* important. Together with the additional benefits these financial resources can generate—when linked to utter ruthlessness of purpose and unconstrained by moral or legal concerns—a second- or third-generation gang can afford the best talent, whether lawyers, accountants, and computer specialists, or extortionists, murderers, and mercenary soldiers. At the same time, a gang can bribe government officials, hire thugs to intimidate (Mexico's high rate of kidnapping immediately comes to mind) those who cannot be bought, and kill those who cannot be intimidated. The profitable gang can also afford the best military and transportation equipment and communications technologies. And, of course, many gangs have larger budgets than do the nation-states within which they operate.[55] Deep pockets and flat organizational structure also mean that gangs and TCOs can move, shift, diversify, and promote operations at will. Consequently, with these advantages, the gangs can establish status, acceptance, credibility, and de facto legitimacy in parastates (criminal free-states) within the Mexican nation-state.[56]

Where the Gang Phenomenon's Pursuit of Wealth Leads

Threats from the gangs and other TCOs at work in Mexico come in many destabilizing forms and in a matrix of different kinds of challenges, varying in scope and scale. If they have a single feature in common, it is that they are systemic and well-calculated attempts to achieve implicit political ends, that is, to create political space from which to move and act without governmental or any other kind of hindrance. This requires the erosion of Mexican democracy and of the nation-state itself, as exemplified by two emerging criminal free-states: Quintana Roo on the southern border with Belize and Guatemala, and Sinaloa in the north.

The Erosion of Mexican Democracy. The policy-oriented definition of democracy that has been generally accepted and used in U.S. foreign policy over the past several years is best described as "procedural democracy." This definition tends to focus on the election of civilian political leadership and, perhaps, on a relatively high level of participation on the part of the electorate. Thus, as long as a country is able to hold elections, it is considered a democracy—regardless of the level of accountability, transparency, corruption, and ability to extract and distribute resources for national development and the protection of human rights, liberties, and security.[57]

In Mexico, we observe important paradoxes in this concept of democracy. Elections are held on a regular basis, but leaders, candidates, and elected politicians are regularly assassinated; hundreds of government officials considered unacceptable by the gang-TCO phenomenon have been assassinated following their election. Additionally, intimidation, direct threats, kidnapping, and the use of relatively minor violence on a person and/or his family play an important role *prior* to elections. As a corollary, although the media is free from state censorship, journalists and academicians who make their anti-narco-gang opinions known too publicly are systematically assassinated.[58]

Consequently, is hard to credit most Mexican and Central American elections as genuinely "democratic" or "free." Neither political party competition nor public participation in elections can be complete in an environment where armed and unscrupulous nonstate actors compete violently with legitimate political entities to control the government both before and after elections. Moreover, it is hard to credit Mexico as a democratic state as long as elected leaders are subject to corrupting control and intimidation or to informal vetoes imposed by unprincipled nonstate actors. As a consequence, Ambassador David Jordan argues that Mexico is an "anocratic" democracy. That is, Mexico is a state that has the procedural features of democracy but retains the characteristics of an autocracy, in which the ruling elites (good or bad) face little or no scrutiny or accountability. Regardless of definitions, the persuasive and intimidating actions of the gang-TCO phenomenon in the electoral processes have pernicious effects on democracy and tend to erode the will and ability of the state to carry out its legitimizing functions.[59]

The Erosion of the State. The Mexican state has undergone severe erosion on two general levels. First, the state's presence and authority is questionable over large geographical portions of the country. Second, the idea of the partial collapse of the state is closely related to the nonphysical erosion of democracy. Jordan argues that corruption is key in this regard and is a prime mover toward "narco-socialism."[60] In the first instance, the notion of partial collapse (erosion) refers to the fact that since the elections in 2000 and the political defeat of the previously all-powerful PRI (Institutional Revolutionary Party), there is now an absence or only partial presence of state institutions in many of the rural areas and poorer urban parts of the country. Also, even in those areas that are not under the direct control of a gang-TCO alliance, institutions responsible for protecting citizens' security—notably, the police and judiciary—have been intimidated and coerced to the point where they are unable to carry out their basic functions. Indicators of this problem can be seen in two statistics. The first is the murder rate, which is among the highest in the world along the northern and southern borders of Mexico—coupled with the grisly and consistent murder and decapitation of police in those areas.[61] Not surprisingly, there are never any witnesses to these atrocities.[62] These indicators of impunity strongly confirm that the state is not adequately exercising its social-contractual and constitutional-legal obligations to provide individual and collective security within the national territory.

The second statistic centers on the widespread, deeply entrenched, and pervasive issue of corruption, a form of nonphysical erosion of the state. As one example, Jordan cites an interview given by an advisor to Mexico's attorney general under the Salinas administration. This advisor also served as president of Mexico's Association of Journalists and was a member of the executive committee of Mexico's Socialist Party. He stated, "The narcotics traffickers have penetrated not only the federal government, but the state governments and municipalities." In another interview, President Salinas's former secretary of finance stated, "[The narco-gang phenomenon] has penetrated the legislative, executive and judicial power of the country. . . . [It is] the most powerful economic organization in the world today, the world's most important multinational organization. . . . [The narcos have penetrated] all of the structures of power of Mexico, to the point that, without any euphemisms, the country does what the narco-traffickers want."[63] Clearly, the reality of corruption at any level of government favoring the gangs and / or the drug cartels mitigates against responsible governance and the public well-being. In these terms, the reality of the high rate of corruption brings into question the reality of effective state sovereignty.

Thus, even though Mexico and its ally the United States have recently agreed on a $700 million antinarcotics assistance package,[64] Mexico's violent nonstate actors remain relatively strong and very wealthy.[65] At the same time, positive political sovereignty, democracy, socioeconomic development, territory, infrastructure, stability, and security are quietly and slowly being destroyed.

The Emergence of Criminal Free-States in Quintana Roo and Sinaloa. The intent of the gang-TCO alliances in these states appears to be removing the cartels and gangs from the constraints of Mexican state authority—and replacing that authority with their own. Rather than competing with the state for political-economic dominance, the gang-TCO alliance resorts to corruption and co-optation to achieve the desired objective. As a result, Quintana Roo and Sinaloa have been viewed for a long time as "hotbeds of co-opted government and corruption" and are said to "have become narco-states."[66] Networks of government protection support those states' gangs and drug cartels; as one example, police protect drug shipments and other illicit commerce (humans) moving north to the U.S. market. Within this corrupt environment, there is increased violence between co-opted factions of the police, enhanced employment of mercenaries, devaluation of currency, and increased migration.[67]

This environment, which affects everyone and everything within these criminal free-states, has been described as feudal or medieval. Local gangs and TCOs maintain their own self-determined system of law and order, "tax" residents and businesses, enjoy complete immunity from their illicit actions, and have a safe haven from which to operate. Such a world has been known to see its values derived from norms based on slave holding, sexual activity with minors and their exploitation in prostitution, the "farming" of humans for body parts, and the killing and torture of innocents for political gain and personal gratification (as sport). Concepts such as due process of law, right to jury trial, individual privacy, and human and women's rights do not exist.[68] It is a feudal environment defined by patronage, bribes, kickbacks, cronyism, ethnic exclusion, and personal whim.

Implications of Adaptation to Criminal Forms of Behavior

The gang-TCO phenomenon is more than a law enforcement problem. And when gangs and TCOs become de facto government, it is more than a national security problem. As they become more and more deeply involved in politics, real estate, and religious and community organizations, gangs and their allies become social actors. These social actors, who are also criminal-soldiers, are changing social, economic, and political organization and violently "barbarizing" accepted values and modes of human behavior. A future vision of larger and larger parts of the global community adapting to criminal forms of behavior would be—at the least—"unsettling."[69] In the meantime, the present vision of the human capacity to treat the gunshots and terrified screams from down the street as mere background noise to unexceptional everyday life should create something more than a vague unease. This is effectively a clash of civilizations' values.

In the Western Hemisphere's "new wars," commercial enrichment appears to remain the primary motivation for the various destabilizing gangs and their criminal allies. The gangs are not yet *directly* challenging governments for control of the state, nor are they sending conventional military forces across national borders. As a consequence, most political leaders are still thinking in traditional terms and have not caught up with reality. They do not appreciate the extent and nature of the threat to political order and responsible democratic governance being raised by the slow-moving clash of two types of values: one serving cruel criminal greed; the other seeking the general well-being of the people.[70]

THE PROCESS OF STATE FAILURE

Solutions to the problems of stability, security, and illegitimate sovereign governance take us back to the threat of state failure. State failure is a process—not an outcome. It is a process by which the state loses the capacity and / or the will to perform legitimizing security and governance functions. It may also be a process by which the state responds to the fact that it had never developed those capabilities in the first place. In any event, there is ample evidence to show that gangs and other TCOs develop out of, and prosper in, "ungoverned" or poorly governed areas, and it follows that gangs and postmodern war are the products of the state failure processes.[71] Thus, the ultimate threat of destabilizing gang activities is not instability or even criminal violence. Instead, it is either state failure or the coerced imposition of a radical socioeconomic-political restructuring of the state and the style, method, or means of state governance. In either case, failed states do not simply go away.[72] Sooner rather than later, the global community will have to deal with the problem—and pay. Neighbor nations and international organizations will pay in terms of their own quality of governance, security, and stability, as well as blood and treasure.

KEY POINTS AND LESSONS

- Gangs and other TCOs contribute significantly to national, regional, and global instability. As they evolve, they generate more and more terror, violence, and instability over wider and wider sections of the political map.
- Gangs, with their TCO allies, are far from being apolitical and unique. They are becoming more and more similar to their politicized insurgent and warlord cousins. They maintain a practical logic that is a continuation of regional politics by other means.

- Gangs and other TCOs use highly sophisticated political-psychological (as well as purely violent) ways and means to achieve their objectives.
- These objectives are primarily freedom of movement and action within and across national boundaries. The unintended or intended results impinge on the effective sovereignty and security, as well as the liberal democratic values, of countries and peoples.
- The primary motives of gangs and other TCOs center on group survival and personal gain. Beyond this, there are no rules.
- To dismiss the above realities as too difficult or impossible to deal with is to accept the inevitability of unattractive alternatives.

Sun Tzu reminds us that we do not need an abundance of warfighters, specialized equipment, and financial resources to deal effectively with an enemy such as the protean gang phenomenon. "What is of supreme importance in war is to attack the enemy's strategy . . . and his plans. . . . Next best is to disrupt his alliances."[73] This kind of effort does not require several pages of "actionable" and "measurable" tactical-operational recommendations, or more equipment and training, or more money for the salaries of "civil servants"—although all that would be helpful. Sun Tzu's winning strategic-level recommendations, more than anything else, require the application of "brain power." The alternative is to see Mexico and Central America further engulfed in a chaos of crime, corruption, and lack of legitimacy.

CHAPTER 5

An Unorthodox Military Movement into and out of Power

Preventive Insurgency and Democratic Transition in Portugal, 1974 and Beyond

The story of the 1974 collapse of Antonio de Oliveira Salazar's forty-four-year civilian dictatorial regime in Portugal begins with disaffected military officers who were fighting the colonial insurgency wars in Angola, Mozambique, and Guinea-Bissau in the 1960s and early 1970s. A former Portuguese commander in Guinea, General Antonio de Spinola, and some fellow officers staged a coup d'etat that would take down the regime that Salazar established after 1930. Then, in the first free elections in half a century, these officers allowed the Portuguese people to be the judges of their insurrectionary action and to set the political direction for a new government. To be sure, the role of the military in Portuguese Africa is an interesting prologue to the narrative of Salazar's downfall, but that is only of peripheral relevance. The real story was within the entire officer corps, the prevention of a countercoup, and the Portuguese transformation from a failing state in Western Europe to a market democracy within the global community.[1]

Thus, this chapter combines three stories in one. First, it is the story of the 1974 coup that deposed the dictatorship. Then, there is the story of the subsequent subnational civil-military-political struggle that was, in fact, a preventive insurgency against the Portuguese Communist Party's (PCP) attempt to take political control of the Portuguese state. Finally, this chapter outlines the process of Portugal's transition from a failing state to a model for postconflict transition. These are the stories that make up the larger story of the Revolution of 1974. What makes this story salient beyond its political-military context is that noted scholar Kenneth Maxwell and others recognize the Portuguese Revolution of 1974 as "a precocious forerunner of the largely peaceful transitions from authoritarianism to democracy in Spain in 1975, and then in the late 1980s in Latin America and Eastern Europe."[2]

CONTEXT

The current international security dialogue goes beyond traditional national policy objectives of defending against probable military threats from other nation-states, as it comes to focus on relative national and global well-being. Increasingly, national security implies protection—through a variety of military and nonmilitary means—of more-ambiguous political, economic, social, and ideological interests.[3] Additionally, the contemporary security dialogue stresses that threats to the national and global well-being are generated by a lack of security and development and by the resultant poverty, violence, and instability.[4] The primary implication of this broadened concept of security is that modern conflicts are far more likely to be internal civil-military matters than to be clashes between opposing countries. Internal discord and turbulence are likely to arise in countries suffering from poverty, a highly unequal income distribution, recent decolonization, and ineffective or repressive police forces and governments. These are the conditions that encourage nonstate actors such as terrorists, insurgents, narcotraffickers and other organized criminals, warlords, gangs, and radicals/neopopulists to attempt to either control or radically change a given government.[5] Thus, to better understand contemporary conflict, one must understand some fundamentals of subnational (intranational) conflict.

The Theoretical Context

In its broadest terms, subnational conflict involves the ways in which governments and nonstate political actors—functioning within and across national borders—interact and affect the defense of the security of states and their citizens.[6] This level of analysis involves the personal security and well-being of the individual citizen. It then extends to protection of the entire population from violent internal nonstate actors and external enemies. In some situations, such as the Portuguese case from 1974 to 1976, it involves the protection of the collectivity against repressive, misguided, insensitive, corrupt, and/or dictatorial regimes. The security problem ends with the establishment of perceived firm but fair control over the entire national territory and the people in it.

More specifically, the security problem within a nation-state requires a basic understanding of what is now interchangeably being called fourth-generation conflict, asymmetric conflict, postmodern war, irregular war, terror war, partial war, or a "war of all the people." Whatever it is called, contemporary intranational conflict is the product of weak or collapsing nation-states and the emergence of new organizing principles. The primary organizing principle is that of asymmetry—or the use of disparity between the contending parties to gain advantage. Strategic asymmetry has been defined as "acting, organizing, and thinking differently than opponents in order to maximize one's own advantages, exploit an opponent's weaknesses, attain the initiative, or gain greater freedom of action. It can have both psychological and physical dimensions."[7]

Thus, what is required more than manpower, weaponry, and technology are lucid and incisive thinking, resourcefulness, determination, imagination, and a certain disregard for convention. This kind of conflict thus is based on perceptions, beliefs, expectations, legitimacy, and the political will to challenge a strong opponent. In short, this kind of conflict is based primarily on words, images, and ideas.[8] It will not be won by seizing specific territory militarily or destroying specific buildings, cities, or industrial capability. Fourth-generation war is won by altering the political-psychological factors that are most relevant in a targeted culture.

The Portuguese officers and men who planned and implemented the Revolution of 1974 understood insurgency war within the framework of fourth-generation war. As a result of their experiences in Africa, they understood the importance of Clausewitz's warning that in internal war, the centers of gravity are not the enemy's military force or the enemy's ability to prepare for and conduct a conventional state-versus-state conflict.

Rather, in intrastate war, the centers of gravity are the personalities of the leaders and public opinion.[9] Thus, a "new" set of lessons—some with what might be considered politically incorrect implications—arise from the analysis of the effectiveness of shifting the center of gravity. The Portuguese experience demonstrated that a nation's armed forces can conduct preemptive or preventive insurgency, as well as counterinsurgency. At the same time, it might be the forerunner of new solutions to much of the intranational political turbulence emerging out of the growing neopopulist disillusionment with the generally poor performance of "democratically elected" governments.

First and foremost, this case emphasizes the implications that an incumbent government may itself create a serious threat to the stability, security, and well-being of the state. The inability or unwillingness—for any reason—of a regime to provide basic personal and collective security and perform its governance functions responsibly must be considered a first-priority threat. The well-known U.S. diplomats Stephen Krasner and Carlos Pascual warn us, "Left in dire straits, subject to depredation, and denied access to basic services, people become susceptible to the exhortations of demagogues and hate-mongers" and radical populists.[10] The question that then arises is What is to be done? Will this be allowed to reach crisis proportions, or should it be dealt with earlier in a preemptory or preventive manner? Most leaders in the world today are reluctant to talk publicly about preemption or prevention. Nevertheless, the general rule would be that decision makers and policy makers must carefully calculate the costs and benefits, prioritize, and when the situation warrants, act earlier rather than later. If a required action is taken sooner rather than later, this implies the initial and intense use of much-less-disruptive and less destructive nonlethal "soft power." If taken later, action in this kind of situation normally requires the initial and intensive use of "hard" military power to respond to a losing situation. Ultimately, however, the only viable test for preventative or preemptive actions is whether there is a clear and present danger to the nation and its well-being.

John Locke reminds us that, in addition to the clear danger of being attacked by a foreign power, "[t]here is one way more whereby a government may be dissolved, and that is, when he who has the supreme executive power neglects and abandons that charge [to provide governance and concomitant security] so that the laws already made can no longer be put in execution. This is demonstratively to reduce all to anarchy, and so effectually to dissolve the government."[11] As a consequence, it is incumbent on the international community and national friends and allies to help channel preemptive or preventative actions in positive and democratic directions. Portugal, then, is not merely an example of a successful revolution that took down a long-term dictator. Nor is Portugal merely an example of how to deal with internal instabilities and turbulence perpetrated by militant nonstate actors. Instead, Portugal is an example of successfully managing the state-failure process and providing a viable democratic model of postconflict transition. That country was three times fortunate.

Additionally, this case stresses that insurgencies may be aggressive nonstate-actor generated, counterinsurgency state organized and implemented, or preemptive state or institution generated; the extremely political-psychological-social nature of insurgencies; the importance of public opinion and leadership as controlling centers of gravity, to be attacked *and* defended; the need for careful planning and implementation of a long-term ends, ways, and means strategy to ensure the desired outcome; and the important role of transnational (external) actors.

Political-Historical Background

After World War I, Portugal suffered the worst inflation in its modern history.[12] That economic calamity was matched by the political turmoil brought on by sixteen years in which there were no fewer than forty-five governments. Moreover, in that same period from 1910 to 1926, only one president of the republic served out his full term of office.[13] With no apparent end of the chaos in sight, the Portuguese armed forces intervened and formed a "military government." That new government appointed a professor of economics, Antonio Salazar, as minister of finance. Subsequently, Salazar took over the Ministries of Interior and Colonies, became prime minister in 1932, and, in 1936, assumed the portfolios of foreign affairs and war. The "Salazar regime" was exactly that.[14]

Salazar was an old-school conservative mercantilist, a corporatist, a populist, and a strongly Roman Catholic clericalist. Moreover, he was obsessed with balancing the budget and did not spend money on investments, infrastructure, or imports. He believed that piety and hard work were good for the soul and that "excess income" and material things would only corrupt the individual.[15] Any one of these regime characteristics would probably have been enough to cause ample socioeconomic and political problems, but all together and over time, Portugal was locked into poverty and lack of development, largely dependent on the export or re-export of cheap primary commodities from the African and other colonies.[16] Most of the population worked on small family farms in the north of the country, on large privately owned landholdings (*latifundios*) in the south, or as "guest workers" in Europe. The general standard of living in Antonio Salazar's Portugal was, therefore, more characteristic of Africa than Europe. Per capita annual income in 1960 was only $160. Over the years, these socioeconomic problems fermented to the point where the regime had to rely more and more on the "secret" political police to protect it from its detractors.[17]

External Interests

But domestic politics are not determined by internal factors alone. External interests can play important roles as well. This is as important in understanding Portugal's political-historical context as is anything else. Portugal includes two sets of islands—Madeira and the Azores—plus the mainland. That space in the eastern Atlantic Ocean constitutes a strategic triangle of over 150,000 square miles. This huge area is crossed by air and sea lines of communication connecting Europe to much of the rest of the world. Over 60 percent of the raw materials, hydrocarbons, other strategic minerals, and finished products essential to Western economies—and security—pass through this strategic triangle every day.[18] Accordingly, since the 1873 alliance with Great Britain and through Portugal's present participation in the North Atlantic Treaty Organization (NATO) and in the European Community (EC), Europe and the United States have valued that country's full and unwavering commitment of facilities and other resources to Western security. Thus, despite internal turbulence and instabilities—or too much imposed stability, for too long—one should not have been surprised when European and other Western interests came to play a significant role in the Portuguese Revolution of 1974.[19]

THE INTERNAL PROTAGONISTS

Portugal's internal conflict situation between 1974 and 1976 was shaped by a complex mix of protagonists—each with a specific motive and programs to take control of or radically change the state. The main players who produced the 1974 Revolution included the officer corps of the armed forces, the "secret" society called the Armed Forces Movement (MFA), the political parties, and the Portuguese people. The internal conflict included the coup, the counterstruggle to restructure the state, and the transformation of the country into a viable market democracy, all driven by these protagonists and their objectives.

The Major Players and Their Basic Motives

THE PORTUGUESE OFFICER CORPS AND THE ARMED FORCES MOVEMENT (MFA)

The Portuguese armed forces were underpaid, poorly equipped, and obligated to serve extralong tours of duty abroad. Nevertheless, the Salazar regime generally enjoyed the passive loyalty of the officer corps. That professional attitude began to erode in 1961 when India forcibly annexed Portugal's Goa territory. The humiliating loss of Goa was a blatant illustration of the unpreparedness and vulnerability of the armed forces—and invited armed revolt first in Angola and then throughout all the African provinces.[20] It also provided the incentive for Indonesia to take possession of Portuguese East Timor. As a result, by the beginning of the 1970s, Portugal's colonial wars were consuming over half the annual defense budget of Europe's poorest country. One in every four men of military age were being conscripted to serve in Africa—and after 1967, for a compulsory minimum tour of four years. By 1973, 11,000 officers and men had died in Angola, Guinea-Bissau, and Mozambique—"a mortality rate considerably higher, as a share of national population, than that suffered by the U.S. Army at the height of the Vietnam War."[21]

As they fought those thankless guerrilla wars for thirteen years on behalf of an unpopular government, the armed forces felt more and more isolated, forgotten, and resentful. Yet the insurgents had been fought to a stalemate by 1974, and there were some strong indicators that they were defeated militarily. That bit of good news and the military's grievances were made irrelevant virtually overnight by one misguided and insensitive dictatorial act. In July 1973, a series of decrees (the Rebelo Decrees) were issued that encouraged young men with a university education to enter the Portuguese officer corps. That, in itself, was not the problem. The problem lay in the provisions for financial incentives that the regular officers were not offered; for quick promotion and seniority on a faster track than the regular officers were allowed; and for the very real possibility that a *miliciano* (a militia officer) could come to outrank a regular officer under whom he had previously served.[22] Thus, it was not disaffection with the government per se or any kind of sympathy with the insurgents' leftist political orientation that caused the Portuguese government to lose the officer corps. Rather, the break between the government and the military was the result of the insulting implication that the regular officers had failed in their duty and were being supplanted by "the second team."[23]

As a consequence, neither the Portuguese military nor the African insurgents won or lost the wars in the overseas provinces. As in many other counterinsurgency campaigns, the final political outcome was decided elsewhere. Africa provided the catalyst, however. The immediate response to the Rebelo Decrees was the formation of a secret society of regular officers—the Movimento das Forcas Armadas (MFA). Less than a year later, on April 25, 1974, officers and men of the MFA stationed in Portugal ousted the incumbent government. Under the leadership of General Spinola, the MFA established a provisional government dedicated to economic reform, decolonization, and democratization (free elections). Additionally, the secret police unit was abolished, all political prisoners were released, freedom of the press was granted, and political leaders of all persuasions were encouraged to return from exile.[24] The implementation of the coup was virtually flawless. It took less than a day to accomplish; only a few people were hurt, and only four were killed; no executions took place; and "the transfer of power resembled more the abdication of a senile monarch than a military overthrow."[25] Thus, the governmental and economic systems established by Salazar after 1930 came to their end "after so many years, in so few hours, and with so little blood shed."[26]

THE MAIN PLAYERS

Immediately after the transfer of power within Portugal, nearly fifty parties emerged to exercise their new "freedoms" and destabilize the political process. Innumerable demonstrations, strikes, and factory and school takeovers were organized and carried out. Landless farmers, particularly in the south of Portugal, forcefully took control of the latifundios they and their families had been working for generations. At the same time, the new government nationalized banks, insurance companies, and basic industries. All these individual and governmental actions induced an exodus of a "brain drain" and an exodus of capital, while at the same time large numbers of Portuguese emigrants and soldiers returned "home" from overseas. That contributed to an unemployment rate of over 15 percent—as a result, domestic and foreign investment quickly dried up.[27]

These rapid and increasingly radical social, economic, and political changes put the moderate General Spinola and his more-left-oriented colleagues at odds, and he resigned as president of the provisional government. For the next year, Portugal appeared to be moving toward a full-scale Marxist-Leninist revolution. The main political players in this instance included "radicalized" officers in the MFA who had been returning to Portugal from Africa, and the Leninist-oriented Communist Party of Portugal (PCP). With Spinola resigned and in exile, the MFA purged its more-moderate members and publicly called for democratic centralization (central control of the state exercised by MFA and PCP leadership), public ownership of the major means of production and distribution, and a classless society. The PCP was very much in accord but openly called for the cancellation of the long-promised elections for a constituent assembly (parliament). The leader of the PCP, Alvaro Cunhal, stated categorically, "I promise you that there will be no parliament in Portugal."[28] With that, a series of events amounting to a preventive insurgency began to unfold.

THE PEOPLE

Nationalization of industry, banking, and other means of production and distribution (socialism) was popular in the cities, towns, and rural areas in the south of Portugal. Likewise, the collectivization of agriculture was popular in the south. But these same ideas and practices in the center and north of the country—where the land was already divided into small, family-owned holdings—were decidedly unwelcome. At the same time, throughout the entire country, people of all classes were becoming more and more uncomfortable with the machinations of the self-proclaimed MFA-PCP "vanguard of the proletariat."[29] Through the expressions of "public opinion"—and the activities of centrist political parties and moderate military officers still in the MFA—the people demanded their long-awaited elections. The left backed down, and free elections for a constituent assembly were held in April 1975.[30]

Of the eligible electorate, 90 percent voted. Portuguese voters indicated a strong preference for moderation, and under the campaign slogan of "Socialism, Yes! Dictatorship, No!" the Democratic Socialists gained the largest single block of votes (37.9 percent); the relatively conservative Popular Democratic Party came in second with 26.4 percent; and the Communists (PCP) were held to only 12.5 percent of the popular vote.[31] Thus, the elections for a constituent assembly began the discrediting of the left but did not alter the thinking of its main leader. Again, Alvaro Cunhal openly stated that if the parliamentary path to political power in Portugal was blocked, a violent alternative might be taken.[32] But after free and fair elections in which the people made their position clear, Cunhal's militantly blatant attitude caused most of the ideologically left-oriented officers in the MFA to withdraw their support from the PCP.

Against a backdrop of increasing social turbulence and public concern, and an important miscalculation of the amount of support remaining within the MFA, the PCP formed an alliance with the hard-line military ideologues and advocated insurrectionary objectives. Matters came to crisis proportions in November 1975. The constituent assembly was besieged by militant workers, and for two weeks there were rumors of an imminent "Lisbon Commune." Then, on November 25, groups of radical soldiers attempted to reenact the 1974 overthrow of the government. Initially they had the support of the PCP, but when it became clear that the bulk of the armed forces and the MFA were opposed to an undemocratic and violent overthrow, the PCP's Alvaro Cunhal was forced to recant.[33]

The fact is that the moderates and the ideological leftists in the officer corps and the MFA had also been organizing. When the hard-line left and the PCP attempted to seize power, the military counterattacked. The result was a demonstration of palpable power and a clear victory for the moderates. But that was not the end of the issue. The Portuguese people were to be heard from again. The constituent assembly wrote a new constitution that mandated the popular election of both the parliament and the president of the republic. Subsequently, in these elections, the Democratic Socialists and the Popular Democrats again emerged as the strongest political parties. The key moderate military figure in the post–April 1975 political maneuvering, General Romalho Eanes, was elected president. Thus, the first popularly elected government since the 1920s was sworn into office on July 15, 1976. That new government was strongly democratic and anti-totalitarian; direct control of the military was given to the National Parliament, and armed forces were made legally responsible to the minister of defense. With the resultant political stability, Portugal's mixed economy (capitalism and some government ownership of business and industry) began to flourish.[34]

Motives and Linkages

The revolutionary motives of the main protagonists were straightforward: to effect fundamental changes in the government, economy, and society. To accomplish that would necessitate taking down the Salazar dictatorship and replacing it with something else. But there was no agreement among the various players as to what that "something else" might be; each of the players had a specific concept of a desired end state and a particular idea regarding how to achieve that political objective.

The Officer Corps and the MFA

A majority of the officer corps understood that Portugal's future lay with Europe, the West, NATO, and the global economy. Thus, they were interested in a new government and an economic system that were compatible with the governments and economies of the global West. Those centrist, or moderate, officers saw no theoretical socialistic contradiction between the free election of parliamentary representatives of the people and the idea of the dictatorship of the proletariat. After all, a parliamentary majority vote is binding on both the "yeas" and the "nays." Moreover, these officers understood that many of the freedoms associated with Western democracy—freedom of speech, selection of leaders, press, vocation, and association—are necessary for human liberty. No society in which these freedoms are not respected is really free, whatever its form of government.[35] As a result, any participant or observer of the Portuguese political scene in the years immediately after the 1974 coup could not help but see that only the hard-line left was involved in purges, exiles, and jailing those who were not in agreement with them. Only the hard-line left was willing to violently deny the right of the people to elect their representatives.[36]

Most of the members of the MFA were in accord with those moderate and Western views. To be sure, there were many officers who were classified as ideological sympathizers with the left. Nevertheless, over time and when the ugly and violent face of Marxist-Leninist reality showed itself, many of those "radicalized" officers withdrew their support from the PCP and renewed their linkages with their more-moderate brethren. It was not the MFA that needed the PCP, but the other way around. The PCP had not had time to develop a military arm of the party and needed the usable military power of the armed forces to circumvent the will of the people and impose the party's will on the country.[37]

The Major Political Parties and the People

The Democratic Socialists and the Popular Democratic Party were firmly linked with the governments of Western Europe and committed to the ideas of Western nontotalitarian democracy. Likewise, the armed forces had similar military-to-military linkages with their fellow officers in Western Europe and the United States. In these terms, those legitimate political representatives of the large majority of the people—and the armed forces—had additional subtle but effective channels of expression and informal means of influence that could be brought to bear on the Portuguese political process. Thus, all the electoral advantages were on the side of the moderate majority political parties. Even though the PCP had received considerable support from the Soviet Union and had its followers, it was definitely a minority party. The Portuguese people therefore appear to have been better represented and more influential in political decision-making processes than a casual observer might have thought.[38]

Political turmoil and civil unrest did not end, however, with elections and the expression of public opinion. An intense struggle among the various players ensued. The change and renewal promised by the Revolution of 1974 and reaffirmed in the preventive insurgency of 1975 did not take place at that time.[39] Instead, a broader consensus within the leadership of the political parties and the armed forces slowly evolved. Over time, the moderate centrist parties and the MFA stopped bickering over trivialities in the definitions of "freedom" and "democracy" and "social progress" and accepted the notion that a pluralistic democracy was a good in its own right. By 1987, the parties and the armed forces had finally realigned themselves to provide majority rule.[40]

This left the PCP politically and psychologically isolated from the political mainstream. And rapidly diminishing support from the Soviet Union during the late 1980s further weakened the militant left. Moreover, the PCP did not accomplish most of the other things required for revolutionary success, as articulated by Lenin and others; as an example, Alvaro Cunhal was unable to convince the Portuguese people that the Communist Party was instrumental in waging a just war against the dictatorship. Additionally, the PCP did not develop a cadre for a revolutionary armed force, did not build and lead a broad national front (political coalition), and did not develop adequate external support from the peoples of "brother countries."[41] The PCP sometimes made political process difficult and slow and sometimes diverted the revolutionary process that had been initiated by the Portuguese armed forces, but it simply did not have the palpable power to impose its Leninist political vision on the rest of the country.[42]

The Poder Moderador

The political realignment of the centrist parties and the isolation of the PCP did not take place by chance. The main players in the Portuguese Revolution were not equals: the military were "more equal" than the other protagonists for three reasons. First, as guardians of the revolution, the armed forces could and did exercise their putative and real power when it was considered necessary. Second, the military institutions were and are very competent at planning, organizing, and implementing nonlethal as well as lethal operations. Again, they exercised those creative talents when necessary. Third, the officers and men of the armed forces most involved in the political process after 1974 understood asymmetric insurgency war and the important role of public opinion in it; the military was never far away from the political arena. Thus, the critical factors contributing to the ultimate success of the prodemocracy forces in Portugal in the preventive insurgency processes after 1974–75 included prudent operational actions, careful planning, and cogent public diplomacy—not luck.[43]

From the 1974 coup through turning power over to the elected government in 1976 and somewhat beyond—despite several tactical setbacks—the Portuguese armed forces always retained the strategic and operational initiative. The organization that provided those advantages to the armed forces and masterminded the decisive unity of effort was the Council of the Revolution. That council acted as an advisory organ of the presidency and was intended to guarantee the progressive continuity of the 1974 Revolution. It was composed of nonelected representatives of the armed forces and exercised a right of veto. In those and more traditional Luso-Brazilian terms, the armed forces acted as the *poder moderador* (moderating power derived from the military's position as the king's essential constituency) in the political process.[44] Thus, against all expectations, the leadership of the armed forces—using the poder moderador—enabled Portugal to avoid both a "White Terror" and the "Red Terror." That is, the repatriated colonials never succeeded in forming a far-right party of embittered nationalists and the landowning aristocracy; the hard-line Leninists never succeeded in forming a viable leftist coalition of radical military officers and other left-of-center political actors.[45]

OUTCOME: WHERE THE PODER MODERADOR TOOK PORTUGAL

The military leadership that exercised the poder moderador in Portugal after 1974 understood that the fulfillment of a holistic legitimate governance and national stability and security imperative consists of three principal efforts. Together, these efforts provided the educational and conceptual, the tactical and operational, and the strategic and political bases necessary to bring the state and the armed forces together into a congenial and legitimizing relationship. In this Portuguese postconflict situation, the poder moderador led down two almost-parallel paths that merged in the long term: the transformation of the state and the transformation of the armed forces.

Transformation of the State

These diverse but highly interrelated efforts centered on providing a foundational understanding of the relationship between security, stability, development, democracy, peace, and sovereignty; providing a preliminary end-state plan outlining the major political objective and the steps or phases necessary to accomplish it; and providing a comprehensive and actionable strategic-level political program to build institutions that would respond to the needs and desires of a society and facilitate legitimate governance. Thus, in addition to directing the state and the armed forces toward a common objective, these three elements—operating together under the influence of the poder moderador—explain the remarkable political continuity demonstrated by the major protagonists during the revolutionary period since 1974.

The Relationship between Security, Stability, Development, Democracy, Peace, and Sovereignty

General Antonio de Spinola (the leader of the MFA coup that toppled the long-standing Portuguese dictatorship and the first provisional president of the new government), his fellow officers, and civilian colleagues understood that democracy is a long-term process. These leaders and their successors in the elected governments since 1974 also understood that neither proclamations nor elections created a democracy, and they knew that the new institutional structures they had established after the 1974 coup were fragile at best. Moreover, they were aware that populist forces of the left and the right operating in Portugal were perfectly willing to bypass the newly established democratic institutions and resort to direct political action to reshape the state in the populists' preferred image.[46]

Those leaders who exercised the poder moderador understood that sustainable solutions to the problems of stability, well-being, and fragile or failing states involve the circular nature of the interdependent relationships among security and peace, stability and development, and democracy and effective sovereignty. Solutions to these problems begin with the provision of personal security to individual members of the society. It then extends to protection of the collectivity from violent internal nonstate actors and internal authoritarian governments, as well as from external enemies. Additionally, security depends on the continued and expanded building of a country's socioeconomic infrastructure. In the context of socioeconomic development, facilitated by the establishment and maintenance of legitimate law and order, a governing regime can begin to develop sustainable stability, peace, and prosperity. In this context, the inherent stability of responsible democracy and concomitant political legitimacy are based on the moral right of a government to govern—and the ability of the regime to govern with moral rectitude. Finally, the insecurity problem ends with the establishment of firm but fair control of the entire national territory and the people in it, which takes us to the concept of effective sovereignty. That is, without complete control of the national territory, a government cannot provide protection against violence or sustain an effective judicial system, rule of law, long-term development, responsible democratic processes, or a lasting peace.[47]

These interdependent conceptual elements provide the foundational bases necessary to strengthen the state and to create an environment within which responsible democracy can flourish. But anticipating, averting, and responding to conflict, postconflict, and / or the failing-state process require a more comprehensive level of conceptualization, planning, and organization that would lead to end-state planning, or *linha de accao* (line of action).

End-State Planning (linha de accao)

End-state planning starts from Clausewitz's truism that conflict is a continuation of politics by other means, but that concept needs to be accompanied by two qualifying arguments. First, military violence is required only when the conditions or changes sought cannot be achieved through political-diplomatic, social-economic, or informational-psychological means. Second, end-state planning advocates synchronization of all national or international civilian and military instruments of power to gain the most synergism from the interaction of the variables selected for action.[48] Thus, end-state planning allowed Portuguese decision makers, policy makers, and planners to think logically, in synchronized phases, about the conditions they sought to create. The strategic-level key was to understand precisely what had to be achieved, understand how it could realistically be achieved, and understand exactly what human, physical, and nonmaterial resources would be required for the effort.[49]

Perhaps the most fundamental element in developing an appropriate and viable linha de accao was to conduct the planning and operationalization of the plan with an eye that looked beyond the immediate objective and toward the kind of peace ultimately desired. For example, General Spinola wanted "*un Portugal renovado, democratico, livre e progressivo*" ("a Portugal modernized, democratic, free, and progressive"). He also understood that, to achieve that ultimate political objective, social cohesion had to be rebuilt.[50] As a consequence, the transition model was divided into four overlapping phases. Because reality is usually more complex than models, these phases—or steps—did not proceed sequentially. In the Portuguese postconflict transition situation, the phases of the linha de accao proceeded sometimes inconsistently and sometimes concurrently but always slowly and deliberately—depending on political-economic-social-moral issues that acted to dictate given responses. Nevertheless, the general plan proceeded as envisioned.[51]

Stabilization. The first phase of the linha de accao was stabilization. It was considered to be the most critical societal requirement of the moment, and it required taking immediate action to enforce law and order, feed people, restart basic public services, generate local employment, and reintegrate refugees and soldiers returning from abroad. These were the actions that provided "security" to every member of the Portuguese society, and that was the primary basis upon which stabilization, popular allegiance to the state, and societal cohesion were built. At the same time, these were the essential elements that had to be in place to regenerate the economy.[52]

Regeneration of the Economy and Addressing the Root Causes of Instability and Possible State Failure. The second phase of the plan was even more comprehensive than the first. Regenerating the economy and providing meaningful work—and pay—to individuals is fundamental. This need not (and cannot normally) lead to immediate prosperity, only to a reasonable hope for things to steadily improve, especially for one's children. Providing meaningful work provides another strong sense of security and gives people a stake in their society and governing institutions. Therefore, socioeconomic safety nets for the unemployed, pensioners, and repatriates were created to prevent social tensions from undermining the regeneration and modernization processes.[53]

Root cause factors were also addressed early in the transition process. Such factors included private exploitation of public and human resources, political exclusion, corruption, lack of health and education facilities, and degradation of the environment. All these causes of poverty, disease, and violence were clearly understood to frustrate and obstruct political, economic, and social development. At the same time, it was understood that the sum of the parts of a desired countereffort to deal with major internal security threats required more than regenerating the economy and dealing with root causes of instability and possible state failure. What was also required was the ability and willingness to exert effective, discrete, and deadly force against those individual men and women who were willing to violently exploit instability and state failure for their own ideological purposes. However, for ultimate effectiveness and the requirement for rebuilding social cohesion, security forces were required to deal with the violent internal opposition on the basis of the rule of law.[54] In these terms, the need to restart the economy and to deal with root causes of instability is an obvious continuation of the stabilization process.

Creation of Laws and Institutions for a Market Economy. Socioeconomic development without political development clearly is not sufficient to generate long-term stability, which requires political competence that can and will manage, coordinate, and sustain security and economic and political development. To accomplish this set of tasks, two things must be in place. First, there must be a competent and uncorrupted public administration. Second, legislation for reenfranchisement and democratic electoral processes, legislation guaranteeing civil rights, legislation guaranteeing security for persons and property, and legislation to underpin the rule of law, courts, police, and penal systems must be in place. In the Portuguese situation, the promulgation of democratic institutions and laws was accomplished relatively easily and quickly.[55]

The promulgation of laws and institutions for a market economy was considerably more difficult and slow. The problems of developing new and more-appropriate tax systems, regulatory policies, and other economic reforms to enable a market economy were exacerbated as a result of the initial postrevolution nationalization of important parts of the economy. The intent was to eliminate the corporate nature of the economy that Salazar had established. As a consequence, much of the nationalized economy had to be privatized. Opening up the economic system challenged vested interests and political elites. Holding former oppressors accountable for public and human exploitation strained barely functioning economic institutions. Shutting down bankrupt state enterprises created unemployment. All in all, there were many political objections and obstacles to the development of laws and institutions for a market economy. But by 1986, a viable market economy had emerged, and Portugal formally joined the European and global communities.[56]

Cultivation of a Civil Society. Popular perceptions of the moral rectitude of political leadership are key to rebuilding social cohesion and public confidence in government. In turn, popular perceptions depend on the proverbial transparency and accountability of government. An independent media is crucial to this process—to help educate the population, to reflect public opinion, and to help keep government officials honest. With these building blocks in place, a legitimate civil society can become a real possibility. The intent of all this is to generate the societal acceptance and support that governing institutions need to manage internal change and violence adequately—and to fairly and effectively guarantee individual and collective well-being.[57] This takes us back to where we started: the stabilization phase of the transition process. It is a circular process that defines, more than anything else, progress toward viable national security. This is the long-term process through which Portugal moved from dictatorship to a market democracy.

The Comprehensive Postconflict Implementing Program to Achieve the End State

The comprehensive program of political-economic-social-security action designed to lead to a viable market democracy in Portugal was written by General Spinola's provisional government after the April 1974 coup.[58] It was made public in May 1974. Nevertheless, not until the late 1980s and early 1990s did the plan come to fruition. It did not develop exactly as planned but remained remarkably coherent despite having been submitted to a free democratic process.

To begin with, once relative stability and security were finally established, the succeeding provisional and elected governments found that they had to address four intervening problems: (1) Salazar's debilitating policies of low investment in productive and human resources; (2) the long mercantilist reliance on colonies to provide cheap raw materials and revenue to buy (not produce) manufactured goods; (3) the postcoup disruption of agricultural and industrial management and investment; and (4) attaching more importance to NATO and the EC than to the former colonies. None of these problems could be dealt with easily, and to one degree or another, they continue to be works in progress.[59] By the early 1990s, however, enough progress had been made on these basic deficiencies, as well as on other problems that were noted in the end-state planning process, to work toward the completion of the eight major sets of tasks outlined in the comprehensive program.

In 2006, one could examine and begin to evaluate the progress made on achieving the Spinola government's comprehensive program. The general tasks were (1) the reorganization of the state; (2) civil liberties; (3) economic and financial policies; (4) security of persons and property; (5) social policy; (6) foreign policy; (7) policy regarding former colonies; and (8) education.[60] These major goals in completing Portugal's transition to a viable market democracy were not achieved easily or quickly, or without digressions. However, over time, the slow and sometimes contentious democratic processes proved effective and set a firm foundation for the future.[61]

Without going into excruciating detail, suffice it to say that the successive Portuguese governments over the past twenty-five to thirty years have, for the most part, implemented the program, that the country has achieved a viable market democracy, and that Portugal is now a contributing member of the global community. One indicator of these achievements is seen in the Centre for Global Development's 2006 annual index of seven policies that measure international commitment: national contributions to foreign aid, trade, investment, migration, environment, technology, and security (policing sea lanes, peacekeeping, and so forth). The Netherlands ranked first in the world. The United States ranked thirteenth. Portugal followed at sixteenth—ahead of Italy, France, and Spain;[62] not a bad placement for a country that other Europeans had once called "Africa's only colony in Europe."[63]

CONCLUSIONS: PARADIGM CHANGE

The realities of national and global security environments and the fundamental tasks of reform and regeneration required to move from a dictatorial failing state to a viable market democracy called for nothing less than a paradigm change. The primary challenge, then, was to come to terms with the fact that contemporary security, at whatever level, is at its base a holistic and long-term, strategic-political-level civil-military effort to preserve individual and collective security and stability. The corollary was to change from a singular tactical-operational-level military or law enforcement approach to a multidimensional, multiorganizational, multinational strategic-political transition paradigm that addressed the legitimate and meaningful preservation and strengthening of the state.

The paradigm that led from dictatorship to legitimate governance in Portugal derived its just powers from the consent of the governed and generated a viable political competence that managed, coordinated, and sustained security; social harmony; social, economic, and political development; and stability. These are the necessary fundamental elements that define the "social contract" between a people and their government and give a regime the moral right to govern. These are also the very pragmatic foundations for national and global well-being and stability. The achievement of these goals required a conceptual framework and an organizational structure to promulgate unified civil-military planning and implementation of the multidimensional concept.

Transformation of the Armed Forces

Despite the success of the Portuguese officer corps and the MFA of facilitating the building of a relatively smooth path from dictatorship to democracy, the armed forces were radically changed and weakened. The process was slow and simultaneously one of military modernization and political disengagement. Military modernization required three elements: the reconstruction of hierarchy and authority; a significant reduction in size; and a major change of roles and missions. In turn, political disengagement was dependent on the implementation and success of military modernization.[64]

Hierarchy and Military Authority

First, after the 1974 coup, the older members of the officer corps were replaced by a younger, politically motivated, left-of-center generation that took control of the government as well as the armed forces. Many of these officers later became purge victims and were replaced by others of even stronger political motivation. In turn, these ideologues—having gone too far to the left—were ousted in favor of more-moderate officers who were less politically inclined and more technically competent.[65]

Reduction in Size

When the more moderate majority of armed forces officers regained control of the government and the military after 1975, the priority task was to replace political standing and orthodoxy with military discipline and hierarchy. With those basics reestablished, a major modernization and training program was initiated. That part of the modernization process was financed by the United States and the Federal Republic of Germany (West Germany).[66] During that part of the military modernization process, the armed forces were drastically reduced in size. Total military strength plunged from over 300,000 at the height of the wars in Africa in 1974 to under 60,000 by 1977. By the early 1990s, the total strength of the armed forces had fallen to the generally present level of approximately 45,000.[67] Virtually overnight—between 1974 and 1977—the Portuguese armed forces diminished from a major first-rate counterinsurgency force to a nucleus around which a conventional "NATO quality" force might be constructed. As a consequence, present roles for the armed forces emphasize air force and naval protection of sea lanes and Portuguese territory in the eastern Atlantic Ocean (the strategic triangle). The army has conformed to a NATO configuration, and battalion and smaller elements are currently performing NATO and European Union (EU) missions in Afghanistan and Bosnia, respectively.[68]

The Change in Roles and Missions

With the major components of military modernization in place—hierarchy and discipline, diminution, and new roles and missions—the newest generation of officers have completed the return of the military to the proverbial barracks.[69] There is no longer a Council of the Revolution with direct ties to the president of the republic and a formal role in exercising the moderating power. As noted above, direct control of the armed forces has been taken from the president and placed under the National Parliament and the minister of defense. Ironically, the military has gone full circle; that is, the armed forces that organized and conducted the revolutionary process are once again—as they were in the 1920s—politically insignificant, small, ill-equipped, relatively poorly paid, and almost incapable of performing their assigned defense missions.[70] But the Portuguese armed forces are rightfully and firmly in the twenty-first century and are fully committed to the market democracy that they played such a large role in organizing and establishing.

Conclusions: Political-Military Disengagement

Portugal's political-military transition from mercantilist dictatorship to market democracy was indeed a model of relatively peaceful and managed change. It was, thus, an example of the use of indirect and soft intellectual power, as opposed to direct and brutal physical power. The metaphor that explains this, and the slow but sure process through which the armed forces achieved a market democracy, can be seen in the Portuguese bullfight. Unlike the better-known Spanish bullfight, in which the matador ("bull killer") kills the bull with his sword, the Portuguese bullfighter has a completely different task; the Portuguese bull is constantly outmaneuvered and brought to a state of natural exhaustion by the skillful horsemanship of the Portuguese bullfighter.

The Portuguese officers and men who served in Africa understood that their revolutionary undertaking was much like their national bullfight. The revolution would lie in the demonstration of skillful political-psychological-military actions that would physically exhaust the enemy and bring the conflict to a point at which the enemy could not move. These officers and men also understood that their revolutionary undertaking was, in Leninist terms, "partial war."[71] Partial war, insurgency war, asymmetric war, fourth-generation war, irregular war, or any other name attached to contemporary postmodern war includes a wide and complex variety of nonlethal actions such as deception, concealed penetration, subversion, psychological mind games, the adroit exploitation of every conceivable form of division that might be found within a small or large targeted entity, and, generally, *not* "fighting fair." In our metaphorical terms, these kinds of unconventional efforts—in their many combinations and forms—constitute the "skillful horsemanship" of the Portuguese bullfighter.

Thus, even though the Portuguese military was radically changed and weakened, that may not be an altogether bad thing. In the context of contemporary irregular war, will, resolve, knowledge of "partial war," and the ability to innovate effectively in a crisis environment are all proven qualities. The Portuguese armed forces maintain these and other similar attributes as a result of their unforgotten experiences in Africa. Such qualities are invaluable in virtually any current and future political-military conflict scenario. Perhaps, however, the most salient quality of the Portuguese armed forces is its formidable example as a force for democracy in the volatile and dangerous new world disorder.

Conclusions Regarding the Transition of the State and the Military

Contemporary war is not a kind of appendage (a lesser or limited thing) to the comfortable vision of conventional war. Contemporary conflict is a great deal more. As long as opposition exists that is willing to risk everything to depose a government, destroy a society, or cause great harm to a society by violent means, there is war. This is a zero-sum game in which there can only be one winner—or, perhaps, no winner. It is, thus, total. As a consequence, it must be considered and implemented as a whole. Today (and in the future), confrontation between belligerents is transformed from the level of military violence to the level of a complex multidimensional struggle for the proverbial "hearts and minds" of a people. Within the context of people being the ultimate center of gravity, antagonists can strive to achieve the Clausewitzian admonition to "dare to win all"—the control or overthrow of a government or another symbol of power.[72]

In connection with the idea of warfare as a whole, the military role goes beyond the traditional warfighting to nontraditional conflict—and to help consolidate success by providing security and support to partners, other government agencies, and nongovernmental agencies in the aftermath. In these terms, military forces provide the capabilities needed to consolidate battlefield success and turn it into strategic victory. Thus, strategic victory requires not only the defeat of an enemy military force but also a multiagency effort to change the society, culture, economy, and political system that undergirded the problems that brought on the crisis in the first place.[73] Furthermore, the international community is increasingly expected to provide the leverage to ensure that legitimate governance—once regained—is given to responsible, incorrupt, and competent leadership that can and will address the political, economic, and social root causes that created the conflict. In turn, that is intended to lead to democratic transition and to a sustainable peace.[74]

The officers and men of the Portuguese armed forces who conducted the various aspects of the 1974 Revolution understood the absolute requirement for an organizational structure and a political-military strategy to accomplish a holistic, long-term, national capability–building "game plan" to achieve a market democracy and a durable peace. They also understood that the organizational requirement for a unity of effort would be crucial to the final outcome of their political-strategic efforts. That unity of effort, therefore, would have to be directed by the Council of the Revolution. As a result, there was a strong and consistent quest for moral as well as de facto legitimacy. There was a serious political-psychological effort to isolate the violent opposition (PCP) from the rest of Portuguese society. There was a vigorous political commitment to deal with root-cause problems, stay the course of the revolutionary project, and take it to its desired end state. And there was a coordinated campaign of intelligence gathering around which to conduct the kind of public diplomacy that would act as the key to the development of public opinion and subsequent support for the revolution. These are proven strategic-level dimensions for success in contemporary war and clearly were well used in the Portuguese situation.[75]

The application of these dimensions (factors) of success was a holistic implementation of direct and indirect "offensive" (proactive preventive diplomacy) and "defensive" (generally military-police) actions. Offensive action was generally mid- to long term. It was primarily civilian and political-economic-psychological oriented but often had to be coordinated with indirect and direct short-term defensive (military) measures. It focused on prevention of crises and—when appropriate—was followed up with military enforcement of law and order and control of violent actors. Additionally, offensive action involved coordinated political-economic-social efforts to diminish or remove the social, economic, and political root causes of instability and its resultant violence. The intent was to foster legitimate civil society, economic prosperity, and a sustainable peace. The specific mix of independent variables that constituted offensive actions was moral and de facto legitimacy; political-military unity of effort; political-psychological isolation of the PCP; political-economic-social actions to stay to the course and to achieve the desired end state; and intelligence and information in support of public diplomacy efforts. The one defensive variable in the Portuguese postrevolution security scheme involved the threat or application of military-police power to a violent or potentially violent situation.[76] In short, a legitimacy approach, appropriate use of soft and hard power, and an organizational structure to direct and ensure the achievement of a desired end state are not radical relics of another time. These dimensions of success are basic foreign policy and military asset management.

The accomplishment of these political-strategic purposes on the part of the officer corps was made much easier by the inadvertent help of the PCP. Because of the messianic knowledge of its theoretical Marxist-Leninist correctness, the PCP did not actively seek popular support for its cause and legitimacy; the PCP also did not create a broad national political coalition to provide political, logistical, and armed support or to help mobilize the masses. Instead, the PCP relied almost completely on the political and military support that it could get from the left wing of the MFA. And because of its political-psychological isolation, the PCP ultimately found itself fighting alone—without much internal support and with diminishing external support from the Soviet Union. In short, the PCP did not follow any of the time-honored rules noted in the paragraphs above or the similar but more limited Marxist-Leninist (Maoist) "factors of success" that were derived from the war in Vietnam.[77] As a consequence, the theoretical "correlation of forces" did not come together for the PCP in Portugal.

All this has not gone unnoticed. The very positive political accomplishment of transforming the state—amid the various negatives that were acting in the Portuguese security environment—is considered to be a forerunner and a model of contemporary solutions to transition from authoritarianism to democracy and from failed-state status to a viable market democracy.[78]

KEY POINTS AND LESSONS

- Despite common wisdom to the contrary, there are and can be such things as civilian dictatorships. There are also such things as democratically oriented military institutions that can prevent or take down a totalitarian regime.
- The Portuguese experience demonstrates that a nation's armed forces may act as a very unorthodox kind of insurgency. That is, a nation's armed forces can conduct preemptive or preventative insurgency, as well as counterinsurgency.

- The Portuguese case serves as an example of successful management of the state-failure process and provision of a viable democratic model for postconflict transition.
- The Portuguese military conducted a long-term, disciplined, and relatively bloodless political-psychological campaign to depose a long-existing dictatorial regime, prevent the "radicalized left" from mounting a countercoup, and propel the country toward a viable market democracy.
- The Portuguese used patience; the instruments of "soft power"; and the words, images, and ideas of fourth-generation asymmetric war to influence the centers of gravity most relevant in that situation—public opinion and leadership.
- This case provides an example of armed forces institutions acting as a force for democracy and a forerunner of new solutions to much of the intranational turbulence emerging out of the growing popular disillusionment with the generally poor performance of contemporary "elected" governments.

The Portuguese experience in conducting the processes of the 1974 revolution reminds us that there is an alternative that is far superior and opposite to military and totalitarian solutions to left- (or neopopulist) and right-wing populist dictatorships and state failure. Sun Tzu makes the point judiciously: "Those who excel in war first cultivate their own humanity and justice and maintain their laws and institutions. By these means, they make their governments invincible."[79]

CHAPTER 6

From Defeat to Power in Four Hard Lessons

The Uruguayan Tupamaros' Sea Change, 1962–2005

The attempt by the Tupamaro (Movimiento de Liberación Nacional, or MLN [National Liberation Movement]) to bring down the democratically elected Uruguayan government was nurtured by many of the same forces at work in the creation of the New Left in Western Europe, the United States, and other parts of the Americas during the 1960s and 1970s.[1] The basis of discontent was working conditions. Resentful militant workers (blue and white collar) were overseen by autocratic employers who could discipline, humiliate, or dismiss their employees at will. Moreover, even though there were widespread calls for greater worker initiative, more professional autonomy, and shared management schemes, most employees' opinions were disregarded.[2] This sense of exclusion from decision making—and from power—was also reflected in the political processes. As in the United States and other major Western pluralist democracies, Uruguayan politics were controlled by relatively moderate right- and left-of-center majorities. These long-standing arrangements had ensured political stability and continuity in Uruguay but by the 1960s tended to exclude the more radical opposition on both the right and the left. Thus, radical university students, the new knowledge-based proletariat, and the liberal professions appointed themselves to be the new working class (proletariat) and the extraparliamentary opposition. In this way, politics moved from the legislature into the streets.[3]

In Uruguay, these politics of exclusion were influenced by the teachings of Che Guevara. Taking exception to the wisdom of Lenin regarding the conditions necessary to mount a revolution, Guevara argued that an insurrection in itself could create the conditions necessary to generate a revolution.[4] Such an insurgency could be organized by a relatively small but mobile group of guerrilla fighters—the *foco* (focus). A government's inability or unwillingness to eliminate the insurgents would force it to overreact against the general population. The foco would then act as a catalyst for the alienation of the people and for a popular insurrection that would stem from government repression.[5] Che Guevara's revolutionary philosophy was deeply engrained in the MLN's Argentine (Montonero and Revolutionary People's Army [ERP]) allies, who went so far as to advocate that organized violence was the *only* way to achieve the changes required in the modern world.[6]

Another revolutionary writer, Abraham Guillen, though less well known than Guevara, also exercised some influence on the Uruguayan Tupamaros. Guillen was a Spaniard who had fought on the losing side of the Spanish Civil War and subsequently immigrated to South America, ultimately to Uruguay. There he became an intellectual mentor and councilor to the MLN in 1962–72. Guillen taught that "[t]he strategy of revolutionary war is essentially political. . . . It is imperative to obtain the support of the great mass of the population [to achieve victory]."[7] Additionally, the young Tupamaros were influenced by the romanticized ideas of the Brazilian guerrilla leader, Carlos Marighella. He stated unequivocally, "To join the armed struggle and to become today's terrorist ennobles the spirit. It is an act worthy of all revolutionaries engaged in armed struggle against . . . dictatorship and its monstrosities."[8]

Some from Uruguay's political left argue that as a consequence of these teachings, the university students, the young people from the liberal professions, and the rebellious petty-bourgeois youth who made up the rank and file of the MLN were quite confused regarding what they were supposed to be doing—but they are quite likely to have felt "ennobled" as they were captured and tortured, killed, or exiled.[9] In any event, to cite Lenin, "To start a revolution in a country [like Uruguay] that has produced a democratic culture and organization provided to everybody—to do so without long and careful planning and preparation would be wrong, absurd."[10] The Tupamaros were wrong, and the effort was illogical at best.

To the credit of the Tupamaros, however, they were among the first contemporary guerrilla groups to operate in a major metropolis. Their model of urban guerrilla warfare has made its mark on post–World War II history and on contemporary conflict in the Middle East.[11] Accordingly, as the New Left continues to clash with the new globalism and with poor and insensitive governance, MLN organization and tactics in the first phase of revolutionary war will likely be a model for now and a long time into the future of insurgency.[12] But the brilliance of the early Tupamaro organization and tactics was not matched by its later strategy and politics.

A more competent strategy and realistic political approach to revolutionary change would come only after a devastating military defeat and long years of repression, rethinking, and reorganization. In the period from defeat in 1972–73 to the democratic achievement of legitimate political power in 2004–2005, the circumstances of their failed revolution took some of the MLN leadership back to Lenin and back to Uruguay's own reformist political philosopher, Jose Enrique Rodo.[13] In Lenin's later writings and speeches, there is a notion indicating that after some sort of failure, "The central feature of the situation . . . is that the vanguard (leadership) must not shirk the work of re-educating itself, of remolding itself."[14] Rodo argued that one should not wait for failure to begin a renewal process. Rather, renewal is a lifelong effort directed at attaining "real liberty."[15] This applies to the state as well as to the individual. "Nations that enjoy liberty change their thought, their tasks, and their goals—they struggle with their past to get away from it."[16] Importantly, interestingly, and ironically, this suggested "retooling," and the resultant sea change, turned the Tupamaro program from something that it was not into something that it could and should be. That regenerative effort created another model that has not gone unnoticed (most notably, in contemporary Ireland, Spain, and Nicaragua):[17] a model for now and the future that takes us beyond the use of armed violence to a peaceful democratic approach to revolutionary change.

ADDITIONAL CONTEXT

Based on long-held opinions about provincial Uruguay on the more sophisticated side of the River Platte estuary, Argentine Porteños (residents of Buenos Aires) have been known to explain the beginnings and endings of the general insurrectionary situation in Uruguay as follows: "Everything is so isolated from the rest of the world that when something does happen, it is turned into an event—that it is not."[18] If there are other characteristics that help a Porteño clarify any given event in Uruguay, they would include the fact that if anything happened, it happened slowly; whatever it was, it had to happen first in Argentina; and in Uruguay, the event was more trivial.[19] Thus, the political-historical-ideological context of the Tupamaro insurgency follows a traditional pattern—slowly doing the same thing that happened in Argentina, and making it into something that it was not. There is some basis to that cynicism, but one must remember that Uruguay is one of the few countries in the world that has over 130 years of experience in representative democracy, peaceful stability, and inclusive political processes.[20] That political culture gives Uruguay advantages and possibilities for political development that are not trivial or well understood outside La Banda Oriental del Uruguay (the easternmost province of La Platte Viceroyalty, which bears the modern name of Uruguay).

As a consequence, in explaining the Tupamaros and the other political actors involved in the Uruguayan insurgency from 1962 through 1974—and beyond—two additional contextual realities are critical: the strong influence of the Tupamaros' Argentine Montonero and ERP insurgent friends and allies; and the political-economic-social situation and tradition in Uruguay at the time. Only then can one better understand how and why the MLN and the civil-military leadership lost touch with their political aims, and how and why the insurgency and counterinsurgency projects became more and more extreme and erroneous. At the same time, with an understanding of the Uruguayan political tradition, one can discern how and why the Tupamaros and the Uruguayan civil-military leadership reclaimed their political objectives, and how and why the insurgency and counterinsurgency projects eventually came together peacefully and democratically.

The Argentine Montoneros, 1955–1979

In Argentina, Juan Domingo Peron is credited with beginning the country's national liberation.[21] After taking power in 1946, he and his first wife, Eva, initiated the nationalization of the major means of production and distribution in the country and gave political voice and dignity to organized labor. This socialist transformation continued until a military coup restored the traditional Argentine oligarchy to power in 1955. What followed the coup that deposed Peron was political deadlock. Peronist resistance to the new government made sure that rule would be impossible without Peron. Peron's opponents in government and society did all they could to outlaw Peron and Peronism and prevent his return to power. Thus, the only way for either side to attempt any kind of political action was through either popular or state violence.[22]

During the subsequent eighteen years of exile, Peron used the Montonero insurgents as a primary means of breaking the political impasse. He also used them as a political bridge to worker-based mass movements and as a bridge to rebellious youth movements. This strategy ultimately proved successful. The military was nudged out of government, and fair elections were called that put a Peronist, Hector Campora, into the presidency in 1973. Those elections paved the way for Peron to return to Argentina.[23] During Peron's exile—and shortly after his return to power—Montonero strategy centered on a Peronist-populist-nationalist political-psychological war to liberate Argentina from foreign economic domination and dependency. In that connection, the Montoneros focused their early efforts on the oligarchy, who were acting in behalf of foreign interests.[24]

Peron had argued that insurgent violence in Argentina would disappear once the Peronist electoral victory had been secured. On his return to Argentina and to political power, a general political amnesty was proclaimed. Additionally, Peronist Montoneros were given important posts in the government and in the national universities. As a consequence, there was a major political opportunity to abandon the armed struggle and cooperate peacefully in a stable new government. Some Peronists claimed victory and took advantage of the situation. Others, however, never abandoned their vision of taking military control of the state. They conducted several covert operations and, after Peron's death in 1974, openly renewed hostilities. Thus, the armed struggle did not end.[25] At that point, the insurgents began to argue that they were liberating Argentina from the military and police, who were acting in behalf of the oligarchy. In these terms, the Montonero vision of the "Peronist Motherland" could only be achieved by building an insurgent army capable of defeating the Argentine Army.[26]

Thereafter, more sophisticated, daring, and spectacular operations were conducted directly against the Argentine security forces. The political objectives assigned to military operations were gradually forgotten, and operations were increasingly designed to show military strength. As a consequence, by 1976, the public mood had begun to change. The insurgents were no longer "the proletariat in arms"; they were providing inconsequential conventional military responses to political situations, and they were bent on emulating the regular armed forces. The people who were supposed to bring national and social liberation to Argentina had developed into an ideology-bound, bureaucratized, isolated, cynical, mirror image of their "enemy." In a moment of belated revolutionary self-criticism, a former Montonero leader reflected, "When you become like the enemy, you end up being the enemy. . . . The enemy has defeated you because he has managed to transform you into him."[27] Accordingly, in December 1976, the Montonero leadership quietly followed its erstwhile Marxist-Guevaraist allies (ERP) into exile but continued to direct operations in Argentina until the debacle of the final "Popular Counter-Offensive" of 1979.[28]

The Argentine government's counterinsurgency response came in the form of unprincipled societal repression and the "Dirty War." One by one, the ERP, the Montoneros, and other revolutionary organizations had been outlawed. These legalities, however, were irrelevant. Captured insurgents and known or suspected "subversive delinquents"—or people who just happened to be in the wrong place and the wrong time—were killed or imprisoned without trial. The state security forces were killing and imprisoning suspected Peronist and Marxist activists literally by the truckload. Over the last year of the insurgency, the Montonero leadership found that there was "no one and nothing" to lead.[29] Thus, the state response went far beyond neutralizing and eliminating the Montoneros and their revolutionary allies. The Argentine state response was total (not limited) and could accurately be described as state terrorism.

The Montoneros illustrate some important points regarding contemporary insurgency. First, they demonstrate the efficiency and effectiveness of mobilizing a mass support base within urban space. Second, they show that insurgents—whether urban or rural based—need not be Marxists, Maoists, or Guevaraists, or even religious fundamentalists; populists and nationalists may also become major players in the insurgency arena. Third, the Montonero experience illustrates that once an insurgent movement achieves a certain momentum, its leadership is not likely to accept peace as a viable alternative to armed struggle. At the same time, the Peronist Montonero insurgency and the Argentine governmental response to it are prime examples of how not to conduct an insurgency and how not to conduct a counterinsurgency.

The Political Tradition and Economic Situation in Uruguay, 1962–1974

From independence in 1830 until the mid-1960s, Uruguay had been a model of democratic politics and socioeconomic development. The prosperity that had underpinned democracy and development came to an end, however, when world demand for the country's main product—wool—began to decline in the late 1950s. From 1954, in a steady downward economic spiral, Uruguay's gross domestic product (GDP) declined, and inflation and unemployment escalated. Also, labor unrest and social violence began to increase. Additionally, ubiquitous corruption in a bloated government bureaucracy exacerbated the decline of the political-economic-social situation in the country.[30]

This situation came into being after more than a century of experience with the institutionalized practice called coparticipation. In that political framework, regardless of which of the two traditional parties—the Blancos ("Whites"; conservatives) or the Colorados ("Reds"; liberals)—was in power, there was always a coparticipative role for a given opposition.[31] Diego Abante credits three factors for the long-lasting success of that political practice: (1) Uruguay's steady rate of economic growth, which allowed the political system to respond successfully to increasing demands from different sectors of the society; (2) the institutionalization of the political reality of a somewhat fragmented society in the law of party designations (*ley de lemas*), in which a voter is allowed a great deal of choice in terms of candidates and parties—and can clearly see in the results of an election that his or her vote was counted; and (3) most important, that the traditional Uruguayan political culture was tolerant and inclusive, not exclusive.[32]

The major premise around which that inclusive political culture was constructed is the recognition of the fundamental freedom of the individual. It comes from a deep, abiding faith in the worth of the individual and a faith in human reason. Thus, every belief or every opinion has the right to be stated and published without hindrance, and the intelligence of the individual is sufficient to distinguish truth from error and to treat harmful or antisocial ideas as they deserve. Moreover, Rodo taught that the government of a free country respects the rights of groups as well as individuals. The two types of rights are not completely separate from one another; rather, the rights of speech, association, political choice, and other individual freedoms are associated with responsible democratic governance. Uruguay's distinctive system further required a combination of intellectual honesty and willingness to compromise. This political culture was well enough engrained in the Uruguayan population to enable it to survive insurgency war and the subsequent military dictatorship.[33] That did not happen easily, however.

The inclusive political tradition and the legal basis for it began to change in the mid-1960s. As living standards declined, bureaucratic corruption increased, strikes and lockouts became commonplace, and social violence escalated, the government reacted repressively. In 1967, President Jose Pacheco Areco acted unilaterally to curb the rising clamor of public criticism against the government. By decree, he closed six left-wing newspapers and banned several left-of-center political parties. In June 1968, the president declared a state of emergency (a suspension of virtually all civil and political rights) in response to militant trade-union activity and student rioting. At the same time, Areco began to take steps to improve the resources and effectiveness of the police and armed forces.[34]

Up to that time, the general relative prosperity of Uruguay and the lack of an external threat to the country precluded the need for anything but token police and military forces. Both institutions were totally subordinated to the will of the democratically elected government but ill prepared to face any kind of security threat. They were small, poorly equipped, and not trained to deal with the rising unrest and militancy of a formerly law-abiding and undemonstrative population. Measures to improve the security situation did not address these unconventional issues but were primarily those that would increase the size and firepower of the police and the military. As predicted by such revolutionary writers as Guevara, Guillen, and Marighella, the result was a blanket and violent response to the general security threat, directed against Uruguayan society. It was not a careful, discrete concentration of effort on the minority that was causing trouble.[35]

That incompetent and violent response of the state, the increasing political repression, and the dramatic decline in living standards in the early and mid-1960s provided the motivation from which the Tupamaro insurgency developed. Those factors operating together also generated a political-cultural crisis in which the long-accepted forms of inclusive democratic government were undermined and the principles of liberal democracy were discarded.[36] In essence, the failing Uruguayan state heedlessly degenerated into a "draconian state" (military dictatorship) in its attempt to save itself.

That Uruguayan experience, even though it is a prime example of how poor judgments on the part of guerrilla leadership can make an insurgency go awry in its early stages and how a government should not conduct a counterinsurgency, also reminds us that there are long-term, far superior, and opposite alternatives to insurgent violence and state repression. At the same time, that experience reminds us that the "enemy military" is not the center of gravity (hub of power) in irregular insurgency war; as Carl von Clausewitz noted in reference to small internal conflicts, popular opinion and the personalities of leaders are the centers of gravity.[37] Abraham Guillen elaborates on this general observation with two points. First, "[Che Guevara's] *foquismo* (reliance on armed encounters and military action) is petty bourgeois in origin as well as outlook. Actually, it is an insurrectional movement for piling up cadavers, for giving easy victories to repressive generals."[38] Second, because of the political orientation of revolution, obtaining the support of the people is critical.[39] Thus, the Uruguayan case is a prime example not only of a "new jungle" within which insurgents can operate but also of popular opinion acting as a primary center of gravity in internal conflict.

THE MAIN INTERNAL PROTAGONISTS

The internal conflict situation in Uruguay between 1962 and 1973 was relatively straightforward. The government had failed to maintain the economic and political underpinnings of peace and prosperity. Insurgency, terrorism, and their associated asymmetry emerged in the form of the Tupamaro National Liberation Movement (MLN), in direct response to that organization's perception of economic and social injustice, governmental corruption, and political repression. In this case, the government found itself fighting to survive the criticism of its citizens and the assault from the Tupamaros. Thus, the main players in this drama included the MLN, the government, and the Uruguayan people. These were the protagonists that shaped the insurgency of 1962 to 1973, the restructuring of the state through the military dictatorship from 1973 to 1985, and the stage-by-stage restoration of security and stability and the renewal of democracy from 1985 to 2005.

The Tupamaros

The first step in the formation of the MLN was taken in 1961 by Raul Sendic. He was a thirty-six-year-old law student from Montevideo who had led a group of sugar farmers from the Paysandu area in a protest against low pay and poor working conditions. After a term in prison for his role in that public demonstration, Sendic and a group of his friends moved back to the sprawling capital city of Montevideo—home to about 70–80 percent of Uruguay's 2.5 million people. They considered the urban setting a more suitable base location for guerrilla warfare than Uruguay's sparsely populated interior, which has no possibilities for mountain or jungle sanctuaries. According to a comrade, Luis Baumgartner, Sendic's purpose at that time was simply to "generate conscience, organization, and conditions for revolution." Moreover, he began to cultivate relations with other insurgent groups in South America—including the Peronist Montoneros and the Marxist-Leninist-Guevaraist ERP.[40]

Thus, Raul Sendic's Tupamaros did not rush into military action. Not until December 1966 did they confront police in an armed action. And the MLN did not publicly announce its political objective of deposing the Uruguayan government until 1968. In the meantime, this group of approximately twenty individuals cultivated a "Robin Hood" image by conducting a series of bank robberies and seizures of money and food that were distributed to the poor. As a result, a poll in 1971 showed that 59 percent of the Uruguayan people thought the Tupamaros to be an organization motivated by social justice and altruistic motives.[41] During the early 1960s, the MLN began to organize into five- to seven-person cells and to recruit new members. Recruits tended to be young men and women primarily from the middle class, including high school and university students. In 1965, there were five hundred fully proven Tupamaro guerrillas and more than five thousand sympathizers who provided various types and levels of support and sustenance. The organization appeared to be a truncated pyramid. At the base were the unproven new recruits; at the next higher level, the five- to seven-person cells; at the top—or flat—part of the pyramid, the political-military command, with which each cell was in contact. The political-military command directed rigorous and strict military training and discipline, prescribed a spartan lifestyle, and centered the organization's outside efforts on Robin Hood–like good deeds.[42] The effort was considered worthwhile, challenging, and even fun. It was good to be a Tupamaro at that time.

The purpose of the initial notion of "generating conscience, organization, and conditions for revolution" was to prepare the way for the "revolution,"[43] even though nobody seemed to know exactly what that would involve. Guillen argued that the general membership of the MLN had only a vague notion of what a revolution would or should bring. Moreover, the leaders were not particularly concerned "because they [like their Montonero and ERP comrades in Argentina] anticipated that taking down the government and seizing political power would resolve everything."[44] As a consequence, there seems to have been no vision of what a "nationalistic, socialistic, and popular democracy" might be. The motive of the Tupamaros became revolution for revolution's sake.

With the long-term political aims of the insurgency beginning to fade, the Tupamaros became more and more arrogant and increasingly militaristic. Robberies and kidnappings increased. Killings and confrontations with the police increased. Taxes on the well-to-do middle class and businesses were increased. Jailbreaks were planned and implemented. Money that had gone to provide for the poor went to the purchase of businesses and weapons. Attacks on military targets became more sophisticated and frequent. And the MLN also created "people's prisons" in which the Tupamaros interrogated, held, and executed their own captured or kidnapped prisoners. In all, the revolutionaries were beginning to run a parallel government and a parallel system of repression in Montevideo and other parts of Uruguay.[45]

As the Robin Hood image of the Tupamaros waned, the public began to turn against the movement in increasing numbers. People began to provide information to the security forces that heretofore had not been forthcoming, and people began to help the authorities trace and find Tupamaro members. Accordingly, MLN ratings in the polls went down, and the attempt in the 1971 elections to support a Frente Amplio (Broad Front) coalition of Christian Democrats, Socialists, Communists, and other left-of-center political parties failed.[46] Thus, in that period of increased arrogance and increased violence, Guillen and the MLN leadership parted ways. In Guillen's terms, the Tupamaros had become overly professionalized, militarized, and isolated from the people. "Their organization is closer to resembling a parallel power—perhaps a Mafia—contesting the legally established [government]," he observed, "rather than a movement of the masses." Furthermore, he thought that "surely, there is little point in defeating one despotism only to erect another in its place."[47]

Not long after losing sight of its political objectives, the MLN began to suffer severe reversals that ended in its complete defeat in 1972–73—and the initiation of an extremely repressive military dictatorship that lasted for a decade before beginning to succumb to the center of gravity again, finally yielding a legally established government in Uruguay once more. The overall timeline goes like this:

1972—The Uruguayan armed forces began to replace the National Police in dealing with the MLN.
1973—Within six months, the military had defeated the Tupamaros, and that organization essentially ceased to exist.
1973–84—The military took control of the state.
1985–2005—Democracy was gradually renewed.[48]

The Government

In the early 1960s, the Uruguayan government comprised a constitutionally determined number of elected officials and an unconstrained and growing number of appointed or hired bureaucrats. The number of bureaucrats was estimated to be equivalent to 20 percent of the entire Uruguayan population.[49] The declining economy was unable to sustain such an unbalanced drain on public finances. Moreover, that bloated bureaucracy was never credited with paying much attention to the needs of the state or the society. Government had become, at best, a personal enrichment process. At its worst, some individuals held two or three government jobs at the same time (with no accountability, depending on one's relationship with a given chief of section). Those unmonitored jobs in the bureaucracy would allow an employee to come and go at will and to collect two or three relatively lucrative government salaries; and after only a few years, one could *jubilarse temprano* ("retire early").[50]

As a result, members of the "political class"—along with their brothers- and sisters-in-law, cousins, and other retainers—were unwilling to give up the easy lifestyle and secure future. The motive, simply, was greed. Consequently, in the mid-1960s, the government and its bureaucracy mobilized the legal-constitutional and political-military institutions and resources of the state for their own purposes. That action took the country into another downward spiral of instability, insecurity, social violence, and further social, economic, and political degradation. The resultant malfeasance in office exacerbated the processes, leading to failing-state status. That status could be seen in government inability and/or unwillingness to provide basic services, to maintain decent roads, education, health, and other public services for most of the Uruguayan society. Failing-state status could also be seen in the inability or unwillingness of government to provide basic personal and community security and a legal system that protected the tradition of societal equity. Additionally, state failure could be seen in the thuggish and brutal repression of basic human and political rights.[51]

The process of state failure is seen in a succession of government actions that took the country from democracy to dictatorship:

1966—A new constitution voided the old *colegiado* executive department of government and provided for a single president. (In the colegiado system, all executive power had been vested in the National Council of Administration. The council comprised six members: four seats went to the majority party, and two seats were reserved for the minority party.)

1967—President Pacheco Areco unilaterally banned six leftist newspapers.

1968—The president decreed a state of emergency, in which most civil and human rights were curtailed.

1970—The president initiated a newspaper censorship process and closed those newspapers that would not accept censorship.

1972—The president made a Declaration of Internal War and gave the armed forces *carta blanca* (a free hand) to deal with the Tupamaros.

1973—All left-wing political activity (including the MLN) was eliminated. Parliament was dissolved and replaced by a Council of State handpicked by the armed forces. By the end of the year, Uruguay had become a military dictatorship.

1973–84—All political parties and activities were banned. The national university was closed. All worker's organizations were outlawed. Repression, jailing, killing, and torture continued without constraint.[52]

The Uruguayan People

Uruguay was and still is a small country of approximately 2.5 to 3 million inhabitants. Most of the population are of European stock, and 70–80 percent live in or near the capital city of Montevideo. The interior of the country is very thinly populated and developed into large sheep and cattle ranches and other agricultural enterprises. The socioeconomic pattern was developed in the last quarter of the nineteenth century, when a large influx of Spanish and Italian immigrants boosted the nation's workforce and also expanded the strong middle-class section of the population. Between 1903 and 1915, the government of Uruguay was in the hands of men of considerable political skill and reforming zeal (including Jose Enrique Rodo), and it was at this time that the bases of the country's political freedom were consolidated.[53]

In the 1960s and 1970s, economic development and almost universal prosperity came to an end. The precipitous decline in living standards incited public demands for economic and governmental reform. The state response is noted in the section above, and the Uruguayan people were left defenseless against government repression and subsequent military dictatorship. Nevertheless, the Uruguayan political tradition of elections, plebiscites, and referenda exerted itself, and the people began to fight back the only way they could—with their votes.

Specific results showing the popular mood toward the Tupamaro insurgents and the corrupted governmental bureaucracy are seen in a succession of polls, elections, plebiscites, and mass rallies that, over the years, demonstrated the political resolve of the Uruguayan people. That resolve, or will, was the operative element that took the country from insurgency through military dictatorship and back to responsible democracy, along the following general timeline:

1962–71—The government initiated a series of repressive measures designed to control popular criticism of corruption and other malfeasance in office. Within this political milieu, the MLN was organized. At the outset, polls indicated that 59 percent of the Uruguayan people accepted the Tupamaros as left-of-center social-economic-political reformers with altruistic motives.

1971—A reversal of popular mood was seen in an electoral defeat of a left-of-center political coalition supported by the MLN. This political defeat came after a disturbing increase in Tupamaro violence and the apparent militarization of their revolutionary effort.

1973—The Tupamaros had been defeated by the Uruguayan armed forces, and the military established a dictatorship.
1981—A plebiscite defeated a referendum to approve a new constitution that would reinstate the traditional Blanco and Colorado parties but greatly restrict political activities of nontraditional political parties.
1982—The Blanco and Colorado parties were allowed to organize internal elections to be held the following year.
1983—Antigovernment (nontraditional) political factions won over 70 percent of the votes in that election. In mid-1983, the military government had increased levels of political repression and press censorship. The result was a series of mass political demonstrations demanding an immediate return to democracy.
1985—Elections were held, and a civilian government under President Julio Maria Sanguinetti reinstated civilian rule. The new government promulgated a blanket amnesty, pardoned Raul Sendic, and allowed the Tupamaros to reemerge as a legitimate political party.
2005—The Tupamaro candidate, Tabare Vazquez, was elected president of the republic.[54]

A Cautionary Note

State failure is an evolutionary process, not an outcome. This process is often brought on by poor, irresponsible, and insensitive governance and leads to at least one other very fundamental reason why states fail. That is, state failure can be a process exacerbated by nonstate groups (insurgency, transnational criminal organizations, or civil-military bureaucracies) that, for whatever reason, want to depose the established government or exercise illicit control over a given country. Through murder, kidnapping, corruption, intimidation, destruction of infrastructure, and other means of coercion and persuasion, these violent, internal, nonstate actors compromise the exercise of state authority. The government and its institutions become progressively less capable of performing the tasks of governance, including exercising fundamental personal security functions.[55]

At the same time, democracy is likely to erode. Crediting elections or government as "democratic" becomes problematic when armed and unscrupulous nonstate actors compete violently to control government by murdering, kidnapping, intimidating, and/or corrupting candidates and other office holders before and after elections. The same is true when corrupt civilian and military politicians and bureaucrats favor themselves or another political actor rather than the public they are supposed to serve. In either of those two situations, the state cannot, in the end, control its national territory or the people in it. The political actor that will succeed in taking control of the state in that kind of an instance is the one with the best arms, the best organization, and the greatest resolve.[56]

However, the dysfunctional nature of a failed or failing state, as it lingers and goes from bad to worse, has an impact on the rest of the global community as the criminal elements become more effective than or take control of the erstwhile government and the conditions within which people live degrade. The consistency of this experience throughout the world, and over time, inspires confidence that these lessons are valid.[57] Uruguay proved no exception to this generalization. But over the long term, Uruguay was more fortunate than many states that have found themselves in a similar situation.

FROM DEFEAT TO POWER: THE TUPAMAROS' METAPHORICAL LONG MARCH, 1972–2005

The outcome of the actions of the Tupamaros, the government, and the Uruguayan people between 1962 and 1972, and then from 1972 through 2005, engendered a series of four obstacles and lessons. These lessons focus on the course of action chosen by a small minority group of "heretical" MLN leaders after the Tupamaro defeat at the hands of the Uruguayan armed forces in April 1972. It was a hard decision to make, but it was the only way to survive and to continue the revolutionary struggle. That is, there were only two paths for the Tupamaros. The first was to adapt their revolutionary socialist program to the Uruguayan reality, and live. The other was to continue experimenting against reality, and die. The complex implications of that first path in the "long march" to success in 2005 were also personally heart and mind wrenching for those who made the decision to reject the armed struggle in favor of a peaceful process to achieve their political objectives.[58]

The actions required to achieve those objectives would generate a sea change in outlook and behavior. The first step in that process was to separate from the main MLN group, reject violent revolution, and pursue peaceful democratic approach to fundamental change. Thus, in addition to turning their backs on lifelong comrades and years of Marxist-Leninist-Guevaraist ideological training, the "traitors" had to negotiate a torturous road to vindication, acceptance, and success. That metaphorical "long march" took that minority MLN faction through three more sets of obstacles and lessons. Once the decision was made to pursue peace, they had to overcome their inflammatory leftist rhetoric and transform their primary political objective from violent revolution to democratically achieved legitimate governance. Next, they had to overcome over a decade of isolation from the rest of Uruguayan society and organize a coalition of other political parties that could eventually win free and democratic national elections. To do so required the development of a long-forgotten attitude of tolerance toward society and other parties—and other people, in general. Last, and perhaps most difficult, the Tupamaros had to revise their long-held ideological concept of a rational political-economic system; the "new" Tupamaros had to overcome the theoretical contradiction between capitalism and democracy. They also had to accept the reality of a European type of mixed economy (some capitalist features mixed with some socialist features). That required the acceptance of pluralist democracy and the rejection of democratic centralism (the dictatorship of the vanguard of the proletariat).[59]

In all, that "long march," with its twists and turns and bumps and obstructions, took over thirty years to accomplish. But the Tupamaros are now being accepted as themselves—as real people, not the "proletariat-in-arms." To be sure, the new Tupamaros are not the same people they were three decades ago, but they are subtly gratified. They are convinced that they are making changes that are possible in a country where revolution is "impossible."[60]

Step One: Deciding on a Peaceful Political Approach

In 1971, the dialectic of increasing governmental repression and escalating Tupamaro military action began to come to a synthesis. The MLN—

with a militant expectation of forcing a "climate of governmental collapse"—stepped up the number of murders, kidnappings, robberies, and cinema, factory, and other business takeovers. During this period, a U.S. Agency for International Development (AID) official named Dan Mitrione was murdered and British ambassador Geoffrey Jackson was kidnapped and held captive for almost a year. The Uruguayan government declared a state of internal war and brought the armed forces, unconstrained, into the counterinsurgency effort. By April 1972, a ruthless and unexpectedly effective military campaign had succeeded in virtually eliminating the Tupamaros in Uruguay. The armed forces uncovered the insurgent network, captured tons of equipment and ammunition, arrested three thousand activists, and killed over one hundred of the leaders. The synthesis came in June 1973 when the armed forces closed the parliament and replaced it with a handpicked Council of State (a military dictatorship) that lasted until 1985.[61]

Tupamaro leader Luis Alemany, who had had command of a unit that was training in Cuba for a counteroffensive against the Uruguayan military government, recounts his understanding of the events leading to another dialectic, that is, a split in the MLN between "hardliners" and "traitors." He had gone to Buenos Aires for a meeting with other Tupamaro military commanders who were training in Chile and Argentina and with representatives of the Argentine ERP. The intent of the meeting was to make the necessary coordinating arrangements for a counteroffensive being planned for early 1973. The Argentines and some of the other MLN commanders wanted to create "another Vietnam" in Uruguay, but that idea began to unravel when Alemany argued that the invasion of Uruguay and subsequent counteroffensive against an unexpectedly good army would be a disaster.[62] In a subsequent meeting in Chile, a comrade, Efrain Martinez Platero, supported Alemany, saying that "[t]hose columns that attempt the counteroffensive will be cannon fodder" and that the effort would turn Uruguay into a "*carniceria*" ("butcher shop").[63]

The minority ("traitors") went on to argue that the column training in Chile would likely be unavailable for the counteroffensive because Chilean president Salvador Allende would probably need the MLN column to help him survive the expected military coup being planned to oust him from office. As a result, the counteroffensive would be weakened seriously.[64] "There was no other alternative than to pursue other, peaceful, means of continuing the revolutionary struggle."[65] To add emphasis to the argument that the counteroffensive was untenable, Alemany, Martinez Platero, and a few others argued that they had evidence that the MLN had been compromised and that Uruguayan Army Intelligence knew all about the planned counteroffensive.[66] The majority responded that if that were the case, it was the fault of the "traitors."[67]

The ultimate result of this debate, of course, was the rupture within the MLN. The movement split into a hardline *tendencia proletaria* ("proletarian tendency") and the traitorous *tendencia nuevo tiempo* ("modern-age tendency"). The modern-age tendency separated itself from the main group, stating that they did not want to continue the armed struggle in any way but that "we will not be traitors to our ideals. . . . We will continue fighting for development, against poverty and tyranny, and [for] the things that all Uruguayans want."[68]

There are echoes of Abraham Guillen in that statement of rupture. Early on, he had counseled his Tupamaro pupils that "[r]evolutionary war is an act of political violence undertaken when the political ends of the people cannot be effectively pursued through peaceful means . . . [but] revolutionary war does not propose to decide anything by arms. . . . [It] operates politically in the name of the general interest in order to win support from the entire population."[69] This first step toward the peaceful pursuit of revolutionary aims was fundamental—and certainly not trivial—and probably the most difficult obstacle that the individuals of the modern-age tendency had to overcome.

Step Two: Overcoming Leftist Revolutionary Rhetoric

Like the Argentine insurgency, the Uruguayan case illustrates a strategy aimed at the destruction of the incumbent government and replacing it with the dictatorship of the proletariat. Achieving that level of political power would be accomplished through the progressive discrediting of public institutions that eroded their ability to perform their juridical functions for society. That kind of action also erodes the basic public trust that government could and would provide individual and collective security, along with other legitimizing functions prescribed by the Uruguayan political tradition. Thus, revolutionary violence became the highest possible good in the process of overthrowing the dictatorship of the governing class and foreign exploiters. Revolution, then, advanced from revolution for revolution's sake to the "exalted instrument of liberation." But the concept of "liberation" still did not define in positive terms exactly what revolution was supposed to accomplish. The way the term "revolution" was being used in Tupamaro rhetoric was more as an instrument or method by which fundamental change would be attained. No one really understood what overthrow of the government would lead to—except to the "highest possible good."[70]

In this way, the Tupamaro insurgency followed a familiar pattern: slowly doing the same thing that had been done in Argentina even while making it into something that it was not. As the Tupamaros lost sight of their political objectives, they correspondingly increased their military efforts to make an "impossible revolution." The traditional Leninist conditions for revolution were not in place; the political, social-psychological, and military "correlation of forces" had not been prepared; and the Uruguayan people were not convinced that exchanging the contemporary government dictatorship for a dictatorship of the "vanguard of the proletariat" would bring any great improvement. As a consequence, instead of continuing to replicate the Argentine insurgency and resultant "Dirty War," there were a few (the minority; the "traitors") Tupamaro leaders who understood the need to change the direction of their impossible revolution and make it into something possible—and really significant. These leaders knew that they had to go back, bypass Che Guevara's foco "military shortcut" to victory, and do what Lenin had recommended many years earlier. That is, MLN leadership had to rethink the problem. The results of that renovating analysis were straightforward and cogent. The revolution and the New Socialism of the contemporary period were no longer based on the clash of different parts of society (bourgeoisie versus proletariat). Rather, the new challenge that revolution had to confront was the issue of responsible legitimate governance.[71]

Hard evidence over time and throughout the world shows that poverty, disease, instability, and social violence are the general consequences of unreformed political, social, and economic institutions and the concomitant misguided, insensitive, incompetent, and/or corrupt (illegitimate) governance. Thus, legitimate governance is more than de facto or de jure legitimacy. Responsible and legitimate governance concerns the manner of governing rather than international recognition or that a given regime claims to represent a nation-state. Legitimate governance is defined as governance that derives its just powers from the governed and generates a viable political competence that can and will effectively manage, coordinate, and sustain political freedom, socioeconomic development, security, and personal and collective well-being. No political group or military force can legislate or decree those qualities for itself. It must develop, sustain, and enhance them by its actions over time.[72] As a result, the nuevo tiempo (modern-age) Tupamaros diverged from the "impossible revolution" to something more difficult, something greater—but something possible. By accepting the idea that they had to move from a violent paradigm to a peaceful governance approach to change, the modern-age MLN could replace conflict with cooperation and fulfill the promise that that new political strategy offers.

The modern-age Tupamaros understood that the institutionalization and implementation of the factors contributing to the responsible and legitimate governance paradigm would require a morally acceptable approach to the Uruguayan people; a less militant and more pragmatic rhetoric; and a new, compromising, and tolerant view of the society, other political parties, and even former enemies. This would not be a short-term effort and glorious entry into the offices of government such as that which Fidel Castro had carried out in Cuba in 1959. Instead, this would be a delicate, difficult, and long-term effort in which they would have to give the people the security, stability, and well-being that politicians of all colors had been promising for so long.[73]

Step Three: Overcoming Isolation to Win Elections

As the Uruguayan security forces put more and more pressure on the Tupamaros, the insurgents withdrew more and more into their own compartmentalized organizational structure. That separation from the outside world further restricted access to external reality and the capability to take the MLN message to the people whom the movement was supposed to be "liberating." As a result, the insurgent's view of other people and other parties or movements—regardless of ideological orientation—was that they were "only tools of the bourgeois dictatorial political system" and "capitalist pigs and watch dogs," rather than human beings or brothers-in-intention. Even among themselves, the isolated Tupamaros had spent much too much time arguing as to who among them was "more proletarian" than the other.[74] The modern-age Tupamaros understood this problem and set about to change their behavior and attitude toward the people of Uruguay.[75]

The choice the new MLN had to make was between assimilation into the traditional political parties and transformation from a "mobilized" singular revolutionary entity into a tolerant entity. That was an easy choice: the modern-age Tupamaros would transition and maintain as much of their identity as possible. In those terms, other Uruguayans not of their political orientation had to be accepted as real human beings and *gente buena* ("good folk"). From that point, the new Tupamaros would become a part of a "community of equals" and join with other left-of-center and centrist political groups to create the kind of parliamentary coalition that would eventually win the national elections of October 31, 2004.[76]

That, in turn, would require the new MLN to transition from its very narrowly organized structure to a wider set of coalition-organizing principles. The intent, pragmatically, was to develop a unity of effort. It would not come about automatically by decree of the leadership or with the creation of a committee. The individuals involved—the leaders and their staffers—would need to know how to communicate and deal with a diversity of peoples, organizations, and culture, as well as the media. If they did not know how to do these things, they would have to learn. In that context, the new Tupamaros had to develop an organizing paradigm to assist in generating strategic clarity out of the bewildering political chaos and ambiguity of the many center and left-of-center political factions that were active in Uruguay after the end of the military dictatorship in 1985.[77]

One of the most salient keys to planning and implementing strategic clarity—and ultimate success—was to generate shared goals. The development of shared goals began with the establishment of an organizational mechanism for developing a common vision for ultimate political success (strategic clarity). Those who worked within that mechanism then made a strategic assessment of the political situation. After that, a broad understanding of what had to be done or not done or changed and a common understanding of possibilities and constraints provided the bases for an overarching plan. That plan became the foundation for developing subordinate or more-specific plans that would make a direct contribution to the achievement of the mutually desired end state. Thus, the roles and missions of the various political entities evolved in a unified fashion and deliberately, rather than separately and ad hoc. Lenin made that point when he stated, "This [kind of] problem can be resolved only very slowly, cautiously, in a businesslike way, and by testing a thousand times in a practical way every step that is taken."[78]

The idea of transition to a tolerant society also aims at the acceptance of amnesty for all who participated in the insurgency and counterinsurgency projects. In 1985, President Julio Maria Sanguinetti declared a general amnesty, not only for the people in the security services who had done unthinkable things but also for the Tupamaros who had reciprocated in kind. Many former Tupamaros, former security forces personnel, and other citizens felt that justice had not been done in the pardoning of each group's former enemies.[79] But rationality prevailed and averted the recriminations, the "witch hunts," and the continuing cynicism that—years later—still prevails in post–"Dirty War" Argentina. Today, that country still does not exhibit the harmony that prevails in Uruguay. The Argentine example clearly demonstrates the importance and necessity of the legitimate governance and tolerant-society policies promulgated in Uruguay and finally accepted in 1989. In a referendum held in April of that year, 57.5 percent of the Uruguayan voters essentially said, "We don't want to spend any more time examining our painful past. We must move on."[80]

Despite some understandable reluctance, the modern-age Tupamaros understood that to become a movement that represents the masses (and that can get things done peacefully), they could not follow old ideologies or retain old resentments; they needed to formulate a program stressing that whatever unites the "forces of liberation" should be done.[81] That approach began with the determination to change their behavior and attitude toward the rest of society and work backward to the late nineteenth century and early twentieth centuries and toward a community of equals and a tolerant political culture.

Step Four: Overcoming the Contradiction between Capitalism and Democracy

The previous steps along the road toward a peaceful, democratic approach to fundamental change were only preparatory actions.[82] A reasonable person could see the value of a peaceful versus a violent approach to revolutionary change. In that connection, a knowledgeable person could understand that legitimate governance could accomplish the objectives of revolution. Likewise, a sensible individual could appreciate the meaning of tolerance, cooperation, and compromise with others in terms of winning free elections. Nevertheless, reasonable, knowledgeable, and sensible New Socialists have a problem with the Marxist-Leninist theoretical contradictions between capitalism and democracy in achieving a rational economic system.[83] That is, "new" and other socialists have been taught that a rational national economic system is the product of democratic centralism and state ownership (control) of the major means of production and distribution in a society. That political-economic combination guarantees the interests of the proletariat. In sharp contrast, both pluralist democracy and capitalism pander to the interests of the bourgeoisie—not to the interests of the working "masses."[84] In these terms, pluralist democracy and capitalism were the real obstacles to fundamental change in the new MLN.[85] This takes us back to the idea of legitimate governance.

Another definition of legitimate governance in the New Socialist lexicon involves "direct government," in which the people express their wants and needs to a trusted leader and that leader promulgates those neopopulist desires through the instruments of the state.[86] Similarly, the general Latin American security dialogue is beginning to argue that solutions to the problems of instability, lack of well-being, and inadequate freedoms can be achieved only through responsible democratic governance. Accordingly, a legitimate government must ensure a close, circular linkage among security, stability, socioeconomic development, societal peace, prosperity, and political freedom.[87] All of this does not require a dictatorship of the vanguard of the proletariat or the direct dictatorship of the people through an individual leader. What it does require is transparent, accountable (to the people), and uncorrupted governance that complies with the needs, morals, and mores of the community.[88] A modern Catholic philosopher widely read in Uruguay, Jacques Maritain, takes this concept to its logical conclusion: "Then only will the highest functions of the State—to ensure the law and facilitate the free development of the body politic—be restored, and the sense of the State be regained by the citizens. Then only will the State achieve its true dignity, which comes not from power and prestige, but from the exercise of justice."[89]

The new Tupamaros understood these dynamics and accommodated them. Accepting and adjusting to these extraordinary demands for reform and regeneration, however, was difficult and painful. These dynamics were, nevertheless, far less demanding and less costly in political, economic, social, and military terms than allowing a failing state's illegitimate governance to continue and to generate crises that work to the detriment of all. Moreover, Tupamaro leaders in the post-Uruguayan insurgency period demonstrated extreme courage and astute analytical capabilities. They were able to break away from old comrades who would think only of revolutionary change being achieved by violent military means. And they showed outstanding adaptive and innovative thinking in reeducating and renewing themselves and in developing a paradigm for peaceful fundamental change.

More specifically, the modern-age MLN leadership understood the importance of moral as well as de facto and de jure legitimacy. Nearly every action taken in the long-term effort to achieve political power was intended to directly support the moral legitimacy of their political project. They also understood the organizational requirement for a unity of political effort. In that connection, the new Tupamaro leaders worked hard to develop the ideas of tolerance, cooperation, equality, and compromise for themselves and their subordinates as they built a political coalition that could and would win free and fair democratic elections. At the same time, there was a remarkable public diplomacy effort to isolate the traditional Colorado and Blanco parties from their centrist and moderate leftist constituencies. There was also a vigorous political commitment to deal with Uruguay's root-cause political instability and socioeconomic problems, stay the course of the revolutionary project, and take it to its desired end state. Finally, there was a coordinated campaign of information gathering from which to base the development of public opinion and support for the new people-oriented Tupamaro program.

These are the strategic-level analytical commonalities that have proven, over the years and throughout the world, to generate success in the political conflict environment.[90] They were deliberately and carefully applied in the transformation of the Uruguayan state from insurgency through military dictatorship to responsible democratic governance. And those analytical commonalities provided a pragmatic conceptual framework from which leaders could see a given political conflict situation as a whole and develop the vision necessary for success.

THE TWENTY-FIRST-CENTURY SECURITY ARENA

A map of the twenty-first-century security arena shows 79 low-intensity conflicts, 32 complex emergencies, and 18 ethnic wars overlapping with 175 small-scale contingencies ongoing around the globe.[91] In these conflicts, military institutions, insurgent nonstate actors, and/or populist reform movements—sometimes radical, sometimes moderate, and sometimes quasi-fascist—compete to take control of existing governments. The ostensible purpose is to provide a different (and to each nonstate actor, a better) way of attaining an acceptable balance among political freedom, socioeconomic development, and security. At base, the issue for military organizations, populists, and/or insurgents is that pluralistic democracy is not satisfying the socioeconomic expectations of peoples and that free-market economies are not fulfilling popular aspirations.[92] The consequence of these dynamics is a vicious downward spiral that manifests itself in diminished levels of popular and institutional acceptance and support for a given incumbent regime. The effects of these dynamics can result in further turmoil and violence that are translated into subtle and not-so-subtle struggles for political power and change. In turn, this leads to the slow but sure destruction of governments, societies, and economies. Results of these dynamics can ultimately be seen in the proliferation of weak, incompetent, misguided, and/or corrupt failing or failed states throughout the world.

Lessons from over a half century of bitter experience suffered by governments, military institutions, insurgents, and other violent challengers involved in various destabilizing and bloody internal conflicts show that a given response to a given threat often ends—or continues on and on—in greater misery and violence than was ever anticipated. Too often, this is because too much time, treasure, and blood are dedicated to tactical and operational military efforts as opposed to defining and implementing a strategic political endgame. Thus, it would be a terrible mistake to assume that there is nothing to be learned from past insurgency wars and other internal conflicts. To the contrary, in the savage wars of peace of the current and future eras, the lessons learned from the Uruguayan and other insurgency experiences are all too relevant. The example of the adaptive and innovative thinking of the modern-age Tupamaros led to a benign political-psychological approach to achieve governmental power. This case, then, is a harbinger of the kinds of dramatic change—positive and negative—that one might expect to see virtually anywhere around the globe again in the future.

KEY POINTS AND LESSONS

- Insurgent organizations tend to mobilize when internal economic and political turmoil reach crisis proportions. In the Uruguayan case, the incompetent and repressive response of the corrupt incumbent regime provided the final motivation from which the Tupamaro insurgency developed.
- Regular military forces can—with the application of enough power and little restraint—quickly defeat an irregular insurgent enemy.
- Military defeat of an insurgent organization does not resolve the root-cause problems that brought on the insurgency in the first place. Thus, there are important political and socioeconomic

aspects of the situation that must also be addressed. Otherwise, the prospects for a country and its people are bleak.

- The Tupamaros began their insurgency with good organization and tactics and a positive relationship with the Uruguayan people. Over time, however, they lost sight of their political aims and strategy, and they lost the support of the people. The Uruguayan case is a prime example of public opinion acting as a primary center of gravity in an internal conflict.
- Tupamaro recuperation and renewal (and ultimate political success) came as a result of four obstacles and lessons that, once applied by the Tupamaros, exerted positive effects on public opinion: they had to transform their primary political objectives from violent revolution to peaceful democratic change; they had to reject the idea of the dictatorship of the vanguard of the proletariat and accept the notion of legitimate governance; they had to overcome an intolerant exclusive political environment and create a tolerant inclusive political climate to win free and fair elections; and they had to repudiate the concept that government ownership or control of the means of production and distribution was the only rational model for a national economy. Accordingly, they had to accede to the reality of a mixed economy that incorporated both capitalist and socialist features.

The Uruguayan insurgency model has not gone unnoticed by groups desirous of effecting a change in governance in other parts of the world. The entire Tupamaro experience illustrates that there is a far superior alternative to violent and totalitarian models for fundamental change. Sun Tzu reminds us that "to win one hundred victories in one hundred battles is not the acme of [military] skill. To subdue the enemy without fighting is the acme of skill."[93]

CHAPTER 7

Reflections on the Successful Italian Counterterrorism Effort, 1968–1983

The current threat from the protean asymmetric insurgency phenomenon (irregular political-psychological war) is different in nature and method from that of past conflicts. In the past, what mattered most were military bases, preserving access to sea lines of communication, choke points, raw materials, and territory—and denying those assets to one's enemies. And in the past, the enemy was a clearly discernable military force, backed by a nation-state's industrial capability to create and then maintain that military force outside its own borders. Now, adversaries are aiming directly at achieving or controlling palpable political power. And the enemy is not a traditional recognizable military entity with a "fixed address" and clearly defined traditional military maneuver methods. Rather, the enemy now becomes an elusive state, nonstate, or individual political actor who prefers unconventional and indirect confrontational methods.

This new kind of confrontation cannot be dealt with by infantry, tanks, and aircraft attacking specific territory or destroying buildings, neighborhoods, or cities, although that may be important in a given discrete tactical context. More than anything else, strategic success in contemporary conflict is based on the sophisticated political-psychological application of all instruments of national and international power. In short, this kind of war relies mostly on words, images, ideas, and soft power—

and a certain disregard for convention. We have seen those new asymmetric elements being applied along with terrorist violence, at will and with impunity, by the weak against the strong. Thus, what would be helpful now is a clear-cut example, or model, of success at countering irregular warfare, a strategy that resulted in the failure of one of the most consequential challenges to a nation-state in modern times: the Italian case of the late 1960s through the early 1980s.

CONTEXT

The Italian Experience with the Gang Phenomenon, 1968–1983

In post-Napoleonic Europe, Italy was defined simply as a "geographic expression." In post–World War II Europe, Italy had only advanced to the status of "the sick man of Europe." That "sick" country was experiencing virtually every symptom of "failing state" status. Productivity was down; gross domestic product (GDP) was down. The Italian currency was down and moving further downward. The only statistics moving upward on the charts were labor strife, poverty, crime, and immigration. In that socioeconomic milieu, chronic political instability was illustrated by the succession of thirty-nine governments over the thirty-five years between the promulgation of the 1948 Constitution and 1983. This state of affairs adversely affected societal relations and increased Italy's vulnerability to criminal and subversive designs. As a result, from 1968 through 1983, 297 different "leftist" groups—along with several additional militant separatist, pacifist, anarchist, and monarchist organizations—mobilized and conducted a terrorism strategy to overthrow the Italian state.[1]

The so-called Red Brigades were at the forefront of that campaign and proved to be the most practical, calculating, and cynical of all the Italian "terrorist" organizations at conducting violent political-psychological war. Additionally, the Red Brigades were the theoretical equivalent to a highly politicized third-generation gang supported by outside forces.[2] For example, one can quibble about the difference between the support of the Soviet Union to the Red Brigades versus the support of illegal drug trafficking organizations to Latin American and Caribbean gangs, but support is support. The common denominator in this equation is that both of the "outside forces" were or are completely sympathetic with the objective of overthrowing or controlling the state. As a consequence, we concentrate our attention on the Red Brigades, rather than the more than three hundred additional organizations that made up the total challenge to the Italian government between 1968 and 1983. This is a good example from which to learn how governments might ultimately control—or succumb to—the strategic challenges of the irregular political-psychological war phenomenon.

Additional Contextual Background

Italian "terrorism" was not taken very seriously from the 1960s through the 1970s and was allowed to fester and grow. Not until after the highly publicized 1978 kidnapping, people's trial, and execution of five-time Prime Minister Aldo Moro did the Italian government directly address the issue of instability and violence. The murder of Prime Minister Moro marked the first time in more than ten years of kidnapping, murder, maiming, and bombing that the Italian government decided that the violent actions of the various antigovernment organizations constituted more than a complex law enforcement problem. These various organizations, or gang equivalents, were challenging the integrity of the country's political institutions and creating an unacceptable level of internal instability. Decision makers began to understand that the intent of every one of the three hundred or more leftist, rightist, and separatist antigovernment organizations, including the Red Brigades, was to destroy the political equilibrium of Italy and give impetus to the conquest of political power.[3] As a consequence, the increasing violence and criminality of that decade of 1968–78 were finally defined as a national security problem.

Significantly, Italy's planning and coordination of the response to the irregular terrorist challenge essentially fell to the paramilitary Carabinieri. At the same time, the mandate given to those political, economic, informational, and security instruments of the state that would implement the counterterrorism effort was twofold. First, there would be no "Dirty War" in Italy. Second, there would be no strategic ambiguity—that is, the various political-security instruments of the Italian state would integrate all their actions under the direction of a Carabiniere General. The intent was straightforward: together, these unifying and legitimizing efforts would reestablish the kind of stability that was derived from popular Italian perceptions that the authority of the state was genuine and effective and that it used morally correct means for reasonable and fair purposes. In that context, the Italian experience illustrates the effective "best practices" through which to reverse the impetus toward forced radical change and/or failing- or failed-state status.[4]

THE MAIN PROTAGONISTS: THE RED BRIGADES

Objectives and Vision

The Italian irregular insurgency war (gang) phenomenon emerged from the prolonged protest cycle of the late 1960s. During those years, demands for political, economic, and social reforms were widespread and included elements of the entire society. Extreme left-wing fringe elements, ranging from white-collar workers to industrial workers to university students, organized and became a political force that was often violently confronted by police. Thus, the Red Brigades evolved from demonstrators favoring socioeconomic reforms into militants defending themselves against police repression. As time moved on, the violence of the Red Brigades changed from self-protection to proactive and aggressive actions. Those actions increasingly shifted from demonstrations, sit-ins, and passing out propaganda to direct violence against individuals and property. All these efforts were considered to be part of the war against the state because "the State, its juristic ideology, and its law are nothing other than instruments through which the elites exercise their control over the people."[5]

For the Red Brigadists, these political crimes quickly became acts of justice. At first, they were acts of retribution and vengeance against perceived attackers. For example, Aldo Moro had to be eliminated because he embodied "all that was the most intelligent and the most dangerous in the [governing] regime." Then, progressively, more ordinary individuals were singled out—depending on the "bureaucratic need."[6] "You make a political analysis, but then you need a victim. When you have singled out your victim . . . he is the one to be blamed for everything. In that moment, there is already the logic of a trial in which you have already decided that he is guilty; you only have to decide about his punishment. . . . [Y]ou punish him not only for what he has done but also for all the rest."[7] From that point, together with adventure, action became an objective, a motive, and a reward in itself.[8]

Basic Organization

The Red Brigades were founded in Milan by members of a militant leftist group called the Metropolitan Political Collective (CPM). Some of the organizers came from Marxist-Leninist backgrounds and others from the more moderate Italian left. The CPM quickly spread to Turin, where workers of that major industrial city increasingly became more violently involved with the police. Subsequent organizational splintering, reorganization, ideology, and actions were adapted to the needs of the organizers' militant orientation. As with the MS-13 gangs in Central America and the Jamaican posses, only people who were able to pass a rigorous vetting process and initiatory rites were accepted into the ranks of the Red Brigades. That process carefully evaluated an individual's military courage and group loyalty. Successful recruits were divided into regular and irregular forces. Regulars were the only members who were allowed into the vertical command structure, and they were required to go "underground" and work for the organization full time. Irregulars kept their paying "day jobs" and lived with their families. Their primary tasks were to recruit sympathizers and to help generate support for the movement. At the same time, as is the case for their counterparts in Latin America and the Caribbean, rules on centralization and vertical hierarchy were enforced strictly, and disagreements with authoritative decisions were not tolerated.[9]

The organizational structure of the Red Brigades included a strategic directorate, an executive committee, several "columns," and a number of "fronts." The column was the basic self-sustaining unit of the movement. It was composed of regulars and was given a specific geographic area of responsibility, such as Genoa, or certain neighborhoods of Milan, Turin, or Rome. The columns controlled subordinate brigades, termed "logistical" or "mass," depending on the mission: the logistical brigades provided support, and the mass brigades were responsible for intelligence and operations. Thus, the primary orientation of all recruits was either specifically military or to provide support for the military actions of the group. Because of that political culture, again—like Western Hemisphere gangs—the Red Brigades attracted those individual men and women who understood discipline and were prone to violence.[10]

The Program to Destroy the Moribund Italian State

At the height of Italian terrorism in the late 1970s, when people were asked about the program of the Red Brigades, most citizens would describe their terrorism as ad hoc and arbitrary. Arbitrary perhaps, but ad hoc it was not. The Red Brigade leadership opposed the idea of spontaneity, and all actions of the organization were carefully planned, organized, and implemented.[11] The primary means of attacking the state and the intent of any action conducted by the Red Brigades was simply to disrupt and destroy symbols of (1) whatever the leadership defined as "bad" or as a "threat" to organizational security and (2) whatever would lead to the progressive discrediting of public institutions that, in turn, would erode the basic public trust in the Italian government.[12]

Typical human targets for the mass brigades included representatives of the capitalist system of production, political figures, and members of the judiciary and security agencies. Typical material targets included property in any way related to the types of individuals noted above. Attacks on property either were complementary to attacks on persons or served for the training and testing of recruits. Targeting tactics involved close, long-term observation of targets and the use of explosives, individual weapons, and ambush, raid, or abduction—depending on the difficulty of attacking a specific individual and his or her prescribed punishment.[13] For example, major attacks included (1) the wounding of Gavino Manca in Milan, an executive at Pirelli; and the murder of Pietro Coggiola in Turin, an executive with Lancia; (2) the abduction and murder of the president of the Christian Democratic Party and former prime minister Aldo Moro in Rome; (3) the murder of Supreme Court Judge Ricardo Palma in Rome; and (4) the murder of Assistant Deputy Police Commissioner Antonio Esposito in Genoa.[14]

Interestingly, the degree of public tolerance for terrorist violence did not allow the murder of the five escorts accompanying Aldo Moro to be classified as murder—that is, only "major murders," such as that of Mr. Moro, were counted as murders. In any event, the ratio of woundings to murders generally was consistent over the late 1970s and early 1980s at about 2:1. And the ratio of abductions/kidnappings to murders over the same period was about 3 to 4:1.[15]

Thus, the program of the Red Brigades was straightforward, transparent, and unchanged from the organization's beginnings in 1969 through the early 1980s. The leadership stressed terrorism as a tactic and a strategy in an irregular urban war. Leaders assumed that terrorism would challenge the integrity of Italy's political and socioeconomic institutions and create an unacceptable level of instability. In turn, the resultant instability was expected to erode the basic public trust that must underlie the legitimate functioning of the state.[16]

RESPONSE TO RED BRIGADES' STRATEGY

The Italian experience with urban irregular war was the transition point toward a new age of unconventional conflict, in which the definition of "enemy" became elusive and the use of "power" against that foe became diffuse. Underlying these ambiguous issues was that this war was an intrastate affair: it was Italians versus Italians. All these ambiguities intruded on the traditional Italian and world vision of war and required a new paradigm that would address the addition of a several political-social-psychological-moral dimensions designed to attack the strategy of the Italian gang phenomenon.

Thinking about the New Paradigm

Italian planners generally understood that an ambiguous antigang urban political war was, in fact, a series of "wars" within the general war. These wars would include (1) the more traditional police-military war against the various antigovernment organizations; (2) a "war" for legitimacy and the moral right of the incumbent democratically elected regime to exist; (3) a "war" to unify a multidimensional political-social-psychological-police effort within the fragmented Italian bureaucracy; (4) an information "war" to convince the Italian people of the moral rectitude of the counterterrorist gang campaign; (5) a "war" to isolate the militant organizations from their internal support; (6) a "war" to isolate the militants from their external support; and (7) an intelligence "war" to locate and neutralize the men and women who lead, plan, and execute violent destabilizing actions. The SWORD data, first published in the SWORD Papers and subsequently in *Uncomfortable Wars,* show that these wars represent the major strategic dimensions that determine the outcome of the general war. The data also take into account the "forgotten" Clausewitzian political-psychological-social-economic-moral dimensions of conflict.[17] According to one of Clausewitz's translators, Michael Howard, these crucial "forgotten" dimensions make the difference between winning only the battles and winning the war itself.[18]

Because of the continuing absence of a homogenous parliamentary majority and the resultant political instability, the Italian government could not micromanage the paradigm. The government (fortunately for Italy) was limited to the promulgation of fundamental measures that would facilitate the conducting of a counterterrorist strategy at the national security level. Thus, at the national security level, government leadership understood that the concept of "wars within the war" would be the basis for the new paradigm. This concept was further reinforced by the fact that it is very close to the ideas that both Carl von Clausewitz and Niccolò Machiavelli addressed in their treatises on war and on gaining control of a state. Machiavelli, for example, argues that good laws and good arms allow the leader with *virtu* to master *fortuna* to take—or maintain—effective control of a state.

Superior virtu consists of six related elements: (1) a well-disciplined and trained security force; (2) careful planning for the application of that force before and after power is achieved; (3) the skillful use of spies (intelligence); (4) isolation of the enemy from the various sources of his support; (5) *unison* (unity) of political-military effort; and (6) perceived prudence (*prudenza,* that is, moral rectitude, self-restraint, and justice).[19] Italian strategic leaders also understood that this particular conflict was a situation in which one part of the populace was pitted against another. As a result, there was no way this confrontation could be allowed to degenerate into a simple military conflict. This intrastate war would have to be fought with prudenza, so as to avoid, as much as possible, damage to the future state of peace, prosperity, stability, and security of the country.[20]

Implementing Fundamental Support Measures

At the national security level, it was understood that the conducting of the diverse wars within the general war could not be left to the discordant elements of the Italian state bureaucracy working separately and pursuing their own agendas. An organization would have to be created that was designed to achieve an adequate level of governmental unity of effort (*unison*) and that could be made more effective with the addition of a centralized intelligence capability. As a consequence, the government created a temporary Counterterrorism Task Force. That organization was given the primary responsibility for both intelligence collection and counterterrorist operations. Thus, intelligence, operational planning, and multiorganizational civil-military coordination fell to the unifying Counterterrorism Task Force.[21] In that context, the prescribed mode of operations for the task force was the subtle use of soft power supported by relevant information warfare, careful intelligence work, and surgical precision in removing specific individual male and female terrorists or gang members from the general populace.[22]

Then, at the legislative level, it was agreed that the moral legitimacy of the Italian republic was strong enough to allow the planning, public dissemination, and implementation of a coordinated and legitimized counterterrorist (countergang) policy. State legitimacy also was strong enough to allow the promulgation of a modern criminal code and "hard law" legislation directed specifically against violent antigovernment organizations. This legislation brought the pre–World War II Criminal Code of 1930 up to date and specifically addressed conspiracy and actions taken for the purposes of subverting the democratic order.[23] As a consequence, the concept of national security was expanded to allow the government to confront—morally as well as physically—the nontraditional strategy of the Red Brigades and their irregular allies.

The Manwaring Paradigm (SWORD Model)

THE MORE-TRADITIONAL POLICE-MILITARY WAR

Experience and the SWORD data show that a successful war against an asymmetric, irregular enemy must be conducted by a highly professional, well-disciplined, motivated security force that is capable of discrete, rapid, decisive surgical action anywhere in a given battle space. Moreover, that action must be designed to achieve political and psychological as well as police-military objectives.[24] In Italy, there was a certain reluctance to take the broadened definition of national security to its logical conclusion and correspondingly broaden the role of the military to a controversial internal protection mission. Planners understood that legitimacy considerations required that the role of the regular armed forces should be limited to supporting the major police organizations. As a result, the ever-present but relatively unobtrusive paramilitary Carabiniere was given the mission of conducting the more traditional "police-military war," and Carabiniere General Carlo Alberto Dalla Chiesa was given the mandate to direct that effort.[25]

As an example of this prudent *unison* approach to "the police-military war," the regular Italian armed forces generally assumed routine, inconspicuous, and unobtrusive police functions that allowed the state police, other police forces, and the national Carabiniere freedom to concentrate on the countergang/terrorist mission. The Carabiniere metaphorically replaced the smart bomb aimed at an apartment in downtown Milan with a discrete knock on the door. In doing that, the Carabiniere was able to destroy a Red Brigade cell without destroying the apartment building or displacing its residents. Within the short to mid term, the Carabiniere gained the approval and admiration of the community and contributed directly to the enhancement of the popular perception that government action was used for reasonable and legitimate purposes. That, in turn, generated positive implications for future social peace in Italy. Under General Dalla Chiesa's leadership, long-term and short-term mutually supportive objectives were determined and pursued, and the war was discreetly brought under control as early as 1981–82.[26]

THE LEGITIMACY WAR

The SWORD data show that the moral right of a regime to govern is the most important single dimension in a war against any adversary. The thrust of a program to depose a government relies on grievances such as political, economic, and social injustices as the means through which government is attacked.[27]

Once the Italian parliament had provided the legislation that would allow the prosecution of a serious antiterrorist war, legitimacy was recognized as key to the success or failure for the terrorist gang phenomenon or for the government. The Red Brigades, for example, identified legitimacy as the primary center of gravity in their strategy to destroy the incumbent regime.[28] The Italian bureaucracy understood that popular perceptions of various injustices tended to limit the right—and the ability—of the government to conduct the business of the state. It countered with programs designed to preempt the militants' antigovernment terrorism strategy. The coordination task was to ensure that every policy, program, and action—political, economic, social, opinion making, and security—would contribute directly to enhancing the popular perception that governmental authority did, in fact, serve public needs and was applied in a morally correct manner.[29]

THE WAR FOR UNITY OF EFFORT

This dimension of an irregular—or conventional—war involves overcoming parochial bureaucratic interests, fighting "turf battles," and ensuring that all governmental efforts are focused on the ultimate common goal, survival. That is to say, the government must have the necessary organization to coordinate and implement an effective unity of political-diplomatic, socioeconomic, psychological-moral, and security-stability efforts against those who would destroy the government. And it had to have the ability to accomplish these tasks in a manner acceptable to the Italian people—which equates back to legitimacy. The data clearly show that without an organization at the highest level to establish, enforce, and continually refine a national plan, authority is fragmented and ineffective in resolving the myriad problems endemic to an asymmetric/irregular assault on the state; thus, it will be a failure.[30]

The Italian government understood that lack of *unison* (unity of effort) was a major deficiency in the conduct of the business of the state and in the conduct of the antiterrorist campaign. As noted above, in 1978–79, the parliament passed an emergency national security measure that created a temporary task force composed of state police, finance guard, and Carabiniere personnel. As a consequence, planning and coordination, to the extent that it was achieved in Italy, essentially fell to that task force. Although not perfect or all-encompassing, it was adequate to the task at hand, achieved its objectives, and was responsible for bringing the Red Brigades and the rest of the gang phenomenon under control within just over two years.[31]

The Information War

When the vast majority of the people are willing to support the state and government forces to implement well-motivated counterterrorist actions, a cooperative synergism of trust is created, which makes the state's informational and public diplomacy efforts effective. The ultimate center of gravity of a country (that is, the hub of all power and movement on which everything depends) is made up of its people and their views, or public opinion. People are the country's primary sources of physical, psychological, and moral strength. Legitimate long-term military and other power depend on the proverbial "hearts and minds" of the citizenry. Thus, as shown by experience and the SWORD data, the climate of opinion that might ultimately lead to support rather than hostility or indifference toward the political institutions of the state must be carefully channeled by a legal, democratic, and moral orientation.[32]

In the Italian case, the state and the media embarked on a strong counterterrorist, public diplomacy campaign. The objectives were to expose and exploit the fact that the various left-wing, right-wing, separatist, pacifist, and other groups making up the terrorist gang phenomenon were not popular organizations representing the masses. Rather, these groups were self-appointed elites whose goals were not in line with what the people wanted or needed. In the final analysis, the government's antiterrorist information war demonstrated that to the terrorists, Italians who were not ideological "true believers" were not really people. As an example, the 2,384 victims who had been murdered, maimed, or kidnapped by any one of the gang phenomena in 1979 were not considered to be human beings deserving of personal dignity, according to the public diplomacy campaign. Instead, the victims were considered "tools of the system," "pigs," and "watch dogs."[33] Moreover, the campaign pointed out that Red Brigadists considered everyone else—even other comrades on the left—to be merely "shit."[34] As a result, terrorist violence, regardless of political orientation, began to be increasingly perceived by the Italian public as wanton and well beyond what might be necessary to make a political statement.

The Wars to Isolate the Terrorists from Internal and External Sources of Support

Logic, experience, and the data indicate that the problem here is to isolate politically, psychologically, and militarily the violent irregular and asymmetric opposition from their primary sources of aid—whoever and wherever those may be.[35] Internally, the Italian gang phenomenon was isolated from the rest of the society as a result of the effect of the legitimacy war, the information war, and the physical paramilitary war. As the terrorists withdrew more and more into their highly secretive and compartmentalized organizational structure, they isolated themselves from the rest of the Italian community. That separation from the outside world further restricted access to external reality, the capability to recruit new members, and the ability to organize significant actions.[36]

Support for the Italian terrorists, however, was not necessarily localized within the borders of the country. Italian antigovernment groups, especially the Red Brigades, were known to be supported by the Soviet Union; Soviet surrogates such as Cuba, Bulgaria, and Czechoslovakia; and Middle Eastern and North African states, including Iraq, Iran, and Libya.[37] More specifically, this aid included "Energia bombs" as part of the materials provided by Palestinians and "revolutionary training" as part of the aid provided by Cuba, Libya, and the Soviet Union.[38]

Support for the Italian government's antiterrorist program on the part of external powers, such as the United States and other Western countries, proved to be spotty and ineffective. If credit is given where it is due, the Italian state deserves most of the credit for effectively bringing the gang phenomenon under control; however, that governmental success was at least partly based on a certain level of failure and internal isolation on the part of the various terrorist organizations.[39]

The Intelligence War

Individual men and women lead, plan, execute, and support any given conflict. As a result, a major concern in any kind of war must be individuals. As a key part of the attack against an irregular enemy's strategy, the state's intelligence apparatus must be in place or be created so that it can locate, isolate, and neutralize the adversary's organizational and leadership structure. Again, experience and the data show clearly that the best police or paramilitary forces are of little consequence unless they know exactly who the enemy is and precisely where enemy forces are located.[40]

The Italian government's efforts to find, discredit, and neutralize the Red Brigades and their leadership focused on the activities of General Dalla Chiesa's counterterrorism task force and the Ministry of the Interior's Central Directorate for Crime Prevention.[41] The Central Directorate for Crime Prevention coordinated the operations of the counterterrorism branch offices organic to the state police in every province of Italy. Dalla Chiesa's task force coordinated the entire intelligence collection effort as well as police operations. Thus, an intelligence orientation or mindset was established in combination with an organization that had the capability to strike at times, at places, and in ways that took the terrorist gangs by surprise. The short-term effect was to neutralize a given group. The long-term effect was to shift the balance of power decidedly toward the legitimate organs of the Italian state.[42]

A specific example from this situation is instructive. Because of the self-imposed isolation of the Italian terrorist organizations, they had only little intelligence with which to work. In stark contrast, the state developed a large and increasingly effective intelligence network. Nevertheless, the role played by the legal Italian Communist Party (PCI) was probably the most decisive factor in destroying the Red Brigades and their various political allies. The PCI's capillary structure—strengthened by the many efficient ancillary organizations that had been collecting information on the entire political organizational spectrum for years—was able to identify and locate specific organizations, leaders, and members relatively easily and quickly. The PCI furnished a great deal of this kind of intelligence to the state security organizations and made them appear to be much more efficient and effective than they really were. In any event, timely and accurate human intelligence provided by the PCI considerably enhanced the Italian government's ability to attack the organization and leadership architecture of the Red Brigades' and other antigovernment groups' terrorism strategies.[43]

IMPLICATIONS

Analysis of the central strategic problem in Italy resulted in the identification of three levels of threat—cause, effect, and response. By 1978 and beyond, however, analysts recognized that the greatest single threat to Italian security and stability (closely related to cause, effect, and response) was actually a void, a failure of the government. The terrorist threat was indeed caused, exacerbated, and allowed to intensify because the elected political institutions of the Italian government had failed to provide responsible governance and had failed to recognize and respond to the associated challenge posed by the terroristic gang phenomenon.[44]

The telling points of the above implication focus on the thrust of any given terrorist, insurgent, or other asymmetric program relying heavily on grievances such as political, economic, and social injustices to depose a government. Moreover, these are the primary means through which a government is attacked and destroyed. A counterterrorism campaign that fails to understand its citizens' legitimate grievances and fails to adapt its strategy to deal with public opinion as the key center of gravity in conventional and unconventional conflict is likely to fail.

For Italians, antigovernment terrorism was the most important political phenomenon of the 1970s and 1980s. For the rest of the world, terrorism is likely to be the most important political phenomenon of the twenty-first century. Precisely how an array or combination of threats might be accomplished now and in the future is limited only by the imagination, but the Italian experience dictates that a minimum of two possibilities must be taken into consideration.

First, the Red Brigades and their hundreds of allies demonstrated to the world how the weak could attack the strong. An unlimited number of violent nonstate actors, gangs, and even individual loonies have learned that they can easily and cheaply hold whole nations at ransom. Whether the irregular attackers are sincerely trying to achieve specific political objectives or are merely trying to gain some monetary or visceral satisfaction for carrying out violent acts is irrelevant. Second, nonstate and other political actors in the global security arena are almost certain to use nuclear weapons, chemical and biological weapons, and cyber weapons in current and future conflicts as "equalizers." Given the asymmetry between challengers and the challenged, only the foolish will fight conventionally. These are the realities of power and politics in the contemporary world chaos.

Finally, the Italian case demonstrates that success in countering terrorism and asymmetric war of all kinds in the "new world disorder" will be constructed on the same theoretical bases that supported favorable results in the past. Even though every conflict is situation specific, it is not unique. Throughout the universe of possibilities, there are analytical commonalities at the strategic and high operational levels. In particular, the seven dimensions, or dependent variables (and the numerous independent variables), discussed in the preceding section determine the success or failure of an asymmetric, irregular intrastate war. The paradigm demonstrated in this Italian case (and others) has power and virtue in part because of the symmetry of its application—both for a besieged government and its allies, and for a violent internal challenger and its allies. That is to say, no successful strategy—on either side of the conflict spectrum—has been formulated over the past fifty years that has not explicitly or implicitly taken into account all of those strategic dimensions, or "wars within the war," noted in the SWORD Papers and as applied in the Italian situation.[45]

KEY POINTS AND LESSONS

- In 1978–83, the Italian gang phenomenon included over three hundred politically diverse organizations motivated to the violent replacement of what they defined as a "moribund" state. The resultant antigovernment campaign relied on internal urban terrorist tactics and strategies from which to develop a support base and to act as an ideological substitute for conventional war.
- The primary terrorist organization, the Red Brigades, utilized a vigorous, broad, and violent set of terrorist tactics to implement its objective of bringing down the Italian state. The Red Brigades, a theoretical equivalent to a third-generation gang, illustrated the increasing lack of differentiation between insurgents, terrorists, international criminals, and gangs.
- The Italian government—once it made the political decision to treat the increasing levels of violence and instability generated by the Red Brigades and that organization's militant allies as a national security problem—planned, organized, and implemented a soft multilayered political-paramilitary response. That approach to attacking the violent opposition's terrorist strategy was successful and brought terrorism under control within a surprisingly short two- to three-year period.
- As a corollary, the unwillingness or inability of a government to develop a long-term, multidimensional, and morally acceptable strategy to confront violent internal nonstate actors was recognized as a threat to the stability and sovereignty of the state itself. In these terms, the state has the clear responsibility to take legitimate measures to confront such violent political actors and avoid the intended destruction of the state.

These hard-won lessons learned from the Italian experience with the gang phenomenon are all too relevant in the political-psychological wars of the twenty-first century. Sun Tzu maintained, "Those skilled in war subdue the enemy's army without battle."[46] In that context, he also argues that "the reason the enlightened prince and the wise general conquer the enemy whenever they move and their achievements surpass [and surprise] those of ordinary men is foreknowledge. . . . What is called 'foreknowledge' cannot be elicited from spirits, nor from gods, nor by analogy with past events, nor from calculations. It must be obtained from men to know the enemy situation [and strategy]."[47]

THE CHALLENGE, THREAT, AND MAIN TASKS FOR NOW AND THE FUTURE

A multipolar world in which one or a hundred actors are exerting differing types and levels of asymmetric power within a set of cross-cutting alliances is extremely volatile and dangerous. The security and stability of the global community is threatened, and the benefits of globalism could be denied to all. Thus, it is incumbent on the United States, the West, and the rest of the international community to understand and cope with the governance challenges exacerbated by the destabilizing and devastating political violence generated by the irregular insurgency war phenomenon.

The challenge, then, is to come to terms with the fact that contemporary security, at whatever level, is at its base a holistic political-diplomatic, socioeconomic, psychological-moral, and military-police effort. The corollary is to change from a singular military or law enforcement approach to a multidimensional, multiorganizational, multicultural, and multinational paradigm.

The ultimate threat is that—unless leaders at the highest levels recognize what is happening strategically, reorient thinking and actions appropriately, and are able to educate and lead their various constituencies into the realities of the postmodern world—it is only a matter of time before the destabilizing problems associated with irregular insurgency war will cause the failure of one vitally important actor or another.

The main tasks in the search for security now and for the future are to construct national and international stability and well-being based on the lessons—negative and positive—learned from present and past cases. The consistency of those lessons is impressive. That consistency warrants confidence that success in countering an irregular challenge to the state, and its associated violence, will be achieved as a result of understanding counterterrorist efforts that have proved successful in the past. The keys to success encompassed in the "wars within the war" of the Italian experience include (1) a realistic strategic vision to counter an irregular/unconventional challenge to the state; (2) a management structure to plan, unify, and implement that vision; and (3) the use of appropriate political-economic-social-security instruments of state and international power to conduct the multidimensional wars within the general war. This is nothing radical. It is basic security strategy and national asset management.

Afterword

The Manwaring Paradigm as a Guide to U.S. National Security in Asymmetric Warfare and for Strengthening the U.S. National Security System

EDWIN G. CORR

In the preceding chapters, Max G. Manwaring has applied his paradigm, Robert Yin's "suspense approach," and the case-study method to seven insurgency, terrorism, and crime cases that, though distinct from one another in their nature, overlap to varying degrees in form, tactics, and weaponry (including terror). From the case studies, the nature of the threat of asymmetric warfare to the United States is clear, as are three distinct paths that can lead to effective and accountable governance, which is Manwaring's desired end state for defeating insurgencies, terrorism, and international crime. The seven cases in their totality provide a description of the transnational, nonstate military and political challenges to the United States and the nation-state world system that originate principally from countries and regions where governance of states is weak to nonexistent.[1]

The current turmoil, instability, hostility, and violence in much of the world are not new, but first colonialism and then the cold war contained these phenomena (the latter while the two cold war blocs focused on the threat of nuclear war). Nevertheless, the 1988 Commission on Integrated Long-Term Strategy's Report by the Regional Conflict Working Group points out that at least thirty wars and twice as many guerrilla conflicts in the previous four decades killed more than 16 million people in developing countries, or what during the cold war was called the Third World.[2] However, the protagonists of those conflicts seldom directed destruction at the great powers outside their Third World areas of conflict. Today the situation is different.

The United States and its partners must address these particular threats from the asymmetric war arena while also managing and coping with two other security arenas: "rogue states" trying to develop nuclear weapons that threaten the United States; and the existing nation-state system arena. U.S. foreign and national security policies must simultaneously enhance the U.S. position within the nation-state world system as well as shape the global balance-of-power system that is emerging and will mature over the next couple of decades. This system probably will consist of superpowers (the United States, Europe, China, Japan, India, and Russia), a second tier of twenty or so major countries, and a large group of smaller states varying in wealth and power.[3]

For the United States to cope with challenges to its security and welfare in these three security arenas, it must have an overarching strategy. This multiple-threat scenario, which has come to replace the single predominating threat that existed during the cold war, makes it difficult for the American public and top political decision makers in the United States to focus the nation's efforts.

WHAT THE MANWARING PARADIGM TEACHES US ABOUT ASYMMETRIC WARS

The Threat and Nature of the Enemy

The famed military theorists Sun Tzu and Carl von Clausewitz teach that a fundamental principle of warfare is to know one's enemy. But who is the enemy, and what is it that Manwaring tells us about those who wage asymmetric warfare against the United States and its partner states?

The stated goals of Al Qaeda, its attacks on the United States, Europe, and other states, and its war against the United States in Iraq clearly establish it as a foe. The United States is also the publicly declared target of Venezuelan fourth-generation warfare (4GW) as well as a number of the world's other insurgencies. Al Qaeda intellectuals see their jihad against the United States as essential to reconquering "Islamic lands" and to further territorial extension. Hugo Chavez considers his 4GW to be a long war that will end in the defeat of the United States and the establishment of a Bolivarian twenty-first-century socialist regime throughout Latin America and perhaps beyond. Al Qaeda, 4GW, and their subgroups are illustrative of U.S. enemies in the insurgency-terrorism arena. And, finally, these religious and ideological movements join forces with transnational crime organizations for whom the United States is the major market.

Insurgencies, terrorist groups, and transnational criminal groups exist as local-, state-, and transnational-level organizations. The transnationalization of these organizations is related to the length of their existence and successes and also to their association with religious or ideological movements. These nonstate groups regard states where they reside (but do not control) as their enemies. When they become transnational—in terms of their own activities or because of support from states or from nongovernmental organizations outside the state where they are located—the insurgents, terrorists, and transnational crime organizations (TCOs) usually regard the United States and its partner countries as foes. This is because the United States and its partners generally support a certain level of global order throughout the state-based world system and often provide specific support to the state or states that insurgents and terrorists are attacking.

A major contribution of this book is the singling out of gangs and other TCOs as national security threats, not only to small countries but also to larger countries, such as Brazil and Mexico, and as a growing threat at the local level within the United States. This phenomenon is also a menace to nation-states because the illegal gains from criminal activity often nurture ideological and religious enemy movements and groups.

The motivations for insurgents, terrorists, and TCOs can be ideological (or political), religious, or criminal and are nearly always a mixture of two or more of these. The longer that ideologically and religiously based insurgent groups exist, the more likely they are to move into criminal activity, especially lucrative narcotics trafficking. At the same time, basically criminal groups are likely over time to develop political goals to protect their criminal interests, and they may begin to cloak their criminal activities behind political, ideological, or religious rhetoric and movements. The longer that ideologically and religiously inspired movements exist, the more likely they are to become incrementally politically corrupt and criminal.

Classical insurgencies against a government in a specific country usually consist of multiple nonstate actors, as occurred in Colombia, Italy, and Uruguay. These differing organizations or factions seldom are in full agreement, but they tend to be more so when strong ideological and radical religious commitments are shared. Still, because such movements are not monolithic, there are opportunities to drive wedges among the organizations or factions of the insurgent fronts.

While for the first time in four hundred years transnational nonstate actors (such as Al Qaeda) are seriously challenging the state-based world system, states' support or tolerance of the nonstate insurgents continues to be integral to nonstate organizations' war efforts.[4] Belligerent nonstate movements must control areas or states or have alliances with states or factions of government within states to advance the movements' interests. Though the expressed ultimate goal of Al Qaeda is to reestablish a caliphate and a united Islamic political-religious empire under sharia legal codes, for example, Al Qaeda is clear in its intermediate objective of controlling some states for use in advancement to its final goal. Currently, Al Qaeda is ensconced in the remote border areas of Pakistan and Afghanistan and seeks victory in and control of Iraq to gain another important safe area or stronghold from which to consolidate and conduct war against "apostate" Muslim-populated states (such as Saudi Arabia, Egypt, Jordan) and their allies, mainly Europe and the United States. Hugo Chavez's use of Venezuela's resources and petroleum income for 4GW against the United States and Western Hemisphere governments that are not in the Bolivarian camp is another example of the essential role of states in relation to an insurgent movement.

There is some question as to whether primarily criminal insurgencies actually want overtly to take over governments, since such states are disparaged within the international community and other states are likely to exert strong pressures on criminally controlled states. This was the case with the nefarious Luis Garcia Meza dictatorship in Bolivia, with the removal of Garcia Meza being a condition for the United States' restoring an ambassador there—me in 1981. Criminal groups may prefer to control a weak state indirectly rather than to occupy its government. States supporting transnational insurgent movements or international crime activities know that they are potential targets for the United States, which generally opposes transnational insurgencies, terrorism, and TCOs.

The magnitude, scope, resilience, and potential for growth of insurgencies, terrorist groups, and gangs and other TCOs have resulted in these being a major security threat to the United States and other states of the state-based world system. This cohort of nonstate actors is the most imminent menace to the United States, although it is not yet strong enough to threaten our survival immediately. The threats from these nonstate actors have evolved from local and state levels to prominence in the international arena, and signs are that they will remain a threat into the future.

Though the instruments of war and communication now are very different from those of earlier eras, the expansion of this insurgent threat might be compared with the extended and sporadic invasions of the perimeters of the Roman Empire that converted it into a "failing empire" and led finally to its demise. A parallel comparison to the Roman Empire is the current concern about U.S. government encroachment on civil liberties in the name of fighting terrorism and the Roman Republic's response in 68 B.C. to a threatening league of nonstate pirates. The Senate set aside 700 years of constitutional law, abridged ancient rights and liberties of Roman citizens, and appointed Pompey as supreme commander of the armed forces. Most historians consider this to be the beginning of the end of the Roman Republic.[5]

The Manwaring Paradigm's Three Paths to Effective Legitimate Governance

Manwaring shows through the case studies how application of dimensions of the Manwaring Paradigm in several countries following three different paths led to success, defined as the reduction of insurgencies, terror, and TCOs and the establishment of more-effective legitimate governance. The first of these paths is illuminated by the Italian case, which demonstrates the effective application of the principles of the paradigm in a state-implemented counterterrorism strategy and campaign. It is a "best practices" case for an existing state under attack by insurgents, terrorists, and criminals.

The second path is revealed in the Uruguay case by a major guerrilla faction of the Tupamaros that (after experiencing at least temporary defeat by the Uruguayan military government and after observing the dead end to which excessive violence had led the Montonero guerrillas in neighboring Argentina) transformed itself and eventually captured the government via democratic elections. The Tupamaros were thus able to implement many of their desired political and social reforms, though doing so required a willingness to forgo violence, adapt, negotiate, and compromise. Manwaring says that this path requires a guerrilla group to (1) realize that a peaceful rather than a violent solution is needed; (2) overcome ideological (or religious) rhetoric and move toward the idea of accountable legitimate governance; (3) overcome isolation and create a political platform to win elections; and (4) overcome ideological contradictions between capitalism and democracy, so as to create a viable national economic system.

Manwaring suggests a third successful path to effective and legitimate governance through the Portuguese case. During the cold war, the Portuguese armed forces overthrew a long-existing civilian dictatorship to end the futile colonial wars in Africa. Then, to stymie a takeover by the Communist Party, the armed forces led the country through democratic and social reforms to install an effective, accountable to-the-people, legitimate government.

This example was emulated or carried out in several Third World countries, especially in Latin America, during what Samuel Huntington termed the "third wave of democracy" at the end of the twentieth century. I was directly involved in such transitions in Thailand, Ecuador, Peru, Bolivia, and El Salvador. This process is related to what academics in the 1950s and 1960s labeled the "Third Path," in which the armed forces (as institutions, not by *caudillo* leaders), working with civilian technocrats and military-sponsored political parties, conducted a tutelary transition from authoritarianism to constitutional, democratic government. Unfortunately, many military leaders of Third World countries, for reasons of power and control of the national treasury, kept postponing the actual handover of power. Another concern about this path is the possibility of its being a sham or a slippery slope taken by initially well intentioned military leaders who end up establishing another military dictatorship.[6]

There would seem to be little doubt that the first path is the most desirable when important U.S. interests are at stake. The preferred situation is for the United States to provide civilian and military resources without having to commit combat troops. To commit combat forces, top U.S. decision makers must be sure that U.S. vital interests are in jeopardy, that the United States has the wherewithal, and that there is sufficient public will and support to carry out a well-conceived combined civilian and military campaign that will achieve the goals of both the local nation-states and the United States. Committing U.S. combat forces seems inevitably to become exponentially expensive in terms of economic and political costs and often in lives, both American and others. Military force is often an essential ingredient, but success requires more political and developmental accomplishments than military ones. When the United States commits combat forces, the rule normally is to keep the presence minimal, except when the enemy force is large and lethal. If the United States introduces troops for combat and occupation, then the amount of force should be overwhelming and there should be a clear and early exit strategy.

The second and third paths are complicated and difficult, but they are sometimes necessary; the United States does not have the luxury of dealing only with nation-states still strong enough and with the leadership and will to travel the first path. The United States must also cope with revolutionary situations and military dictatorships and must hone its thinking and tools to deal with them. In all these cases, the paradigm remains valid.

THE PILLARS OF SUCCESS FOR THE UNITED STATES AT WAR

In a chapter in Manwaring's *Gray Area Phenomena* and then again in Manwaring and William J. Olson's *Managing Contemporary Conflict: Pillars of Success* (1996), former ambassador David C. Miller stated that the United

States prevailed against the Soviet Union because of three fundamental strengths: the development of theories of engagement; the development of appropriate weapons systems with safeguards and controls; and the development of an executive branch management structure to implement the theories of engagement, using both civilian and military assets wisely.[7] These three pillars are critical in national conflicts.

THE PARADIGM AS A THEORY OF ENGAGEMENT FOR ASYMMETRIC WARFARE

The Manwaring Paradigm contains the components of an overarching U.S. strategy for dealing with asymmetric warfare, including insurgencies, terrorist groups, and gangs and other TCOs. The Manwaring Paradigm, similar to George Kennan's containment theory of engagement, does not presume that we must militarily conquer or destroy the enemy quickly—rather, the presumption is that we are in a long-term, complex political and developmental struggle. As shown in the case studies, the attacked state and its supporter states' effective application of the paradigm (whether consciously or unconsciously) leads to the reduction (if not destruction) or transformation of these violent movements that threaten peace and public order, and this creates the possibility of establishing effective legitimate governance throughout their territories. One imperative is deliberate elimination of the "gray areas" within which insurgents, terrorists, and TCOs have taken root and from which they have expanded sufficiently to threaten the states where they operate—and in some cases, the United States and U.S. partner countries' interests or territory.

Simply defeating militarily the bulk of an insurgency, capturing major terrorist groups, and locking up gang leaders and crime bosses is not sufficient. Extending the constant presence of the state throughout states' territories, the imposition of law and justice, and social and economic development are the keys to diminishing and defeating this threat over the medium and long term. This is what the "legitimate governance" dimension of the Manwaring Paradigm is about; this makes it the most important dimension of the paradigm, followed in importance by the "unity of effort" dimension. Each of the seven dimensions of the paradigm is an integral part of a whole, but these two variables are the most important.

WHAT THE MANWARING PARADIGM IMPLIES FOR THE UNITED STATES ABOUT ITS NATIONAL SECURITY STRUCTURE

The bureaucratic structure and agencies concerned with national security and the way in which the president makes, coordinates, and implements foreign and national security policies need to be fixed. Application of the Manwaring Paradigm and the "suspense approach" to the U.S. national security system simultaneously reveals how the United States has failed to adapt enough to the changed security situation and suggests necessary reforms in the national security system for the optimum conduct of U.S. foreign policy and the protection of the United States.

The Suspense Approach and U.S. National Security Structure

Where We Are

In 2007, a growing number of observers and commentators described U.S. involvement in Iraq as a mistake. Resentment was directed chiefly against the president, the vice president, the secretary of defense, active duty general officers of the armed forces (for being too reticent to offer dissenting advice to superiors), and high-level officials in the Department of State (for allowing themselves to be sidelined in the decision-making process). However, few critics to date have focused on the national security system in terms of process, organization, and relative strengths and balance among the departments involved with respect to resources and people; nor has the overdependence on private-sector contractors and nongovernmental organizations (NGOs) been critically assessed. The Manwaring Paradigm helps us to do that.

For most Americans, war is the province of the military (perhaps even more so, now that there is an all-volunteer, professional army and no draft); increasingly, of "for profit" private-sector contractors; and to some degree, of humanitarian "do-good" nongovernmental organizations. Other civilian Americans are presumed to be only marginally involved in wars today. Additionally, even though one life lost in war is tragic, the level of American military deaths in Iraq has remained relatively low in comparison with other wars. There are growing concerns about the economic costs of the Iraq War, but current American living standards have not yet been greatly affected. In contrast to the World War II domestic situation, in the United States today there is little sense of deprivation, much less of sacrifice. There is, nevertheless, citizen frustration about how we got into the Iraq War, the lack of preparation for the occupation, and the immense costs of occupation.

Out of this frustration, calls for changes in national security policy making and structure are heard. There have been reforms during the past decades in components of the national security structure, but as yet, there has been no comprehensive overhaul of the system, as the United States did successfully with the 1947 National Security Act when faced by a new kind of enemy and the nuclear threat. We confront a new kind of enemy today in nonstate global insurgencies.

Briefly, critics have said that the United States' overall national security system is badly impaired, if not broken, because of (1) an inadequate intelligence capability; (2) relatively weak civilian departments and agencies for diplomacy and development; (3) a disproportionately funded and staffed Department of Defense, armed forces with a questionable internal distribution of resources and personnel, and the Department of Defense and armed forces creeping incrementally into almost every function of national security regardless whether they are the most effective bureaucratic organization for the tasks; (4) overreliance on private-sector contracted companies to carry out national security functions and development for which they are not designed and have not proven capable; (5) overreliance on nongovernmental "not-for-profit" organizations for development projects; and (6), last but perhaps most important, the weakness of the decision-making process and the command and coordinating structure for the president's use in managing foreign policy and national security. Adding to the challenge of fixing this situation, changes in the system are resisted by Congress because congresspersons' personal careers and political largesse are connected to supporting the executive departments and agencies that they oversee through their committee assignments.

Where We Came From

In the Declaration of Independence (1776), one of the "injuries and usurpations" that our founders listed against the king was that he had "affected to render the military independent of, and superior to the civil power."[8] From the Revolutionary War period through World War II, the United States principally used conscripted soldiers in times of war; when the nation was not at war, the armed forces were relatively small in number and were meagerly funded. The armed forces were important in the westward expansion but aside from this were not a major influence on other aspects of American politics, the economy, or the bulk of American lives. George Washington in his 1796 Farewell Address had warned against "overgrown military establishments," which "under any form of government, are inauspicious to liberty, and which are to be regarded as particularly hostile to republican liberty."[9] Safe behind two oceans and with nonthreatening neighbors to the north and south, the United States followed this founding father's advice until the country was thrust upon the stage of history by World War II.

Granted, the United States during the nineteenth century expanded across the North American continent with an imperialist outreach in the Mexican and Spanish-American wars and in the early twentieth century embarked on military incursions and occupations in the Caribbean and Central America. However, this happened without either immense growth in the land forces or an increased military influence within society or government. World War II, the cold war, and the United States' role as a superpower altered this state of affairs.

With the enactment of the National Security Act of 1947, the United States revamped and formed a new management and coordination structure and created new civilian agencies and military commands to respond to threats from the Soviet bloc. Although this proved effective, there were questions early on about the impact that the large defense establishment would have on U.S. society and politics. Questions increased because of disenchantment with the Vietnam War and, later, concern over whether the national security structure was adequate for the wars the United States was actually fighting, because of growing U.S.

involvement in low-intensity conflicts around the globe. Nuclear war was avoided, but small proxy wars (with varying results) were not. Concern about the impact of a large influential defense establishment was again voiced by President Dwight D. Eisenhower in his 1961 Farewell Address, in which he warned "that in the councils of government, we must guard against the acquisition of unwarranted influence, whether sought or unsought, by the military-industrial complex."[10]

Because of worries about foreign policy and national security performance and questions about our national security machinery in terms of the proper mix and setting of priorities, during the past half century numerous governmental commissions were created to review the matter and to make recommendations for improvement. Ambassador Miller and I (first in *Low Intensity Conflict: Old Conflicts in a New World* and again in *Managing Contemporary Conflict: Pillars of Success*) listed eleven major reports written between 1958 and 1993, and there have been at least a half dozen more since then, most recently the Baker-Hamilton Bipartisan Commission Report on Iraq.[11] No commission's recommendations have been fully adopted or implemented. Major parts of the national security system were overhauled, but the system as a whole has not been. Improvements in parts of the system sometimes have resulted in greater imbalances and poorer operation of the system as a whole.

Manwaring's Paradigm Applied to Correcting the U.S. National Security System

In this part of the afterword, attention is given primarily to the "unity of effort" and "legitimacy" dimensions. Other dimensions are touched upon only in passing. However, in a thorough analysis of the U.S. national security system, each variable should be examined.

Manwaring's "Unity of Effort" Dimension Applied to the U.S. National Security System

A major concern about the U.S. national security system relates to the Defense Department's continuing movement into areas that I believe would be better carried out by civilian agencies if such agencies existed or existing agencies had more capacity. This judgment should not be taken as criticism of the professionalism and commitment of military personnel. Additionally, the armed forces have an imperative to take charge in violent conflict situations when societies and their governing structures have broken down; however, this should be rare and in keeping with the established procedures by which the president makes an exception by transferring command from an ambassador to a military commander by a presidential finding.[12]

In asymmetric warfare, control should be returned to civilian authority as early as possible because functions relating to foreign civilians and civil institutions are most effectively carried out by U.S. civilian agencies. There are two primary underlying reasons for this: first, the disparate missions for which military and civilian personnel are recruited, prepared, and trained; and second, the way in which this translates into their respective applications of force—the military "to seek and destroy" and the civilians to apply only the sufficient amount of power to halt the violence and then to seek "civil" resolution of the problems. The latter approach is the key to success in asymmetric warfare, since such wars must be fought discriminately, both by individuals and in the selection of what kind of organizations are used for specific tasks.[13]

Because U.S. civilian agencies in the foreign policy and national security system have not kept pace—largely because of lack of sufficient resources—with the military, they need to be overhauled thoroughly. This must begin with increasing their capacity through larger budgets, more personnel, and more-disciplined, professional, and competent civilian organizations within the foreign policy and national security bureaucracy. Some very important steps have been taken by the U.S. government to repair the national security structure. Secretaries of State Colin Powell and Condoleezza Rice fought to increase personnel and to increase training and equipment. Secretary Powell's progress was undone by staffing demands of Iraq, Afghanistan, and elsewhere. In President Bush's FY 2009 budget proposal, he requests an additional 1,100 new positions for diplomats. However, Powell's and Rice's efforts have been mainly for enough people to perform currently assigned tasks, not to increase needed civilian roles in the national security area.[14] Because reform and changes have been stopgap, partial, and focused only on particular parts of the system, they have in some respects diminished the overall system they aimed to improve. The civilian side of the house is, to the total system's detriment, badly in need of revitalization.

To bring unity of effort into such an overhaul, we must first understand the major components that now make up our national security machinery and how these components fit into the total existing system. Any substantive correction in the balance among these components must be based on an understanding of the tasks that need to be done and an assessment of whether one or another element of the national security system could more effectively perform those tasks.

The Defense Department and Armed Forces. The Defense Department (with different names and organization) emerged from World II as a remarkably effective bureaucracy. During World War II, because of the importance of military victory, the Defense Department greatly eclipsed the State Department in terms of power, influence, and prestige.[15] There was a brief period of mass demobilization of our armed forces after the war, but this was curtailed by the Soviet challenge. The United States' role as a superpower competing with the Soviet bloc spurred the Defense Department's growth and further increased its bureaucratic power vis-à-vis the Department of State. The Korean War and the Vietnam War reinforced this relative dominance.

During the 1980s, in my third ambassadorial appointment as the president's personal representative and (by statute) in charge of all U.S. executive branch agencies and employees (including military) in El Salvador—where an intense civil war was in progress—I relied on and worked closely with the commanders in chief of the U.S. Southern Command. Their support, cooperation, and advice were essential to success against the Salvadoran insurgency. An event occurred during that period that affected my thoughts over the years about civilian-military relations within our national security system. Knowing how short U.S. embassies were on funds for travel, one of the Southern Command commanders kindly offered to pick me up in his big Boeing jet (converted to an executive aircraft) to take me to Washington, D.C., where we both had meetings within the executive branch and in Congress about the critical Salvadoran situation. I was somewhat taken aback when I entered the plane's well-furnished executive cabin to see that the commander's chair was one taken from a plane of the fairly recently deposed shah of Iran that had been constructed to replicate the peacock throne! The larger commander's seat asserted wealth and power in comparison to the seats for his, in this case, civilian guests—symbolic of the ample resources of the Defense Department and armed forces in comparison with the Department of State. (The commander, who was an extraordinarily talented, sensitive, and effective person, had the peacock throne seat removed from his plane after that trip to Washington.)

Granted, it takes more money for certain kinds of tasks than others, but the budget and resource differences are out of proportion, both between the military and civilian parts of the U.S. government and among components within the Defense establishment. Comparison between civilian and Defense Department budgets will be made later. Here, I make a comment about the disconnect between some of the remote threats upon which the Pentagon spends much of its budget versus the twenty-first-century wars that the United States is currently fighting. The Defense Department has continued to spend billions of dollars for such items as the Air Force's F/A-22 stealth fighter, the Navy's new DDG-1000 destroyer, Virginia-class attack submarines, the technically troubled V-22 Osprey tilt-rotor aircraft, and the yet-to-be-proved long-range missile defense system. After years of delay, the Department of Defense at last plans to increase ground troops by 92,000 over the next few years. It appears that no single weapon is cancelled in President Bush's proposed 2009 budget.[16]

The imbalance between civilian and defense agencies does not reflect our country's history, professed ideals, alleged emphasis on civil over military rule, or the resolution of problems through peaceful means over military power (while always having force in reserve as an option). Since World War II, the Defense Department and armed forces have evolved in the national security field at the expense of the total national security system's capacity and efficacy. The U.S. position as the world's most powerful nation has thrust it into a leadership role that requires a large, potent and effective military establishment, but the Defense Department must be subordinate to civilian government and not be charged with tasks best performed by civilians for reasons of both cost and effectiveness.

The Goldwater-Nichols Department of Defense Reorganization Act of 1986, drawing on the Packard Commission Report, aimed at making the Defense Department and armed forces more effective, which it certainly did. However, this needed and welcomed reform also further increased the bureaucratic strength of the Department of Defense and armed forces in comparison to that of the civilian agencies. Since this groundbreaking act, there have been countless commentaries that what Congress did for the Defense Department and the armed forces needs to be done similarly for the civilian agencies and for the entire executive branch national security system. However, it should be done systemically rather than piecemeal as we proceed into the future.

The Iraq War has been another stimulus for the Department of Defense and the armed forces to move further into areas that traditionally have been, and I believe should continue to be, functions performed by civilian agencies when conditions permit. Ample and concrete evidence of this is highlighted in a 2006 staff report of the U.S. Senate Foreign Relations Committee, from which some of the following examples are drawn.[17]

Growth into Strategic and Political Intelligence. The Department of Defense's stealthy expansion into the nonmilitary intelligence field first dramatically came to my attention in 1980 while I was the U.S. ambassador in Peru when my embassy received a strong complaint that Peruvian police had picked up a U.S. Army sergeant who amateurishly was carrying out a Department of Defense intelligence operation about which my subordinates and I had not been informed. There is no doubt that the armed forces require battlefield and military strategic intelligence, but I have long been concerned by Defense's push into human intelligence collection in areas and fields seemingly little related to military operational needs as well as in areas that have serious political implications.

Also of concern has been the expanding use of Special Operations forces. I was a member of the advisory "red team" to the first commander of the U.S. Special Operations Command when it was formed. As a former Marine who trained with SEALs and Marine Force Recon, I am a great admirer of the skills and bravery of the men and women from all services who make up this command. Beyond its important combatant roles in Iraq and Afghanistan, the Special Operations Command takes the lead in planning, synchronizing, and executing global operations against terrorists and their networks. However, I am somewhat skeptical about the level of special forces language and cross-cultural skills in terms of some of the missions assigned to them and also about the frequent reliance of special forces on U.S. air support when engaged in enemy terrain, because this too often results in collateral damage to civilians that is counterproductive in asymmetric warfare.[18]

Special forces are vital, but there can be too much of a good thing. The budget of the Special Operations Command grew from $4 billion since September 11, 2001, to almost $8 billion in the 2008 budget. This is about a fifth of the total cost of civilian diplomacy and U.S. development assistance. The Special Operations Command has troops for operations assigned to U.S. embassies in fifty countries, and there is ambiguity and disagreement about the degree to which they are under the U.S. ambassador's control and direction.

Growth in Security Development Assistance. Security assistance to carry out development projects in support of our security objectives has long been an important part of our diplomacy. In keeping with the cardinal principle of civilian control over the military, the U.S. Congress historically has funded security assistance through the foreign affairs budget, the 150 account, which is directed by the secretary of state. Overseas, security development assistance is under the direction of the U.S. ambassador and carried out by the Office of Defense Cooperation of the embassy. For Afghanistan and Iraq, President George W. Bush requested and Congress granted the authority and funding to the Department of Defense to train and equip military and police forces, and to reimburse coalition partners doing the same thing, without going through the Department of State. Subsequently, Defense asked for and got the same program extended to other countries with money authorized through Section 1206 of the 2006 Defense Authorization Act. Defense is now carrying out this program in fourteen countries.

Growth into Economic Development and Humanitarian Assistance. The Department of Defense has also moved more and more heavily into economic development and humanitarian assistance—areas previously regarded as the purview of the U.S. Agency for International Development (USAID) and its predecessor agencies. In Iraq and Afghanistan, purportedly because of USAID capacity limitations and because of the intent to use huge contracts with private-sector companies, Congress initially channeled $22 billion for reconstruction to the Defense Department's Iraq Reconstruction Management Office (IRMO) for its management. The executive also created the Commanders' Emergency Response Program (CERP), using the hundreds of millions of dollars found in Saddam Hussein's coffers. Appropriated funds were then added by Congress to CERP. Subsequently, the Defense Department requested and received authority to carry out development projects in any countries where U.S. military operations (not just combat operations) are being conducted. This has greatly expanded Defense development projects, especially in Africa and in Latin America. There is little question that where there is not violent conflict, these funds would be better administered by U.S. civilian agencies working within host countries' national development plans.

Growth into Public Affairs and Information for Foreign Audiences. The Defense Department now rivals civilian agency information activities abroad through its always-active public affairs and psychological operations programs, turned more and more toward foreign civilian audiences. This is done under a mandate to counter terrorist propaganda in key regions and countries. However, even as the Department of Defense is sending "military information teams" to many U.S. embassies, military information programs are almost universally perceived as propaganda and biased. An effort is being made to put them under the direction of embassy public affairs officers, where the return on the funds would be greater.[19]

Growing Disproportionate Influence on Political and Diplomatic Decisions. Finally, the Department of Defense has had since World War II, and especially under President George W. Bush, a disproportionate voice in diplomatic and national security matters; I believe that, in large part, this is because of its enormous proportion of national security resources and capabilities. A goal of the United States since World War II has been to have our armed forces so well trained, armed, prepared and ready that they deter other countries from attacking the United States. In our quest for this predominance, the United States by some reports now spends as much on national defense as do all other countries combined and certainly more than the next top twenty countries combined. Our success in amassing lethal and destructive battlefield power is one of the reasons our enemies have turned to asymmetric warfare. Victory in asymmetric wars ultimately depends not on battlefield prowess (although this is an essential ingredient) but on changes in societies, economies, and governance, which are best achieved by competent, well-funded civilian organizations.

Because of the bureaucratic weight of the Defense Department and the armed forces, it is the place to which the president naturally turns in times of political and security crises, since it can most easily shift personnel and resources. The Defense Department has one and a half million active-duty service members, 850,000 paid reservists, and 650,000 civilian workers (not counting the thousands of employees of contracted private companies). This is in contrast to the State Department's and USAID's about 21,000 American Foreign and Civil Service employees, about 40,000 Foreign Service Nationals, and several thousands of USAID-contracted private-company employees. President Bush's FY 2009 proposed budget to Congress requests $515.4 billion for the Department of Defense, which does not include either war spending in Iraq and Afghanistan or the cost of nuclear weapons (funded through the Energy Department) or homeland defense costs (funded through the Department of Homeland Security). The proposed budget asks for only $70 billion to finance war spending until October 1, 2008, expecting the new president to request supplemental war spending, which in FY 2008 totaled about $190 billion. Straight-line projection of current spending would put the figure at $170 billion for FY 2009. The total Defense Department budget for 2009 should therefore be about $700 billion: when adjusted for inflation, the highest level since World War II. (However, when the base Pentagon budget, nuclear weapons, and warfighting costs are combined, they total just over 4 percent of the current economy, which is less than during the Korean War, 14 percent, and the Vietnam War, 9 percent.) This $700 billion is in comparison with about $40 billion for the combined annual budget of the State Department, USAID, and U.S. contributions to international institutions and U.S. economic development assistance to developing nations.[20] The ratio of the military budget to the civilian budget for foreign policy and national security is more than 17:1. I would not suggest that the civilian side of the national security system should approach the Defense Department and armed forces in personnel or budget; however, the civilian agencies should have enough personnel and resources to empower them with the capacity not only to do their regular peacetime jobs but also for adequate training of personnel and for surges during times of crises.

In addition to the enormous differences in budget and personnel, the American peoples' attitude toward the armed forces is overwhelmingly positive, while its attitude toward civilian bureaucrats, especially diplomats, is often negative. The image of soldiers, sailors, pilots, and Marines risking their lives, as in charging up a hill under direct fire, rightfully evokes respect and admiration and a feeling of obligation by Americans to ensure that members of the armed forces have every possible advantage that money can buy. In contrast, the American image of diplomats is often one of effete males in striped trousers holding a cocktail glass and conducting their (devalued) work behind closed doors. More important, the State Department has nothing to match the huge amount of Department Defense dollars for outsourcing huge contracts to private companies or the economic importance of military installations and military manufacturing plants to U.S. communities, both of which translate into congressional budget support for the Defense Department budget.

Department of Homeland Defense. The Department of Homeland Defense, established in 2002, grew out of Al Qaeda's September 11, 2001, attack on U.S. soil. The department still has many bureaucratic problems but is filling a vacuum that the Department of Defense had increasingly been called upon to fill to assist in our now decades-old "war on terrorism," efforts to reduce illegal immigration across our borders, and narcotics control. The creation of the Department of Homeland Security may be a brake on the Department of Defense's expansion into yet another area of civil governance.

The Intelligence Function. After erroneous intelligence reports that Saddam Hussein had weapons of mass destruction and was in partnership with Al Qaeda, Congress in 2005 created the Directorate for National Intelligence (DNI), pursuant to the Intelligence Reform and Terrorism Prevention Act of 2004. The need for this critical reform, especially as it relates to a sharing and vetting of intelligence by U.S. government agencies and to the definition of roles and coordination of these myriad agencies (for both foreign and domestic security), has long been recognized. One hopes that the situation is being improved by the DNI. The tradition of U.S. intelligence agencies being providers of information and not policy advocates is pretty well established. The major issue is definition of roles among intelligence agencies, especially the huge intelligence organizations within the Defense Department. Another important intelligence issue is in-house capabilities versus outsourcing to private companies that will be addressed later.

The Department of State, USAID, and Information Programs. The Department of State, USAID, other development agencies, and the civilian information programs (the old U.S. Information Agency, or USIA) all need to be evaluated and changes enacted to strengthen and expand them. All should report to the president through the secretary of state, just as the myriad defense and armed forces units report through the secretary of defense. An overhaul is needed of the civilian agencies similar to what the Goldwater-Nichols Act did for the Defense Department in 1987, what the creation of the Department of Homeland Defense did for domestic security in 2002, and what the Intelligence Reform and Terrorism Act of 2004 did for the intelligence community in 2005. However, the review of the civilian side of the national security system must include a reexamination of the roles of all components of the system to establish the proper balance and assignment of functions among them. It should also look at the roles of the private-sector contracted companies and NGOs.

USAID in the 1960s had a superb, large public safety program staffed chiefly by recently retired civilian police from U.S. municipal police departments. The program, which was terminated by Congress, was truly effective in building foreign civilian police departments, including instilling more-humane treatment of citizens and prisoners. The United States would be better off today with a restored high capacity USAID Public Safety Program training police around the world instead of having handed the bulk of this mission to our armed forces or largely ignoring this vital task in developing countries where our interests are at stake.

If one goes back forty years, USAID had in-house capabilities to carry out development projects. It had its own agronomists, engineers, educators, health experts, and so forth. Today, USAID has evolved primarily into a planning, project evaluation, and contracting operation with private-sector companies and NGOs. Notwithstanding this, USAID still has knowledgeable professional development officers equal to any in the world and clearly superior to those in the Defense Department. I have little doubt that a superstaffed and well-resourced USAID would have done a much better job in the reconstruction and development efforts in Iraq than has the Pentagon's Iraq Reconstruction Management Office. This agency is much criticized over its scandalous mismanagement of tens of billions of dollars in projects farmed out to private companies, many of whom had little macro-development expertise and insufficient language and cultural knowledge.

The president's 2008 proposed budget further slashed the USAID economic development account. This administration may be bent on dismantling USAID and depending mainly on the narrowly focused U.S. Millennium Challenge Account and the HIV/AIDS prevention program for U.S. development efforts. This is a mistake. What is needed is to rebuild USAID and give it a surge capacity to deal with unexpected crises, rather than depending on Defense for future reconstruction and development efforts.

The current rush of the armed forces into public affairs is another mistake. While ambassador in El Salvador during the civil war, I was frustrated by the inability to secure sufficient funding for Salvadoran civilian public affairs programs supported by the embassy's very capable USIA public affairs counselors. Some of the funds that the Southern Command poured into Salvadoran military broadcasting programs and psychological operations would have been better used on the civilian side of the Salvadoran government.

The same thing is being repeated today with the military information support teams that regional commanders are dispatching to U.S. embassies. After the cold war, with the intent of strengthening the secretary of state's hand in foreign affairs and national security, USIA was abolished as an agency and its people and tasks were assigned to the State Department's Bureau of Educational and Cultural Affairs, where those functions had been carried out prior to the cold war. Consideration should be given to reestablishing USIA with its director reporting to the secretary of state. Information functions the Department of Defense is assuming that have civilian targets in noncombat environments should be assigned to this agency.

These are just a few examples. A rapid, concerted effort is required to reorder and greatly expand the civilian departments' capabilities in resources and personnel. Expenditures for this will be more effective yet will remain but a fraction of what we spend on the Defense Department, including the armed forces, for the performance of civilian tasks best done by civilians.

With this, there must also be a restoration of commitment to duty and, when need be, to sacrifice by the Foreign Service at all levels. Foreign Service officers are commissioned officers of the president. They have joined what is by law a disciplined organization in which its officers are available for assignments worldwide. The number of posts deemed too dangerous for U.S. diplomats to be accompanied by their families in 2007 reached twenty-one, and the number of posts where employees receive danger pay is twenty-six.[21] Those who are unwilling to serve in such posts should be removed from the service.

Private-Sector Contractors. Bear in mind that the fundamental purpose of the national government is to protect the people of the state from external enemies and to maintain order within the state. The government is accountable to the nation as a whole. The fundamental purpose of private companies is to earn a profit for its owners or stockholders, and it is to this constituency, not the state as a whole, that they are ultimately accountable. This I know from eight years of experience on corporate boards.

The American public was shocked upon learning that private-company contracted personnel were interrogating Iraqi prisoners in Iraq and that in cases of interrogator mistreatment of prisoners there was no applicable law under which such interrogators could be held accountable. I was amazed when a friend of mine told me that his Marine colonel son, commanding a regiment in Iraq, was frustrated because he had to rely on the Kellogg, Brown and Root (KBR) Company for rations and supplies sometimes needed immediately for an operation. Too often, the rations were not available within the time frame needed.

During the current Iraq war, the contracted services include security companies, such as Blackwater, Triple Canopy, and DynCorp International, that perform military and diplomat protection missions and train Iraqi and Afghan soldiers and police, areas previously considered the domain of the armed forces (and, earlier, of USAID). On my visits to Iraq in December 2003 and in 2004, soldiers and Marines complained to me about the "mercenary" privately contracted employees of private security companies, the Defense Department's response to not having enough troops to get the job done. Most security contractors' employees were former U.S. soldiers that the U.S. armed forces trained; upon completion of their enlistments, rather than re-upping, they went to work for security companies. They earn several times what U.S. soldiers receive and, early in the occupation, had better body armor and Humvees. Blackwater guards shot and killed seventeen Iraqi civilians on September 16, 2007. Investigations seem to show that there had not been provocation and have judged Blackwater normal comportment to be counterproductive in terms of U.S. goals and to have complicated military operations.[22]

There are roughly 180,000 private contractors working for U.S. government agencies in Iraq doing everything from traditional military and intelligence duties to reconstruction projects. There are about 160,000 U.S. military in Iraq. KBR alone has 50,000 workers there. There are at least 177 private security companies employing 48,000 workers in Iraq, of which 30,000 are heavily armed guards. Security costs account for 16 to 22 percent of reconstruction projects and account for much of the overrun costs on projects.[23] For the most part, the traditional offensive combat tasks of the armed forces have not been farmed out, but the use of private security companies for defense of personnel and site protection illustrates that the erroneous belief so popular in much of America since the 1980s that government is almost uniformly inept and that the private sector is superior in carrying out almost any task has now been extended to our armed forces.[24]

The intelligence community also has been privatized, with private contractors now accounting for 70 percent of the intelligence budget. In a number of our key and most delicate intelligence units, more than half of the personnel are contracted from the private sector. Among contractor companies' personnel and individually contracted persons alike, a very high percentage are former U.S. government or military employees trained at U.S. government expense. They represent an expensive "brain drain" from the government and receive salaries (paid indirectly or directly by the U.S. government) significantly superior to what they were paid as government employees.[25] To compete and retain personnel, the armed forces since 2007 have had to offer huge bonuses for reenlistment of soldiers, especially of special forces troops.

Moreover, among both military and civilians, there is lack of continuity in dangerous places because of short tours and frequent turnover of personnel. I commented after a trip to Dubai in 2007, where I conferred with four Iraqi ministers of government and U.S. embassy officers from our Baghdad embassy about assistance projects, that not only did the U.S. government not know the situation in Iraq before we invaded, but also, because of lack of continuity of personnel, only recently have we gotten a grasp on what has happened and what we have done since we got there.

Using private companies is complicated by the competitive bidding process and by the need to explain why sole-source contracting is justifiable, both of which are slow and cumbersome. Reliance on private companies to be deployed rapidly with joint preplanning for unseen crises is difficult, if not close to impossible. One of the challenges of restructuring and improving our national security system will be determining to what extent private contractors should be used. As the Government Accounting Office reports and congressional hearings continue to review how effectively companies performed, the future use of private companies in dangerous, complex situations may be seen as less viable. If so, the rejuvenation of civilian departments and agencies will be even more important.

Nongovernmental Organizations. Some of the comments about private-sector companies' contractual employment in national security campaigns and in development programs to help strengthen threatened friendly governments are also applicable to NGOs. This is even more true if the NGOs have contracts with the U.S. government or receive substantial assistance from the U.S. government to help them implement government-promoted and -endorsed programs.

There are numerous NGOs that do not have contracts and have little or no dependence on U.S. aid for their programs. Some of them actually eschew U.S. support and stridently oppose U.S. government policy in the country or geographical areas where they are working. In El Salvador, this was sometimes the case, especially by human rights organizations and some grassroots development programs. As an example, there were two U.S. based Sister-Cities organizations operating in El Salvador—one in support of towns in government-controlled areas and one in areas where the FMLN insurgency was strong. Another complicating factor is the new government policy of contracting with and supporting "faith-based" NGOs' development efforts, since this can complicate matters in conflicts where religion is an important element of the struggle.

The protection of citizens working in conflict zones is challenging. Trying to coordinate development efforts with contrary NGOs is more difficult. Nevertheless, working with responsible NGOs is a must for U.S. national security planning and coordination. NGOs have increasingly undertaken measures to establish norms for performance and accountability, but greater thought must be given to how private-sector contractors and NGOs can participate in planning and training with U.S. civilian and military authorities.

Manwaring's "Legitimacy" Dimension Applied to Correcting the U.S. National Security System

Applied to the U.S. national security system, legitimacy refers primarily to the American public's backing of U.S. government decisions and operations to intervene militarily in a situation. This depends in large part on the U.S. government's ability to ensure that it is strong in the three areas set forth by David Miller as the pillars of success needed to win conflicts or wars.

During the Reagan administration (as the end of the cold war approached) and particularly during the administrations of Presidents George H. W. Bush and Bill Clinton, there was much discussion about new threats, the search for a new theory of engagement, and the criteria for the commitment of U.S. forces into combat. Examples were debates over the Weinberger Doctrine, unilateral versus multilateral military interventions, reexamination of just war theory, and the doctrine of overwhelming force. The George W. Bush administration entered office with the announced intention to decrease U.S. involvement in the international arena but—following the September 11, 2001, attacks on America—had to change focus. The administration pronounced its doctrine of preventive strikes, and Secretary of Defense Donald Rumsfeld espoused a smaller, more agile and lethal military force to replace the doctrine of overwhelming force. Discussions and debates on strategy and the proper use of force need to be reopened.

Charismatic leadership, public affairs management, and "spin" are all important factors, but no matter how good an administration is in these areas, it can only sell faulty decisions and flawed implementation for a limited period. Edsels were hard to sell! The decision-making process, the decisions themselves, and the implementation must be sound to maintain public support. The process must be based on vital national security interests and the process designed so as to minimize the dangers of "unintended consequences."[26]

UNITY OF EFFORT AND FINAL REMARKS

Because of the outcome thus far of the administration's decision to invade Iraq and our inadequate preparation for the occupation phase there—based on faulty information and incorrect assumptions—and because of the growing threats to our security and vital interests in the three global security arenas outlined earlier in this afterword, the United States needs to analyze and remake its national security system for success against the threats that confront it. The Manwaring Paradigm is a guide to the conduct of U.S. national security in asymmetric warfare and for assessing and strengthening the national security system.

Max Manwaring has cogently described the nature of the very present threat to the United States and its partner states generated by nonstate actors operating out of "gray areas," where states do not exercise sufficient presence and effective legitimate governance. His paradigm also provides the essence for a theory of engagement or strategy for U.S. foreign policy and actions with respect to insurgencies, terrorism, and transnational crime. (To cope with rogue states and the emerging global balance of power system, the United States must practice the realpolitik and idealism that served it well in the past.)

To be effective in the support of a fellow state under attack by nonstate actors and movements, the U.S. government must be able to demonstrate to its citizens that U.S. legitimate and vital interests are threatened; must know the enemy culturally, linguistically, and historically; and must comprehend the nature of the war that the adversary is waging. In addition, the U.S. government must understand the enemies' support from internal and external private groups and other states and must help the targeted state interrupt and reduce such support. In terms of practicing "unity of effort," the U.S. government must have its national security system organized to cope with security threats and to "stay the course." The United States must capacitate, arrange, and have ready for immediate deployment for an extended period of time its own appropriate civilian foreign affairs agencies, military forces, private-sector contractors, and nongovernmental organizations. The U.S. government's strategy, plans, and operations must be aimed at defeating the enemies and establishing the supported government's presence and rule over its territory in a way that will keep the enemies vanquished.

To achieve this, the United States must complete a comprehensive restructuring of the bureaucratic makeup of our national security system to ensure that we have the proper balance and capacity among the system's component parts. It has been said that "if the only tool you have is a hammer, every problem looks like a nail." Success in asymmetric warfare requires more than the hammer of the U.S. armed forces to pound down the nail of armed insurgents and terrorists. We need in our toolbox various tools designed and prepared to take care of specific areas, such as intelligence, reconstruction, unemployment, economic and political development, and creating the rule of law and governance. No one wants to do away with the hammer, but to do the job most effectively and efficiently, we need to create the best set of tools possible for all the required tasks. This includes not only strengthening the government's civilian side of the national security system but also reexamining Department of

Defense budget priorities and the appropriate use of the private sector in our foreign policy and national defense and its integration into the planning and coordination processes.

There are those who, à la John Robb in *Brave New War* (2007), would argue that a call for strengthening the U.S. government's capacity and balance within the national security system and relying less on the private sector flies in the face of current reality. Robb offers an excellent picture of how global guerrillas effectively practice "open-source warfare" in their attack on the nation-state global system. He urges and predicts as the proper response greater resilience and decentralization in societies as the nation-state system evolves into a "market state" that will provide protection for those who can afford it. Open-source warfare has proved effective in the early stage of nonstate actors' attacks on the state, especially in failing and underdeveloped states, but not yet in the stronger and more-sophisticated states. Not even insurgents' "black swan" attacks (those resulting in large casualties) have caused much economic disruption or change in daily life in Europe and the United States. There is also the question of how effective decentralized warfare would be for the nonstate insurgents should they reach the stage of trying to establish and consolidate a caliphate or an extensive twenty-first-century socialist entity.

The demise of the nation-state and the abandonment of those populations not rich enough to provide their own defense and welfare, as proposed by Robb and others, is too far in the future to have a great influence on our immediate strategies and actions. Robb's proposals for defense and success against the transnational guerrillas are of little help to those who want to start fixing things now. The pragmatic course is to make our own national security system flatter, more decentralized, and more capable and nimble while maintaining central overall direction and coordination.

Few of us are willing to accept the "Katrina effect" of government inaction and incompetence, which is what the Robb book suggests for the less fortunate of our society. The long-predicted withering away of the state, whose role is to defend and promote the welfare of all its citizens, is not imminent. Provocative, captivating books such as that by Robb must be assimilated into our thinking, but we must cope with the moment. With proper organization of the U.S. national security system, correct strategy, and effective implementation, the United States and partner nation-states can, during the next couple of decades, defeat the current nonstate actors. The best guide yet for our efforts is this book of Max Manwaring's, plus his and his colleagues' impressive set of literature on this subject (summarized by Manwaring and John Fishel in their other recent book in this series, *Uncomfortable Wars Revisited*). I hope that you and U.S. political leaders and decision makers will quickly incorporate this wisdom and research-based strategy into our nation's thinking about foreign and national security.[27]

Notes

FOREWORD

1. Manwaring, *Uncomfortable Wars.* Max's first major prize-winning book was Manwaring and Prisk, *El Salvador at War* (1988), for which I also wrote the preface.

2. J. Fishel and Manwaring, *Uncomfortable Wars Revisited.*

3. This observation was first published by Kimbra Fishel, wife of John Fishel and a student of mine at the University of Oklahoma, as "Challenging the Hegemon," in a special edition of the journal *Low Intensity Conflict and Law Enforcement.*

INTRODUCTION

1. K. Fishel, "Challenging the Hegemon: Al Qaeda's Elevation."

2. There is no body of international relations literature that effectively addresses nonstate, irregular conflict at the global level. Rather, insights must be drawn from three different types of literature that range from the most broad grand strategy level to a more specific tactical level: hegemonic stability / power transition, traditional terrorism, and revolutionary / asymmetric / insurgent / guerrilla / irregular warfare. For examples of hegemonic literature, traditional terrorism literature, and revolutionary literature, see chapter 3, note 1. All three of these sets of literature focus primarily on the nation-state, and conflict is defined generally in military terms. The one area of divergence in the three literatures is that the terrorism and

revolutionary literatures recognize that nonstate actors can sometimes play more than bit parts in the global security arena. Nevertheless, the mainstream international relations dialogue articulates that nonstate actors are, at base, local law-enforcement problems and do not require the nation-state processes of sustained national security policy attention. See Trager and Kronenberg, *National Security and American Society*; Sarkesian, *U.S. National Security*; and Jordan, Taylor, and Mazarr, *American National Security.*

3. See Qiao and Wang, *Unrestricted Warfare*; and Crocker, "Engaging Failed States."

4. Yin, *Case Study Research,* 140.

5. Ibid., 1–10, 15, 147.

6. Beckett, *Modern Insurgencies and Counter-Insurgencies*; Beckett, "Future of Insurgency"; Ian F. W. Beckett, "Soft Power and Counterinsurgency: Political and Civil Dimensions of Winning Hearts and Minds," paper presented to the Rand Insurgency Board, Washington, D.C., March 8, 2006; Marks, "Urban Insurgency"; and Marks, "Ideology of Insurgency."

7. Yin, *Case Study Research,* 46, 51.

8. Ibid.

9. Laquer, "Postmodern Terrorism."

10. Verstrynge Rojas, *La guerra asimetrica.*

11. Clausewitz, *On War,* 596.

12. Manwaring and J. Fishel, "Insurgency and Counter-Insurgency."

13. Yin, *Case Study Research,* 140, 31–32.

14. Ibid.

15. Manwaring and J. Fishel, "Insurgency and Counter-Insurgency."

16. Ibid.

17. Yin, *Case Study Research.*

18. Dahl, *Modern Political Analysis*; Dahl, *After the Revolution*; Gilpin, *War and Change*; and Smith, *Utility of Force.*

19. Sun Tzu, *Art of War,* 63.

CHAPTER 1. A MULTIPLE CONFLICT SYNDROME

1. Metz, *Future of Insurgency.*

2. Steinitz, "Insurgents, Terrorists," 147.

3. Over the period 1959 through 2006, the author has continuously interviewed civilian and military officials regarding political-military affairs and insurgency in several countries. This and subsequent assertions made in this and later chapters are consensus statements based on observation and interviews. The intent is to allow anonymity for those who object to their names being made public. In subsequent notes, these statements are cited as Author Interviews.

4. Smith, *On Political War,* 3. This encompasses what B. H. Liddell Hart, drawing from Sun Tzu, calls the indirect approach to war. "The perfection of strategy would be, therefore, to produce a decision without any serious fighting.... Thus, those skilled in war subdue the enemy's army without [major] battle. They capture his cities without assaulting them and overthrow his state without protracted [military] operations." Liddell Hart, *Strategy,* 324; and Sun Tzu, *Art of War,* 79.

5. Crenshaw, *Terrorism, Legitimacy, and Power*; and Laqueur, *No End to War.*

6. This concept was formulated and elaborated in Easton, *Framework for Political Analysis.*

7. For a good discussion of this set of points, see Marks, "Ideology of Insurgency."

8. U.S. Army, Field Manual 90–8, *Counterguerrilla Operations.* Also see Field Manual 3–07.22, MCRP 3–33.5, *Counterinsurgency Operations* (draft).

9. Clausewitz, *On War,* 88.

10. See Hodges, *Philosophy of the Urban Guerrilla,* 250.

11. A classic book on this topic is Fluherty, *Dance of the Millions.* Also see Hanratty and Meditz, *Colombia.*

12. Fluherty, *Dance of the Millions.* Also see Restrepo, "Crisis."

13. Author Interviews.

14. Ibid. Also see Rabassa and Chalk, *Colombian Labyrinth*; Eduardo Pizarro, "Revolutionary Guerrilla Groups in Colombia," in Bergquist et al., *Violence in Colombia,* 169–93; and Klepak, "Colombia."

15. Author Interviews. The "Hobbesian Trinity" has created a situation in which life is indeed, in the words of seventeenth-century philosopher Thomas Hobbes, "nasty, brutish, and short."

16. Rosenau, *Turbulence in World Politics.*

17. Author Interviews.

18. Ibid.

19. Ibid.

20. Ibid. Also see Marks, *Colombian Army Adaptation*; Marks, *Sustainability*; and Marks, *Maoist Insurgency since Vietnam.*

21. Rabassa and Chalk, *Colombian Labyrinth.* Also see Larry Rohter, "A Colombian Guerrilla's 50-Year Fight," *New York Times,* July 19, 1999; Larry Rohter, "Colombia Rebels Reign in Ceded Area," *New York Times,* May 16, 1999; Howard LaFranchi, *Washington Post,* February 5, 1999; Gary M. Leech, "An Interview with FARC Commander Simon Trinidad," *NACLA Report on the Americas,* September/October 2000; Clifford Krauss, "Colombia's Rebels Keep the Marxist Faith: Guerrilla Commander Says, 'This Is a Means,'" *Christian Science Monitor,* July 19, 1999; Serge F. Kovaleski, "Rebel Movement on the Rise: Colombian Guerrillas Use Military Force, Not Ideology to Hold Power," *New York Times,* July 25, 2000; Alfred Molano, "The Evolution of the FARC: A Guerrilla Group's Long History," *NACLA*

Report on the Americas, September / October 2000; and *Janes's Information Group,* "FARC: Finance Comes Full Circle for Bartering Revolutionaries," January 19, 2001. The most recent public source for data is "FARC Inc.," *Semana,* available online at semana2.terra.com.co / opencms / opencms / Semana / articulo.html?id+84464.

22. See citations in note 21, above. Also see *Economist,* "Survey of Colombia," April 21–27, 2001.

23. Marks, "Urban Insurgency," 141.

24. Ibid. Also see Author Interviews.

25. Author Interviews. Also see Spencer, *Colombia's Paramilitaries;* Juan Forero, "Colombian Paramilitaries Adjust Attack Strategies," *New York Times,* January 22, 2001; Juan Forero, "Rightist Chief in Colombia Shifts Focus to Politics," *New York Times,* June 7, 2001; and Tod Robberson, "Militia Leader's Revelations Igniting Fear in Colombia," *Dallas Morning News,* December 17, 2001.

26. Porch, "Uribes's Second Mandate," 3.

27. Ibid.; and *Economist,* "Survey of Colombia."

28. Porch, "Uribes's Second Mandate," 7.

29. Author Interviews.

30. Porch, "Uribes's Second Mandate," n.p.

31. Bushnell, "Politics and Violence," 17–19.

32. Ibid.; and Lupsha, "Role of Drugs," 181. Also see Olson, "International Organized Crime."

33. Bushnell, "Politics and Violence"; Lupsha, "Role of Drugs"; Lupsha, "Towards an Etiology"; and Olson, "International Organized Crime."

34. Author Interviews.

35. Ibid.; see chapter 1, note 20, above. Also see "The Statutes of the FARC-EP," chapter 1, article 1 in *El pais que proponemos construer.*

36. Rabassa and Chalk, *Colombian Labyrinth;* and Spencer, *Colombia's Paramilitaries.*

37. Author Interviews.

38. Ibid.

39. Ibid.

40. Ibid.

41. Ibid. Also see Jordan, *Drug Politics,* 165–67.

42. Jordan, *Drug Politics;* Author Interviews; and Crenshaw, *Terrorism in Context.*

43. Kaplan, "Coming Anarchy."

44. An early assertion of this argument was made by Rensselaer W. Lee III in *The White Labyrinth,* 139. Another, by an eminent Peruvian jurist, is Belaunde, "Corrupción y discomposición." For a more recent and thorough discussion of this issue, see Jordan, *Drug Politics.*

45. Author Interviews. Also see Marks, "Ideology of Insurgency" and "Urban Insurgency."

46. Author Interviews; Marks, "Ideology of Insurgency"; and Marks, "Urban Insurgency."

47. Author Interviews.

48. Ibid.

49. Ibid.

50. Ibid.

51. Jordan, *Drug Politics,* 19.

52. Ibid.; and Author Interviews. Also see Ana Maria Bejarano and Eduardo Pizarro, "The Crisis of Democracy in Colombia: From 'Restricted' Democracy to 'Besieged' Democracy," unpublished manuscript, 2001; and Bejarano and Pizarro, "Colombia: A Failing State?"

53. Bejarano and Pizarro, "Colombia: A Failing State?" Ambassador Kaman's comments are from an interview with the author, December 7, 2000.

54. Jordan, *Drug Politics,* 158–70, 193–94.

55. Author Interviews; Inter-American Development Bank, *Annual Report 1999,* 141; and data taken from Rubio, "La justicia," 215.

56. Jordan, *Drug Politics,* 161.

57. Ibid.; and Author Interviews.

58. Jordan, *Drug Politics;* and Author Interviews.

59. Frechette, *In Search of the Endgame.*

60. Frechette, "Colombia and the United States."

61. See discussion of SWORD model in the introduction to this book.

62. Author Interviews. Also see Max Manwaring, "U.S. Too Narrowly Focused on Drug War in Colombia," *Miami Herald,* August 15, 2001.

63. Sun Tzu, *Art of War,* 73.

CHAPTER 2. TRANSFORMING WAR INTO "SUPERINSURGENCY"

1. Smith, *Utility of Force,* 3. Italics added.

2. Ibid., 5.

3. Ibid., 5–28. Also see Colonel Thomas X. Hammes, U.S. Marine Corps (retired), *Sling and the Stone,* 207–15; and General Nguyen Giap, *Peoples' War, Peoples' Army,* 34–37.

4. President Chavez used this language in a charge to the National Armed Forces (FAN) to develop a doctrine for fourth-generation war. It was made before an audience gathered in the military academy auditorium for the "1st Military Forum on Fourth Generation War and Asymmetric War," in Caracas, Venezuela,

and was reported in *El Universal,* April 8, 2005. Also, in January 2005, General Melvin Lopez Hidalgo, secretary of the Venezuelan Defense Council, stated publicly that Venezuela was changing its security doctrine to better confront "*la amenaza permanente de los Estados Unidos*" ("the permanent threat of the United States") and that a document entitled *Pueblo en armas [The People in Arms]* had been published that confirmed the primary military principles of President Chavez. Reported in *Panorama,* April 27, 2005.

5. See previous note (chapter 2, note 4). Also see Urbina and Cirino, *La democracia defraudada;* and Polgatti, *Conflicto y guerra.*

6. "War of all the people" is another translation of Hugo Chavez's words in this context. Thus, my colleagues and I interchangeably use the terms –"fourth-generation war," "superinsurgency," "people's war," and "war of all the people."

7. Hammes, "Fourth Generation Warfare," 40–44.

8. Smith, *Utility of Force,* 375, 415.

9. As an example of this discussion, see Jordan, Taylor, and Mazarr, *American National Security,* 3–46; Sarkesian, *U.S. National Security,* 7–8. Also, these terms are developed in Schoultz, *National Security,* 24–25, 143–330; and Trager and Kronenberg, *National Security,* 47.

10. See previous note (chapter 2, note 9).

11. Esty et al., "State Failure Project."

12. Guzmán, "El discurso del Dr. Guzmán"; Comité Central del Partido Comunista del Perú, *Desarrollar la guerra popular,* 82–88; Comité Central del Partido Comunista del Perú, *Bases de discusión;* and "El documento oficial de Sendero" ["The Official Document of Sendero"], in Mercado U., *Interview with Chairman Gonzalo.*

13. Krasner and Pascual, "Addressing State Failure."

14. J. Fishel and Manwaring, *Uncomfortable Wars Revisited.* Also see Author Interviews.

15. There is a wealth of primary source material regarding statements made by Al Qaeda and Osama bin Laden available to the public. See usinfo.state.gov/topical/pol/terror/99129502.htm.

16. Reported on Radio Nacional de Venezuela, September 27, 2004, and September 28, 2004. President Chavez was quoted in *El Universal,* Caracas, February 25, 2005; *El Universal,* April 8, 2005; and *Europa Press,* Madrid, Spain, April 3, 2005. Also see *Economist,* "The Chávez Machine Rolls On," December 2, 2006, 41–42.

17. Esty et al., "State Failure Project."

18. Author Interviews.

19. Paraphrased from Smith and Zurcher, *Dictionary of American Politics,* 352, 112–13.

20. Author Interviews.

21. Ibid.

22. Ibid.

23. Ibid.

24. Ibid.

25. K. Fishel, "Challenging the Hegemon: Al-Qaeda's Elevation."

26. Clausewitz, *On War,* 596.

27. See introduction, note 2. It is also important to look at Qiao and Wang, *Unrestricted Warfare*; Smith, *On Political War*; and Crocker, "Engaging Failed States."

28. See previous note (chapter 2, note 27). See also K. Fishel, "Challenging the Hegemon: Al-Qaeda's Elevation."

29. Smith, *Utility of Force,* 275–79.

30. Metz, *Future of Insurgency.*

31. Gunaretna, *Inside,* 54, 89; Bergen, *Holy War, Inc.*; and Zuhur, *Hundred Osamas.* Also see primary source material at usinfo.state.gov/topical/pol/terror/99129502.htm.

32. Clausewitz, *On War,* 595–96.

33. Smith, *Utility of Force,* 279.

34. Qiao and Wang, *Unrestricted Warfare,* 123–69.

35. Ibid., 154.

36. Metz and Millen, *Future Wars,* ix, 15–17.

37. Smith, *On Political War,* 3.

38. Qiao and Wang, *Unrestricted Warfare,* 109.

39. General Sir Frank Kitson, *Warfare as a Whole.*

40. Brzezinski, *The Choice,* 28. Also see Boutros-Ghali, "Global Leadership"; and Boutros-Ghali, *Agenda for Peace,* 11, 32–34.

41. Steven Metz, "Relearning Counterinsurgency," a panel discussion at the American Enterprise Institute, in Washington, D.C., January 10, 2005; and Smith, *On Political War.*

42. See chapter 2, notes 4 and 6. Also see Urbina and Cirino, *La democracia defraudada*; and Polgatti, *Conflicto y guerra.*

43. Rousseau wrote, "Quiconque refusera d'obeir a la volonte generale y sera constraint par tout le corps: ce qui ne signifie autre chose sinon qu'on le forcera de'etre libre." ("For whoever refuses to obey the general will and is unwilling to comply with the body politic, there is no other recourse than to force him to be free.") See Rousseau, *Social Contract,* book 1, chapter 7; and Talmon, *Origins of Totalitarian Democracy.*

44. See chapter 2, note 4. Also see Hammes, "Fourth Generation Warfare."

45. "Special Report: Hugo Chavez's Venezuela," *Economist* (May 14–20, 2005): 23–24; Anderson, "Country Report—Venezuela," in *Countries at the Crossroads*; "Venezuela: Politics in the Military, the Military in Politics," *Inter-American Dialogue* (April 2006): 6–8; "The Chavez Machine Roles On," *Economist* (December 2, 2006): 41–42; Shifter, "In Search of Hugo Chavez," 46; "Chavez Victorious,"

Economist (December 9, 2006); Shifter, *Hugo Chavez;* and "Venezuela Lets Councils Bloom," *Washington Post,* May 16, 2007, www.washingtonpost.com/wp-dyn/content/article/2007/05/16AR2007051602547_2.

46. See previous note (chapter 2, note 45); and Author Interviews.

47. See previous notes (chapter 2, notes 45 and 46). Also see Stephen Johnson, "South America's Mad-TV: Hugo Chavez Makes Broadcasting a Battleground," *Heritage Foundation Policy Research and Analysis,* August 10, 2005; Ellner, "Revolutionary and Non-Revolutionary Paths"; "New Regional Voice," *Foreign Broadcast Information Service* (*FBIS*), April 22, 2005; "Expanded Telesur News Coverage Furthers Anti-US Line," *FBIS,* December 22, 2005; "Perspective Audience," *FBIS,* August 5, 2006; and "Telesur's Deal with Al-Jazirah," *FBIS,* February 27, 2006.

48. Reported in *El Universal,* January 5, 2005; *El Universal,* March 8, 2005; *Europa Press,* April 3, 2005; *La Voz,* April 3, 2005; and *El Universal,* April 8, 2005.

49. Patrick Markley, "Venezuelan Forces Start Training to Repel U.S.," *Boston Globe,* March 6, 2006; Andy Webb-Vidal, "Chavez Seeks to Link Putin with Anti US Alliance," *Financial Times,* London, July 27, 2006; Alan Cullison, "Russia Reaches Out to Venezuela," *Wall Street Journal,* July 27, 2006; and Torres, *Impact of "Populism,"* 8.

50. Julio A. Cirino, "Hugo Chavez, un Napoleon en el Tropico," *El Diario Exterior,* March 15, 2007, www.eldiarioexterior.com/noticia.asp?idarticulo=13500; "Venezuela to Buy More Weapons," BBC News, February 6, 2006, www.news.bbc.co.uk/go/pr/fr/-hi/world/Americas/4682488.stm; Shifter, *Hugo Chavez;* and Simon Romero, "Venezuela Spending on Arms Soars to World's Top Ranks," *New York Times,* February 24, 2007, www.nytimes.com/2007/02/25/world Americas/25venez.html.

51. See chapter 2, note 4.

52. Author Interviews; Buzan, *People, States, and Fear.*

53. Verstrynge Rojas, *La guerra periférica y el Islam revolucionario: Origines, reglas, y ética de la guerra asimétrica [Peripheral (Indirect) War and Revolutionary Islam: Origins, Regulations, and Ethics of Asymmetric War]* (Madrid: El Viejo Topo, May 2005).

54. Qiao and Wang, *Unrestricted Warfare* (Beijing: PLA Literature and Arts Publishing House, 1999).

55. Ibid., 21; Verstrynge, *La guerra periférica.*

56. Howard, *Lessons of History;* also see Alvin and Heidi Toffler's discussion of first-, second-, and third-wave war in *War and Anti-War.*

57. More than 2,500 years ago, Sun Tzu warned us, "In war, numbers alone confer no advantage. Do not advance relying on sheer military power" (*Art of War,* 122).

58. See chapter 2, note 6. Also see Liddell Hart, *Strategy,* 333.

59. Kitson, *Warfare as a Whole,* 2; Qiao and Wang, *Unrestricted Warfare,* 109, 123; Verstrynge Rojas, *La guerra periférica.*

60. See previous note (chapter 2, note 59).

61. See chapter 2, notes 6, 59, and 60.

62. See chapter 2, notes 4 and 59.

63. Hammes, *Sling and the Stone,* 207–15; Giap, *Peoples' War, Peoples' Army,* 34–37. The assertions about strategic-level characteristics of 4GW are derived from statistical tests based on interviews with civilian and military officials and scholars with direct experience in sixty low-intensity conflicts (SWORD Papers). The results of this research were first published as Manwaring and J. Fishel, "Insurgency and Counter-Insurgency." Hereafter cited as SWORD Papers.

64. SWORD Papers; also see Urbina and Cerino, *La democracia defraudada,* 103–39.

65. SWORD Papers; Urbina and Cerino, *La democracia defraudada;* chapter 2, notes 4 and 6.

66. Hammes, *Sling and the Stone*; Liddell Hart, *Strategy;* SWORD Papers.

67. SWORD Papers; Liddell Hart, *Strategy;* Sendero Luminoso's leader, Abimael Guzmán, made the statement about the length of time the organization was prepared to fight; see Mercado U., "El discurso del Dr. Guzmán," in *Los partidos políticos en el Perú,* 85–90.

68. Reported in *New York Times,* April 6, 2007.

69. See chapter 2, notes 4 and 6.

70. See chapter 2, notes 4 and 6; Hammes, *Sling and the Stone*; Qaio and Wang, *Unrestricted Warfare;* SWORD Papers.

71. Anderson, "Country Report—Venezuela," in *Countries at the Crossroads 2006;* Iglesias, "Venezuela," 6–8.

72. SWORD Papers; Qaio and Wang, *Unrestricted Warfare,* 152.

73. SWORD Papers; Qiao and Wang, *Unrestricted Warfare;* Hammes, *Sling and the Stone.*

74. Giap, *Peoples' War, Peoples' Army,* 36. Also see chapter 2, notes 4 and 6.

75. Rupert Smith, *Utility of Force,* 282; SWORD Papers.

76. Chapter 2, note 6. Also see Hammes, *Sling and the Stone*; SWORD Papers.

77. See chapter 2, note 4.

78. Guillen, "Philosophy," 231, 249, 253, 283.

79. Ibid., 284, 259.

80. Ibid., 230, 249, 283, 299.

81. Ibid., 232, 251.

82. Ibid., 233, 279.

83. Author Interviews; SWORD Papers.

84. Evidence of President Chavez's expanding horizons may be seen in many different activities. For example, see Fernando Baez, "On the Road with Bush and Chavez," *New York Times,* March 11, 2007, www.nytimes.com/2007/03/11/opinion/11Baez.html; "Iran, Venezuela to Set Up HQ for Joint Cooperation," www.iranmania.com; Steven Dudley, "Chavez in Search of Leverage," *Miami*

Herald, April 28, 2007; and Simon Romero, "Venezuela," *New York Times,* February 24, 2007, www.nytimes.com/2007/03/14/world/americas/14latin.html.

85. See previous note (chapter 2, note 84).

86. Max G. Manwaring, conference brief, "Hemispheric Strategic Objectives for the Next Decade," Strategic Studies Institute of the U.S. Army War College and the Latin American and Caribbean Center of Florida International University, March 2004. The idea of "wizard's chess" is taken from Rowling, *Harry Potter and the Sorcerer's Stone,* 282–84. See also Manwaring, "New Master of 'Wizard's Chess.'"

87. Hammes, "Fourth Generation Warfare."

88. David, "Saving America," 116.

89. The SWORD model dimensions, as applicable to the populace-oriented extension, are the strength or weakness of a country's governmental institutions (i.e., the degree of a regime's legitimacy); the ability to reduce internal and external support of an illegal challenger; the type and consistency of outside support for a targeted government; the credibility of objectives and degree of organization for unity of effort; the level of discipline and capabilities of security forces; and the effectiveness of the intelligence apparatus. See J. Fishel and Manwaring, *Uncomfortable Wars Revisited,* 87–96.

90. Clausewitz, *On War,* 596.

91. Author Interviews.

92. Ibid.; SWORD Papers; Giap, *Peoples' War, Peoples' Army,* 34.

93. Author Interviews; SWORD Papers; Giap, *Peoples' War, Peoples' Army.* Also see Manwaring, *Internal Wars,* 11–13.

94. Gray, "Deterrence."

95. Ibid. Also see Corr and Manwaring, "Challenge of Preventive Diplomacy."

96. Gray, "Deterrence"; Corr and Manwaring, "Challenge of Preventive Diplomacy."

97. Author Interviews. Also see Smith, *Utility of Force,* 368.

98. Author Interviews. Also see Joes, *America and Guerrilla Warfare.*

99. Author Interviews; Joes, *America and Guerrilla Warfare.* Also see Summers, *On Strategy.*

100. See previous note (chapter 2, note 99). Also see "A Populace-Oriented Model for Reexamining Contemporary Threat and Response," in J. Fishel and Manwaring, *Uncomfortable Wars Revisited,* 87–96.

101. J. Fishel and Manwaring, *Uncomfortable Wars Revisited.*

102. Rupert Smith, *Utility of Force,* 279, 375.

103. Clausewitz, *On War,* 92–93.

104. Clark, "End-State Planning."

105. The reality of this assertion is demonstrated in former president Bill Clinton's speech that opened the summit meeting of world leaders at the United

Nations in September 2000. In that speech, he urged the leaders to prepare national and international institutions for a new age in which unilateral and international forces will have to "reach rapidly and regularly inside national boundaries to protect threatened people." Quoted in *New York Times,* September 7, 2000. Also see Komer, *Bureaucracy Does Its Thing;* Manwaring, "Interview with General Galvin."

106. See previous note (chapter 2, note 105). Also see Manwaring and Corr, "'Almost Obvious' Lessons."

107. See, for example, the Phase 1 report authored by Murdock et al., entitled "Beyond Goldwater-Nichols: Defense Reform for a New Strategic Era," available (as are the others) at www.csis.org / isp / bgn / reports.

108. See Locher, *Victory on the Potomac.* The psnr.org website has been restricted, but information may be obtained by writing to the Project on National Security Reform, The Center for the Study of the Presidency, 1020 19th St NW, Suite 250, Washington, DC 20036.

109. Murdock et al., "Beyond Goldwater-Nichols."

110. Ibid.; and "TF [Task Force] Irregular Challenge CSA [Chief of Staff of the U.S. Army] Outbrief," Carlisle Barracks, Penn.: Strategic Studies Institute, U.S. Army War College, June 28, 2005; and "TF Irregular Challenge DAS [Director, Army Staff] Decision Brief on Interagency Cadre Initiative," Carlisle Barracks, Penn.: Strategic Studies Institute, U.S. Army War College, November 27, 2006. Also see preface by General James T. Hill, commander of the U.S. Southern Command, in Manwaring et al., *Building Regional Security Cooperation.*

111. See previous note (chapter 2, note 110).

112. See chapter 2, note 110.

113. See chapter 2, note 110.

114. Sun Tzu, *Art of War,* 122.

CHAPTER 3. A MULTIDIMENSIONAL PARADIGM FOR POLITICAL-TERRORIST WAR

1. The revolutionary literature would include Mao, *On Guerrilla Warfare;* Trinquier, *French View of Counterinsurgency;* Guevara, *Obras completas;* Guillen, "Philosophy"; and Asprey, *War in the Shadows.* See, as examples of hegemonic literature, Morgenthau, *Politics among Nations;* Strausz-Hupe et al., *Protracted Conflict;* A.F.K. Organski, *World Politics;* Organski and Kugler, *War Leger;* Art and Jervis, *International Politics;* and Brown, *New Forces, Old Forces.* As examples of the traditional terrorism literature, see Crenshaw, "Causes of Terrorism"; Crenshaw, *Terrorism in Context;* Gilpin, *War and Change;* Laqueur, *New Terrorism Fanaticism;* Laqueur, "Postmodern Terrorism"; Lemke, "Continuation of History"; and Lemke, *Regions of War and Peace.* The revolutionary literature would include

Mao, *On the Protracted War;* Mao, *On Guerrilla Warfare;* Trinquier, *French View of Counterinsurgency;* Guevarra, *Obras completas;* Guillen, "Philosophy of the Urban Guerrilla"; and Asprey, *War in the Shadows.*

2. See, as examples, Trager and Kronenberg, *National Security;* Sarkesian, *U.S. National Security;* and Jordan, Taylor, and Mazarr, *American National Security.* For a notable exception to this position, see K. Fishel, "Challenging the Hegemon: Al Qaeda's Elevation."

3. See K. Fishel, "Challenging the Hegemon: Al Qaeda's Elevation." Also see Osama Bin Laden, "A Letter to America," November 24, 2002, available online at http://observer.guardian.co.uk/worldview/story/o,11581,845725,00.html.

4. See K. Fishel, "Challenging the Hegemon: Al Qaeda's Elevation." Also see Laqueur, *New Terrorism Fanaticism;* Laqueur, "Postmodern Terrorism"; Qiao and Wang, *Unrestricted Warfare;* Kitson, *Warfare as a Whole;* and SWORD Papers.

5. This statement comes from General Michael P. C. Carns, U.S. Air Force (retired), "Reopening the Deterrence Debate," 8.

6. Esty et al., "State Failure Project"; Homer-Dixon, "On the Threshold"; and Homer-Dixon, *Environment, Scarcity, and Violence,* 133–68. Also see Qiao and Liang, *Unrestricted Warfare;* and SWORD Papers.

7. Lewis, "Revolt of Islam."

8. Sherifa Zuhur provides an excellent discussion of jihad in *A Hundred Osamas.*

9. Lewis, "Revolt of Islam."

10. Ibid. Also, in an interview with Osama bin Laden, Peter Bergen found that bin Laden considered that these are the main problems of the Islamic world. See Bergen, *Holy War, Inc.* For primary source material regarding statements made by Al Qaeda, see http://usinfo.state.gov/topical/pol/terror/99129502.htm.

11. See Bergen, *Holy War, Inc.;* also see Al Qaeda source material cited in previous note (chapter 3, note 10).

12. See previous note (chapter 3, note 11).

13. For an online transcript of the "Declaration of War against America Occupying the Land of the Two Holy Places," see www.pbs.org/newshour/terrorism/international/fatwa_1996.html. Also see Osama bin Laden, "A Letter to America," November 24, 2002, available online at http://observer.guardian.co.uk/worldview/story/9,11581,845725,00.html.

14. David Forte, "Islam's Trajectory," a presentation at the Foreign Policy Research Institute (FPRI) in Bryn Mawr, Penn., May 6–7, 2006, available online at www.fpra.org.

15. Ibid. Also see K. Fishel, "Challenging the Hegemon: Al Qaeda's Elevation," 119.

16. Forte, "Islam's Trajectory." Also see Rich, "Al Qaeda"; and Scheuer, "Al Qaeda Doctrine."

17. Forte, "Islam's Trajectory," www.fpra.org, p. 5.

18. Ibid., p. 8.

19. Cassidy, "Feeding Bread to the Luddites"; Laqueur, "Postmodern Terrorism"; and Hammes, "Al Qaeda: A Transnational Enemy," in Hammes, *Sling and the Stone*, 130–52.

20. Cassidy, "Feeding Bread to the Luddites," 336.

21. Ibid., 337.

22. Ibid. Also see Keegan, *History of Warfare*, 387. This "Eastern tradition" is attributed to Sun Tzu and Mao Tse-Tun. See Sun Tzu, *Art of War*; and Mao Tse-Tun, *On Guerrilla Warfare*.

23. Qiao and Wang, *Unrestricted Warfare*, 123.

24. Ibid., 152–69.

25. Ibid., 118. Also see SWORD Papers.

26. Qiao and Wang, *Unrestricted Warfare*, 157.

27. Ibid. For further elaboration of the Spanish case, see the later section of this chapter.

28. Ibid., 143. Also see Kitson, *Warfare as a Whole*, 69; SWORD Papers; and Brzezinski, *Out of Control*, 28.

29. Kitson, *Warfare as a Whole*, 123–24.

30. Ibid, 35.

31. Ibid., 154.

32. Ibid., 123.

33. Ibid.; and SWORD Papers.

34. K. Fishel, "Challenging the Hegemon: Al Qaeda's Elevation," 121–24; and Scheuer, "Can Al Qaeda Endure?" Also see chapter 3, note 9.

35. Gunaretna, *Inside*, 54. Also see Hammes, *Sling and the Stone*, 149.

36. Cassidy, "Feeding Bread to the Luddites," 348; and chapter 3, note 10. Also see Marks, "Ideology of Insurgency."

37. Cassidy, "Feeding Bread to the Luddites," 348; chapter 3, note 10; and Gunaretna, *Inside*, 89.

38. Rich, "Al Qaeda," 47.

39. "Pledge of Death in God's Path," available at http://usinfo.state.gov/topical/pol/terror/99129502.htm. Also see Ulph, "Mujahideen Pledge Allegiance on the Web."

40. Lenin, "Report on War and Peace" and "Symptoms of a Revolutionary Situation," in *Lenin Anthology*, 545 and 275–76. Also see Mao, *On Guerrilla War*, 2000.

41. K. Fishel, "Challenging the Hegemon: Al Qaeda's Elevation," 121. Also see Peter Bergen, "The Dense Web of Al Qaeda," *Washington Post*, December 25, 2003. Bergen describes Al Qaeda and its supporters as a structure of concentric rings in which different kinds of operations may be conducted vertically and horizontally by different parts of different rings.

42. Michael Scheuer, "Can Al Qaeda Endure?"; Hammes, *Sling and the Stone*, 135; and chapter 3, note 10.

43. Scheuer, "Can Al Qaeda Endure?"; chapter 3, note 10. Also see Gunaretna, *Inside,* 54.

44. Ibid. Also see Cassidy, "Feeding Bread to the Luddites," 338–49; K. Fishel, "Challenging the Hegemon: Al Qaeda's Elevation," 121–25; Hammes, *Sling and the Stone,* 350; and Heffelfinger, "Al Qaeda's Evolving Strategy."

45. Scheuer, "Al Qaeda's New Generation."

46. Ibid.

47. See chapter 3, note 10; and Scheuer, "Osama bin Laden."

48. See chapter 3, note 10; Scheuer, "Osama bin Laden"; and Scheuer, "Al-Qaeda Insurgency Doctrine."

49. See previous note (chapter 3, note 48).

50. See chapter 3, note 48; and Scheuer, "Al-Zawahiri's September 11 Video." Ayman al-Zawahiri is the deputy chief of Al Qaeda.

51. See chapter 3, notes 48 and 50. Also see Heffelfinger, "Al Qaeda's Evolving Strategy."

52. See chapter 3, note 10; Scheuer, "Osama bin Laden"; Scheuer, "Al-Qaeda Insurgency Doctrine"; Scheuer, "Al-Zawahiri's September 11 Video"; Heffelfinger, "Al Qaeda's Evolving Strategy."

53. See previous note (chapter 3, note 52).

54. See chapter 3, note 52.

55. See chapter 3, note 52.

56. See chapter 3, note 52.

57. A copy of the proceedings and charges against the 29 accused is available online at www.elpais.es/static/espiciales/2006/auto11M/elpais_auto.html?sumpag1.

58. Investigations in the United Kingdom regarding the bombings in London in 2005, yielded the information that there was a close relationship between that attack and the one in Madrid a year earlier and, in particular, that Al Qaeda had been more involved in the Madrid bombings than had been originally reported by Spanish authorities. See House of Commons, "Report of the Official Account of the Bombings in London on 7th July 2005," May 2006. This report can be downloaded at www.officialdocuments.co.uk/hc0506/hc10/1087/1087.asp.

59. See chapter 4 of this book for details regarding first-, second-, and third-generation gangs in the Americas. Also see Manwaring, *Street Gangs.*

60. Author interviews with present and former members of Spain's parliament, in Madrid, July 5–8, 2006.

61. See previous note (chapter 3, note 60). Also see http://usinfo.state.gov/topical/pol/terror/99129502.htm.

62. See chapter 3, notes 10 and 60.

63. See chapter 3, notes 10 and 60.

64. See chapter 3, note 58. Also see Block, "Devising a New Counter-Terrorism Strategy."

65. See chapter 3, note 60. Also see Jordan and Wesley, "After 3/11." Note that "3/11," in Spain, refers to the March attacks in Madrid.

66. "Terrorist Threat to UK—MI5 Chief's Full Speech," *Times Online,* November 11, 2006.

67. Mill, "Tangled Webs"; and Jamestown Foundation, "GSPC Joins Al Qaeda."

68. Author Interviews. Also see Jamestown Foundation, "GSPC in Italy."

69. Author Interviews.

70. Ibid.

71. Ibid. Also see Scheuer, "Al Qaeda Doctrine."

72. See, for example, Gelb, "Quelling the Teacup Wars"; "camouflaged war" is a term used by Liddell Hart in *Strategy* (p. 367); and "unrestricted war" is a term coined by Qiao and Wang in *Unrestricted Warfare* (see esp. pp. 10–11).

73. Metz, *Future of Insurgency,* 15.

74. Guillen, "Philosophy," 278–79.

75. Qiao and Wang, *Unrestricted Warfare,* 129–38.

76. Ibid., 133.

77. Ibid., 154.

78. These dimensions are found in K. Fishel, "Challenging the Hegemon: Al Qaeda's Elevation," 118. The original terms are found in Manwaring and K. Fishel, *Insurgency and Counter-Insurgency,* 272–310.

79. K. Fishel, "Challenging the Hegemon: Al Qaeda's Elevation," 119–25. Also see Joes, *From the Barrel.*

80. K. Fishel, "Challenging the Hegemon: Al Qaeda's Elevation," 118–22.

81. Hammes, *Sling and the Stone,* 150.

82. K. Fishel, "Challenging the Hegemon: Al Qaeda's Elevation," 118.

83. Ibid.

84. Ibid.

85. In these terms, Al Qaeda has become representative of the traditional global imperial or revolutionary power discussed by Morgenthau and Gilpin. See Morgenthau, *Politics among Nations;* and Gilpin, *War and Change.*

86. Picco, "Challenges of Strategic Terrorism"; also see Frank Hoffman, "Assessing the Long War," address to the Foreign Policy Research Institute, January 5, 2007.

87. Sun Tzu, *Art of War,* 38–41.

CHAPTER 4. SOVEREIGNTY UNDER SIEGE

1. For early discussions of these phenomena, see Huntington, *Clash of Civilizations;* and Kaplan, *Coming Anarchy.* Also see Easton, *Framework for Political Analysis;* and Easton, *Political System.*

2. Clausewitz, *On War,* 596.

3. Huntington, *Clash of Civilizations;* and Kaplan, *Coming Anarchy.* Also see Easton, *Framework for Political Analysis;* and Easton, *Political System.*

4. Sullivan, "Terrorism"; Sullivan and Bunker, "Drug Cartels"; Manwaring, *Street Gangs.*

5. Sullivan, "Terrorism"; Sullivan and Bunker, "Drug Cartels"; Manwaring, *Street Gangs.* Also see Easton, *Framework for Political Analysis;* and Easton, *Political System.*

6. Manwaring, *Street Gangs.*

7. Easton, *Framework for Political Analysis;* and Easton, *Political System.* David Easton formulated and elaborated the concept of "authoritative allocation of values" as the accepted definition of politics.

8. Sullivan and Bunker, "Drug Cartels."

9. Ibid.

10. Statement made at a U.S. Army War College–Florida International University (USAWC/FIU) conference held at the Center for Strategic and International Studies (CSIS), entitled "New Security Threats in the Western Hemisphere," Washington, D.C., June 29, 2004.

11. Sullivan and Bunker, "Drug Cartels."

12. Mackinlay, "Warlords." Also see Mackinlay, *Globalization and Insurgency.*

13. Mackinlay, "Beyond the Logjam." Also see Sullivan and Bunker, "Drug Cartels."

14. Sullivan, "Maras Morphing."

15. Ibid.

16. Ibid. Also see Rojas Aravena, "Nuevo contexto"; and Contreras Polgatti, *Conflicto en la post modernidad.*

17. Bruneau, "Maras and National Security."

18. Esty et al., "State Failure Project."

19. Crocker, "Engaging Failed States"; Krasner and Pascual, "Addressing State Failure."

20. The author has conducted a series of interviews (cited as Author Interviews) with more than three hundred senior U.S. and Latin American officials and journalists. These interviews took place from October 1989 through July 1994, September 1996, December 1998, November 2000, February 2001, March 2002, February 2003, March and August 2004, and March through May 2006. Also see Griffith, *Drugs and Security;* Lee, *White Labyrinth;* Belaunde, "Corrupción y discomposición"; Flynn, *Transnational Drug Challenge;* and Jordan, *Drug Politics.*

21. Bruneau, "Maras and National Security."

22. U.S. Agency for International Development, "Central America and Mexico Gang Assessment" (Washington, D.C.: USAID Bureau for Latin America and Caribbean Affairs, April 2006), hereinafter referred to as AID Paper, 2006.

23. Arana, "New Battle"; Arana, "How the Street Gangs"; Oscar Bonilla, "Current Situation of Gangs in El Salvador," unpublished paper written for the Consejo Nacional de Seguridad Pública del Salvador, November 2004.

24. Arana, "New Battle"; Arana, "How the Street Gangs"; Bonilla, "Current Situation." Also see Mark Lacey, "Drug Gangs Use Violence to Sway Guatemalan Vote," *New York Times,* August 4, 2007, www.nytimes.com/2007/08/04/world/Americas/04guatamals.html.

25. AID Paper, 2006; see also Manwaring, *Street Gangs.*

26. See www.seguridadpublicaenmexico.org.mx.

27. Londono and Guerrero, "Violencia en América Latina," 22. Also see AID Paper, 2006.

28. AID Paper, 2006.

29. Ibid.; Arana, "How the Street Gangs."

30. AID Paper, 2006; Arana, "How the Street Gangs."

31. Bonilla, "Current Situation."

32. AID Paper, 2006; Author Interviews.

33. AID Paper, 2006; Author Interviews.

34. AID Paper, 2006; Author Interviews.

35. Sullivan and Bunker, "Drug Cartels," 48–49.

36. Ibid.; Manwaring, *Street Gangs,* 9–10.

37. Arana, "How the Street Gangs," 101; Sullivan and Bunker, "Drug Cartels," 45–53.

38. Arana, "How the Street Gangs"; Sullivan and Bunker, "Drug Cartels."

39. Sullivan, "Maras Morphing," 493–94.

40. Ibid., 501.

41. J. Fishel and Grizzard, "Countering Ideological Support," 4; AID Paper, 2006; Author Interviews.

42. J. Fishel and Grizzard, "Countering Ideological Support"; AID Paper, 2006; Author Interviews.

43. In 2007, the United States pledged $4 million to fight street gangs and drug trafficking in the Central American region. That money is to help Central American governments draft a regional security policy. See www.cnn.com/2007/WORLD/Americas/07/19/central.america.gangs.reut/index.html.

44. Reported by the Overseas Security Advisory Council (OSAC), December 12, 2005; see www.osac.gov/Maras/story.

45. Sullivan, "Maras Morphing."

46. AID Paper, 2006.

47. Ibid. Also see Mark Stevenson, "Mexico: Drug Gangs Using Terror Tactics," *Miami Herald,* May 17, 2007, www.miamiherald.com/915/story/110509.html.

48. See previous note (chapter 4, note 47). Also see "Drug Gangs Set Their Sights on the Military," *El Universal,* May 15, 2007, www.mexiconews.com.mex/Miami/vi_24610.html; Kevin G. Hall, "Mexican Drug War Getting Bloodier,"

Miami Herald, March 21, 2007, www.miamiherald.com/579/vprint/story/47875.html; "Mexican Gangs Terrorize Border," CNN, March 1, 2006, www.cnn.com/2006/WORLD/Americas/03/01/mexico.gangs.reut/index.html; and Jordan, *Drug Politics.*

49. See previous note (chapter 4, note 48). Also see Sullivan, "Maras Morphing."

50. George W. Grayson, "Mexico and the Drug Cartels," Foreign Policy Research Institute, August 17, 2007. See www.fpri.org.

51. Sullivan, "Maras Morphing."

52. Ibid. Also see "Mexican Drug Lords Use New Tools to Intimidate," CNN, April 13, 2007, cnn.worldnews.print this.clickability.com/pt/cpt?action+cpt&title=Mexico=drug=lord; and Duncan Kennedy, "Mounting Toll in Mexico's Drug War," BBC News, July 5, 2007, newsvote.bbc.co.uk/mpapps/pagetools/print/news.bbc.co.uk/2/hi/Americas/6250200.stm.

53. Manwaring, *Street Gangs,* 24.

54. Lupsha, "Role of Drugs"; Lupsha, "Towards an Etiology"; and Olson, "International Organized Crime."

55. Lupsha, "Role of Drugs"; Lupsha, "Towards an Etiology"; and Olson, "International Organized Crime."

56. Lupsha, "Role of Drugs"; Lupsha, "Towards an Etiology"; and Olson, "International Organized Crime."

57. Jordan, *Drug Politics,* 19.

58. Ibid.; Arana, "New Battle"; Arana, "How the Street Gangs"; Sullivan and Bunker, "Drug Cartels"; and Sullivan, "Maras Morphing."

59. Jordan, *Drug Politics,* 142–57.

60. Ibid., 193–94.

61. "Five Slain in Nuevo Laredo, Pushing Year's Total over 100," *Houston Chronicle,* May 9, 2006, www.chron.com/disp/story.mpl/world/3852351.html. This is just the first five months of the year, in a city with a population of only 330,000.

62. Stevenson, "Mexico," *Miami Herald,* May 17, 2007; Hall, "Mexican Drug War," *Miami Herald,* March 21, 2007; and Kennedy, "Mounting Toll," BBC News, July 5, 2007. For online access, see chapter 4, notes 47, 48, and 52.

63. Quoted in Jordan, *Drug Politics,* 152.

64. Grayson, "Mexico and the Drug Cartels." For online access, see chapter 4, note 50.

65. Ioan Grillo, "'Cop-Killer' Guns from U.S. Seen Crossing into Mexico," *Boston Globe,* August 19, 2007, www.boston.com/news/world/latinamerica/articles/2007/08/19/cop_killer_guns; Kennedy, "Mounting Toll," BBC News (see chapter 4, note 52); "Armed Gang Kills Mexican Police," BBC News, May 17, 2007, www/newsvote.bbc.co.uk/mpapps/pagetools/print/news.bbc.co.uk/2/hi/Americas/6664215.

66. Mary Beth Sheridan, "Traffickers Move into Yucatan Peninsula," *Los Angeles Times,* August 27, 1998. Also see Sullivan and Bunker, "Drug Cartels."

67. Bunker and Sullivan, "Cartel Evolution."

68. Bunker and Begert, "Overview."

69. Ibid.

70. Olson, "International Organized Crime."

71. Sullivan and Bunker, "Drug Cartels."

72. Esty et al., "State Failure Project"; Dorff, "Strategy."

73. Sun Tzu, *Art of War,* 77–78.

CHAPTER 5. AN UNORTHODOX MILITARY MOVEMENT INTO AND OUT OF POWER

1. Spinola, *Ao Servico de Portugal,* 9–24. Also see Spinola's *Portugal e o futuro,* 130–270.

2. Maxwell, *Making of Portuguese Democracy,* 183. Also see Judt, *Postwar.*

3. As an example of this discussion, see Jordan, Taylor, and Mazarr, *American National Security,* 3–46; and Sarkesian, *U.S. National Security,* 7–8.

4. Krasner and Pascual, "Addressing State Failure," 155.

5. Ibid.

6. Godson, "Transtate Security," 81.

7. Metz and Johnson, *Asymmetry,* 5–6. Also see Hammes, "Fourth Generation Warfare."

8. Steven Metz, "Relearning Counterinsurgency," a panel discussion at the American Enterprise Institute, Washington, D.C., January 10, 2005.

9. Clausewitz, *On War,* 596.

10. Krasner and Pascual, "Addressing State Failure," 153.

11. Locke, *Of Civil Government,* 159.

12. Payne, *History of Spain,* 571.

13. Ibid., 559–69. Also see Oliveira Marques, *History of Portugal,* 162.

14. Anthony James Joes, "Portugal: The Army and the Liberal Revolution," in Joes, *From the Barrel,* 191.

15. This and other assertions made below are the results of interviews with General Pedro Alexandre Gomes Cardoso (retired), Brigadier General Renato F. Marques Pinto (retired), Captain Virgilio de Carvalho (navy, retired), Colonel Paulo Carvalho, Colonel Julio Faria Ribero de Olivera, Colonel Adelino Rodrigus Coelho, Colonel R. D. Schular, Lieutenant Colonel Jose A. Cardiera Rina, and others who prefer not to have their names made public. The interviews were conducted in Lisbon, Portugal, October 17–19, 1985; October 1–4, 1987; February 19–21, 1990; and July 9–16, 2006, by the author. Hereinafter cited as Author Interviews.

16. Author Interviews. Also see Judt, *Postwar,* 510–11.

17. Author Interviews; Judt, *Postwar.* Also see Maxwell, "Emergence of Portuguese Democracy," 233; Wiarda, *Corporatism and Development,* 178–79; and Joes, *From the Barrel.*

18. Admiral Sousa Leitao, "Portuguese Strategic Triangle." Also see Manwaring, "Iberia's Contribution."

19. Interview with Prime Minister Cavaco Silva, reported in *Expresso,* February 3, 1990, 4–11.

20. Author Interviews. Also see Judt, *Postwar.*

21. Judt, *Postwar,* 512. Also see Author Interviews.

22. Joes, *From the Barrel.* Also see Beckett, "Portuguese Army."

23. Author Interviews.

24. Ibid. Also see Joes, *From the Barrel;* Judt, *Postwar;* and Maxwell, "Emergence of Portuguese Democracy."

25. Fields, *Portuguese Revolution,* 200.

26. Joes, *From the Barrel,* 201.

27. Maxwell, "Emergence of Portuguese Democracy," 241–42.

28. Interview quoted in *l'Europeo,* June 13, 1975, and in *Conflict Studies* (September 1975): 28.

29. Author Interviews. Also see Graham, "Military in Politics," 239.

30. Author Interviews.

31. Judt, *Postwar;* and Maxwell, "Emergence of Portuguese Democracy."

32. Judt, *Postwar;* and Maxwell, "Emergence of Portuguese Democracy."

33. Author Interviews. Also see Maxwell, "Emergence of Portuguese Democracy"; and Judt, *Postwar.*

34. Author Interviews; Maxwell, "Emergence of Portuguese Democracy"; and Judt, *Postwar.* Also see Bruneau, "Portugal"; and Manwaring, "Iberia's Contribution," 593.

35. Author Interviews.

36. Ibid.

37. Ibid.

38. Ibid.

39. Spinola, *Ao Servico de Portugal.*

40. Maxwell, "Emergence of Portuguese Democracy."

41. General Nguyen Giap, "Factors of Success," in Giap, *People's War, People's Army,* 34–37.

42. Author Interviews.

43. Ibid.; also see Spinola, *Ao Servico de Portugal.*

44. Manwaring, *Military in Brazilian Politics.*

45. Ibid. Also see Maxwell, "Emergence of Portuguese Democracy"; and Maxwell, *Making of Portuguese Democracy,* 172–77.

46. Author Interviews.

47. Ibid.

48. These observations appear in one form or another throughout the eight books of Clausewitz, *On War.*

49. Author Interviews.

50. Spinola, *Ao Servico de Portugal.*

51. Author Interviews.

52. Ibid. Also see Krasner and Pascual, "Addressing State Failure"; and Spinola, *Ao Servico de Portugal.*

53. Spinola, *Ao Servico de Portugal.*

54. Ibid.

55. Ibid.

56. Ibid.

57. Ibid.

58. Ibid., 437–50. Also see Spinola, *Portugal e o futuro.*

59. Spinola, *Ao Servico de Portugal.* Also see interview with Prime Minister Cavaco Silva, reported in *Diario de Noticias,* February 16, 1989, pp. 8–12; and interview reported in *Expresso,* February 3, 1990, pp. 4–11.

60. Spinola, *Ao Servico de Portugal.*

61. Author Interviews.

62. Reported in *Economist* (August 19, 2006): 80.

63. From interviews with Prime Minister C. Silva cited in chapter 5, note 59.

64. Author Interviews. Also see Maxwell, *Making of Portuguese Democracy,* 172.

65. Author Interviews; Maxwell, *Making of Portuguese Democracy.*

66. Author Interviews; Maxwell, *Making of Portuguese Democracy.* Also see Rupp, "Defense Industrial Assistance."

67. Arms Control and Disarmament Agency, *World Military Expenditures,* 101; and Institute for International Strategic Studies, *Military Balance, 2005–2006,* 88–90.

68. Arms Control and Disarmament Agency, *World Military Expenditures;* and Institute for International Strategic Studies, *Military Balance, 2005–2006.*

69. Author Interviews.

70. Ibid.

71. V. I. Lenin, *What Is to Be Done?* in *Lenin Anthology.*

72. Clausewitz, *On War,* 596.

73. Kitson, *Warfare as a Whole.*

74. Krasner and Pascual, "Addressing State Failure." Also see Boutros-Ghali, "Global Leadership"; and Boutros-Ghali, *Agenda for Peace,* 11, 32–34.

75. Manwaring and J. Fishel, "Insurgency and Counter-Insurgency."

76. Author Interviews. Also see Manwaring and Corr, "Confronting."

77. Giap, *Peoples' War, Peoples' Army.*

78. Maxwell, *Making of Portuguese Democracy,* 183.

79. Sun Tzu, *Art of War,* 88.

CHAPTER 6. FROM DEFEAT TO POWER IN FOUR HARD LESSONS

1. Judt, *Postwar,* 406–8, 420–21.

2. Ibid., and author observation and interviews. From 1955 through 1958, the author was in a position from which to observe personally the political-military-insurgency situation developing in Argentina and Uruguay. Over the period 1959 through 2006, the author has continuously interviewed civilian and military officials regarding political-military affairs and insurgency in those countries and others. Thus, this and subsequent assertions made in this chapter are consensus statements based on observation and interviews (cited as Author Interviews).

3. Author Interviews. Examples in Western Europe would include the Red Army Faction (RAF—also known as the Baader-Meinhoff Gang) in Germany and the Red Brigades in Italy. In the United States, the most notable examples would include the Symbionese Liberation Army, the Black Panthers, and the SDS (Students for a Democratic Society).

4. Lenin argued that armed movements are successful when (1) the oppressed classes have become discontent and indignant; (2) there is more than normal aggravation in the society; (3) there is a considerable rise in the level of social violence in the masses; and (4) the revolutionary class has the capability to take actions that are strong enough to take down an incumbent government. See V. I. Lenin, "The Symptoms of a Revolutionary Situation," in *Lenin Anthology,* 275–76.

5. Guevara, *Guerrilla Warfare,* 15–20.

6. Author Interviews. Also see Gillespie, "Political Violence in Argentina"; and Moyano, *Argentina's Lost Patrol.*

7. Guillen, "Philosophy," 253.

8. Marighella, *Manual,* 40.

9. See, as examples, Guillen, "Philosophy"; Baumgartner, *Cronica desaforada;* Lessa, *La revolucion imposible;* and Rico, *Como nos domina.*

10. Lenin, "Report on War and Peace," in *Lenin Anthology,* 545.

11. Author Interviews. Also see Beckett, *Modern Insurgencies and Counterinsurgencies;* Beckett, "Future of Insurgency"; Marks, "Urban Insurgency"; and Hoffman and Taw, *Urbanization of Insurgency.*

12. See previous note (chapter 6, note 11). Also see Guillen, "Philosophy."

13. According to many Latin Americans, Rodo's writings were widely read and discussed from Mexico and the Antilles to Argentina and Chile. A. Curtis Wilgus has stated that such writings as *Ariel* and *The Motives of Proteus* came to be virtual holy scripture to many of the young men and women of the Americas in the mid-1900s and again in the early twenty-first century. William Rex Crawford observed that *Ariel* became the "pillow book" for Uruguayan and other

South American youth after Rodo's death in 1917. During his residence in Uruguay, Wilgus observed the same phenomenon as Crawford. See Wilgus, *Modern Hispanic-America,* 196–97; Crawford, *Century,* 79; and Henriquez-Urena, *Literary Currents,* 179–90.

14. V. I. Lenin, "Speech to the Congress, April 2" in "Communism and the New Economic Policy," in *Lenin Anthology,* 533.

15. Rodo, *Motives of Proteus,* 6.

16. Ibid., 358.

17. Note the current programs of the IRA (Irish Republican Army), PIRA (Provisional Irish Republican Army), the ETA (the Spanish Basque Independence Movement), and the Sandinista Party in Nicaragua.

18. Author Interviews.

19. Ibid.

20. Abante, "Uruguay—Democracy," 453.

21. Gillespie, "Political Violence in Argentina," 215–23.

22. Ibid.; and Moyano, *Argentina's Lost Patrol.*

23. Gillespie, "Political Violence in Argentina"; and Moyano, *Argentina's Lost Patrol.*

24. See chapter 6, note 23.

25. See chapter 6, note 23.

26. See chapter 6, note 23.

27. See chapter 6, note 23.

28. Author Interviews; also see chapter 6, note 23.

29. See chapter 6, note 23.

30. Author observation; Author Interviews. Also see Beckett, *Modern Insurgencies and Counter-Insurgencies,* 177–78; and Godfrey, "Latin American Experience," 124–25.

31. Abante, "Uruguay—Democracy," 453.

32. Ibid.

33. Jose Enrique Rodo, *El espiritu de la libertad,* in *Obras completas,* 1091–92. Also see Rodo, "La prensa de Montevideo," in *El mirador de prospero,* in *Obras completas* (1928 ed.), 777–83.

34. Baumgartner, *Cronica desaforada,* 116–19; Lessa, *La revolucion imposible,* 13–124; and Rico, *Como nos domina,* 45–52.

35. Baumgartner, *Cronica desaforada;* Lessa, *La revolucion imposible;* and Rico, *Como nos domina.*

36. Godfrey, "Latin American Experience," 129–33.

37. Clausewitz, *On War,* 596.

38. Guillen, "Philosophy," 269.

39. Ibid., 253.

40. Baumgartner, *Cronica desaforada,* 72. Also see Asprey, *War in the Shadows,* 1994 ed., 1073; Beckett, *Modern Insurgencies and Counter-Insurgencies,* 178; and Gross, "Uruguay," 145.

41. Godfrey, "Latin American Experience," 126–27.

42. Ibid. Also see Asprey, *War in the Shadows,* 1994 ed., 1073–74; Gross, "Uruguay," 145–48; and Azeem, "Conceptualisation of Guerrilla Warfare," 121.

43. Baumgartner, *Cronica desaforada,* 103.

44. Guillen, "Philosophy," 272.

45. Ibid., 263–77; Baumgartner, *Cronica desaforada,* 121–23, 131, 141, 180; and Asprey, *War in the Shadows,* 1994 ed., 1074–75.

46. Baumgartner, *Cronica desaforada*; and Godfrey, "Latin American Experience," 132.

47. Guillen, "Philosophy," 273, 267–71.

48. Beckett, *Modern Insurgencies and Counter-Insurgencies,* 178; Godfrey, "Latin American Experience," 128–33; and Gross, "Uruguay," 147–48.

49. Beckett, *Modern Insurgencies and Counter-Insurgencies;* Godfrey, "Latin American Experience"; Gross, "Uruguay."

50. Author Interviews.

51. Ibid. Also see Abante, "Uruguay—Democracy," 457; Baumgartner, *Cronica desaforada,* 131, 158–63, 177; Godfrey, "Latin American Experience," 125–27; and Gross, "Uruguay," 149.

52. See previous note (chapter 6, note 51). Also see Beckett, *Modern Insurgencies and Counter-Insurgencies,* 178; and Rico, *Como nos domina,* 52–60.

53. Godfrey, "Latin American Experience," 125.

54. Abante, "Uruguay—Democracy," 456–58; Asprey, *War in the Shadows,* 1994 ed., 1073–74; Baumgartner, *Cronica desaforada,* 379–401; and Godfrey, "Latin American Experience," 127.

55. Krasner and Pascual, "Addressing State Failure." Also see Crocker, "Engaging Failed States."

56. Guillen, "Philosophy," 239–42.

57. See, as only one example, Esty et al., "State Failure Project."

58. Author Interviews. Also see Baumgartner, *Cronica desaforada,* 401; Lessa, *La revolucion imposible,* 140–43; and Rico, *Como nos domina,* 61–82 and 188–92.

59. See previous note (chapter 6, note 58).

60. Author Interviews.

61. Abante, "Uruguay—Democracy," 457; Asprey, *War in the Shadows,* 1994 ed., 1074; Beckett, *Modern Insurgencies and Counter-Insurgencies,* 178; Godfrey, "Latin American Experience," 126–33; Gross, "Uruguay," 147–48; and Lessa, *La revolucion imposible,* 334.

62. Lessa, *La revolucion imposible,* 369–70.

63. Ibid., 375–76. Also see Vergara and Varas, *Coup!*

64. Lessa, *La revolucion imposible.*

65. Ibid., 377.

66. Ibid. Also see Coronel Sergio Luis D'Oliveira (retired), *El Uruguay y los Tupamaros.*

67. Lessa, *La revolucion imposible,* 373, 385–98.

68. Ibid.

69. Guillen, "Philosophy," 284.

70. Author Interviews. Also see Baumgartner, *Cronica desaforada;* Lessa, *La revolucion imposible;* and Rico, *Como nos domina.*

71. See previous note (chapter 6, note 70).

72. Guillen, "Philosophy," 283–84; and Maritain, *Man and the State.* For a more classical citation, see Rousseau, *Social Contract.*

73. Guillen, "Philosophy"; and Lessa, *La revolucion imposible.*

74. Guillen, "Philosophy," 380.

75. Rico, *Como nos domina,* 174–92.

76. Ibid., 27–43, 174–92.

77. Ibid.

78. Lenin, "Communism and the New Economic Policy," in *Lenin Anthology,* 533.

79. Baumgartner, *Cronica desaforada,* 255–56, 266–69.

80. Ibid., 281.

81. Guillen, "Philosophy," 259.

82. Baumgartner, *Cronica desaforada,* 255.

83. Lenin, "Communism and the New Economic Policy," in *Lenin Anthology,* 518–33; and Lessa, *La revolucion imposible.*

84. V. I. Lenin, "The Right of Nations to Self-Determination" and "The Revolutionary Taking of Power," in *Lenin Anthology,* 160–80 and 295–414, respectively.

85. Author Interviews. Also see Judt, *Postwar,* 421.

86. "Chaves le mete mas presion a Latinamerica, y a USA," *Urgente* 24, August 11, 2005; Julio A. Cirino, "La revolucion mundial pasa por Hugo Chavez," part 1, in *Panorama,* April 20, 2005, and part 2, in *Panorama,* April 27, 2005; and consensuș statement from the conference "Southern Cone Security," sponsored by the Office of External Research, Bureau of Intelligence and Research (INR), U.S. Department of State, in Washington, D.C., July 8, 2005.

87. Consensus statement from the conference "Building Regional Security Cooperation in the Western Hemisphere," cosponsored by the North-South Center of the University of Miami and the Strategic Studies Institute of the U.S. Army War College, in Miami, Fla., March 1–2, 2003. Also see Organization of American States, Draft Declaration on Security in the Americas, approved by the Permanent Council, October 22, 2003.

88. Corr and Manwaring, "Central Political Challenge."

89. Maritain, *Man and the State,* 19.

90. Manwaring and J. Fishel, "Insurgency and Counterinsurgency."

91. See the "World Conflict and Human Rights Map," prepared by Berto Jongman with the support of the Goals for Americans Foundation, St. Louis, 2006; *The State of the World Atlas,* 2006; and genocidewatch.com.

92. Rojas Aravena, "Nuevo contexto."

93. Sun Tzu, *Art of War,* 77.

CHAPTER 7. REFLECTIONS ON THE SUCCESSFUL ITALIAN COUNTERTERRORISM EFFORT, 1968–1983

1. Pisano, *Dynamics of Subversion,* 5–37.

2. A third-generation gang is a mercenary-type group with goals of power and a set of fully developed political aims. See Sullivan and Bunker, "Drug Cartels"; Manwaring, *Street Gangs.* Also see chapter 4.

3. Pisano, *Dynamics of Subversion,* 39–40. Also see testimony of Red Brigadist Antonio Savasta, quoted in Drake, *Aldo Moro Murder Case,* 50; declaration of Red Brigades sent to *L'Expresso* and published as "Le due anime delle Br," March 1, 1987.

4. Pisano, *Dynamics of Subversion;* Author Interviews.

5. Pisano, *Dynamics of Subversion.*

6. Testimony of Antonio Savasta, quoted in Drake, *Aldo Moro Murder Case,* 51.

7. Savasta, quoted in Della Porta, "Left-Wing Terrorism in Italy," 150.

8. Ibid.; Author Interviews.

9. Author Interviews.

10. Ibid.

11. Ibid.

12. Ibid.; testimony of Red Brigadist Patrizio Peci, recorded in Moran, *Rand Note,* 47.

13. Author Interviews; Della Porta, "Left-Wing Terrorism in Italy," 130.

14. Della Porta, "Left-Wing Terrorism in Italy"; these data may also be found in Pisano, *Dynamics of Subversion,* 157–67.

15. Author Interviews; Della Porta, "Left-Wing Terrorism in Italy"; Pisano, *Dynamics of Subversion.*

16. Author Interviews; Della Porta, "Left-Wing Terrorism in Italy"; Pisano, *Dynamics of Subversion.*

17. Author Interviews and SWORD Papers.

18. Howard, "Forgotten Dimensions of Strategy," 109.

19. Machiavelli, *Art of War,* liv–livi, 7–8, 34, 36, 46, 77–78, 171, 179, 202–204.

20. Ibid.

21. Author Interviews.

22. Ibid.

23. Ibid.; Pisano, *Dynamics of Subversion,* 144–51; Della Porta, "Left-Wing Terrorism in Italy," 118–19.

24. SWORD Papers.

25. Author Interviews.

26. Ibid.

27. SWORD Papers.

28. Author Interviews.

29. Ibid.

30. SWORD Papers.

31. Author Interviews; Pisano, *Dynamics of Subversion,* 146.

32. SWORD Papers.

33. Interview with militant quoted in Della Porta, "Left-Wing Terrorism in Italy," 150.

34. Quoted in Fenzi, *Armi e bagagli,* 76.

35. SWORD Papers.

36. Author Interviews; Della Porta, "Left-Wing Terrorism in Italy," 157–59.

37. For a few examples, see Moran, *Rand Note,* 36, 59–60; Pisano, *Dynamics of Subversion,* 119–43; Della Porta, "Left-Wing Terrorism in Italy," 120; *Panorama,* September 15, 1980, 45; Orlando, *Siamo en Guerra,* 195–96; Pisano, "Libya's Foothold in Italy."

38. See previous note (chapter 7, note 37).

39. Author Interviews.

40. SWORD Papers.

41. Author Interviews.

42. Ibid.

43. Ibid.

44. Ibid.

45. SWORD Papers.

46. Sun Tzu, *Art of War,* 77.

47. Ibid., 144–45.

AFTERWORD

1. In earlier books—Corr and Sloan, *Low Intensity Conflict,* and Manwaring, *Gray Area Phenomena*—Manwaring and his collaborators described these threats for Americans and their leaders.

2. U.S. Department of Defense, *Supporting U.S. Strategy,* 1–6.

3. Perkins and Boren, "Summary."

4. K. Fishel, "Challenging the Hegemon: Al Qaeda's Elevation."

5. Charles W. Freeman, "Diplomacy and Empire," speech to DACOR (Diplomats and Consular Officers Retired), February 9, 2007, at DACOR House, Washington, D.C., printed by the Middle East Policy Council, available at www.mepc.org/whats/diplomacy.asp.

6. Huntington, *Third Wave;* Anderson, *Politics and Change.*

7. Miller, "Beyond the Cold War," 154–55; and Miller, "Back to the Future," 14–15.

8. See Stourch and Lerner, *Readings in American Democracy,* 68.

9. Quoted in Bridges, *Freedom in America,* 193.

10. Ibid., 371.

11. Baker and Hamilton, *Iraq Study Group Report.*

12. In the criticisms of the Defense Department and the armed forces that follow, I hope readers will take into consideration that I served for three and a half years on active duty as a U.S. Marine Corps infantry officer, and throughout most of my career in the Foreign Service I worked cooperatively, productively, and in friendship with many military personnel of all ranks.

13. It always disturbed me that in supporting the efforts of Latin American states to return to constitutional and democratic governments from the mid-1970s to the 1990s, because of the limited personnel and resources of U.S. civilian agencies and the ample personnel and resources of U.S. armed forces, military personnel frequently performed tasks that would have better been done by civilians.

14. See "Lame-Duck Budget," editorial, *New York Times,* February 5, 2008. I am currently serving on the American Academy of Diplomacy's "Red Team" for a study to determine what resources are needed to enable the Department of State to accomplish its foreign policy objectives by developing a "Foreign Affairs Budget for the Future," using the current structure of Congress 150 Account. This mandate does not really allow a "from the ground up" approach for funding of civilian agencies of all areas that would best be carried out by civilian agencies.

15. Some have argued that had the military departments not been so strong relative to the Department of State during World War II, better decisions might have been made, such as invading Europe through the Balkans to meet the Soviet forces as far east as possible, thereby reaching a better postwar settlement with the Soviets.

16. Cindy Williams, "Beyond Preemption and Preventive War: Increasing U.S. Budget Emphasis on Conflict Prevention," Policy Analysis Brief, Stanley Foundation, February 2006; "The Iraq War Debate: A Reality Check on Military Spending," editorial, *New York Times,* July 21, 2007; "Lame-Duck Budget," editorial, *New York Times,* February 5, 2008.

17. *Embassies as Command Posts in the Anti-Terror Campaign,* report to members of the Committee on Foreign Relations, U.S. Senate, 109th Cong., 2nd sess., December 13, 2006 (Washington, D.C.: U.S. Government Printing Office, 2006).

18. See Carlotta Gall, "British Criticize Air Attacks in Afghan Region," *New York Times,* August 9, 2007.

19. *Embassies as Command Posts in the Anti-Terror Campaign,* report to members of the Committee on Foreign Relations, U.S. Senate, 109th Cong., 2nd sess., December 13, 2006 (Washington, D.C.: U.S. Government Printing Office, 2006).

20. "The Department of State by the Numbers," *DACOR Bulletin,* April 2007, p. 16; David Stout and Thom Shanker, "Next Years War Costs Estimated at $176 Billion or More," *New York Times,* February 6, 2008; Thom Shanker, "Proposed Military Spending at Its Highest since World War II," *New York Times,* February 4, 2008; Sheryl Gay Stolberg, "Bush Presents Budget That Would Increase Deficit," *New York Times,* February 5, 2008; Andrew Taylor, Associated Press writer, *Norman Transcript,* February 5, 2008; also see President Bush's Fiscal Year 2009 Budget Proposal.

21. Matthew Lee, Associated Press writer, "World Shrinks for U.S. Diplomats as Embassy Security Fear Grows," *Norman Transcript,* July 7, 2007, p. A9.

22. See the series on Blackwater in *Washington Post National Weekly Edition,* October–November 2007; also see David Johnston and James M. Broder, "FBI Says Guards Killed 14 Iraqies without Cause," *New York Times,* November 14, 2007; and John M. Broder and David Rohde, "Use of Contractors by State Dept. Has Soared," *New York Times,* October 24, 2007.

23. Nir Rosen, "Security Contractors: Riding Shotgun with Our Shadow Army in Iraq," April 24, 2007, www.motherjones.com/news/feature/2007/iraq_contractors-2.html; "Accountability on the Battlefield," editorial, *New York Times,* October 8, 2007.

24. Part of the reason for such poor implementation in the Iraq War may be that President Bush has been caught in a paradigm shift from the U.S. government's depending on the armed forces and civilian agencies to fight wars to depending too much on private contractors—caused in part by not having available sufficient personnel and capacity within the government.

25. See Patrick Redden Keefe, "Don't Privatize Our Spies," op-ed piece, *New York Times,* June 25, 2007; and Steve Fainaru and Alec Klein, "Outsourced Intelligence," *Washington Post National Weekly Edition,* July 9–15, 2007, pp. 19–20.

26. The great sociologist Robert Merton in 1936 isolated five contributing factors that singly or in combination can affect adversely the outcomes of collective action or public policy: (1) ignorance of the true conditions pertaining; (2) errors in inference (based on accurate information but distorted by obsession or wish fulfillment); (3) the primacy of immediate interests (where the desire for an outcome is so great that there is a willful ignoring of possible negative effects); (4) the ideological or moral imperative of "basic values" (faith-driven decisions or political ideology); and (5) self-fulfilling prophecy. This or some similar set of guidelines should be part of the decision-making process today, and bureaucratic processes should be established to ensure that they are taken into account within the national security system. The list was taken from Allawi, *Occupation of Iraq,* 6–10.

27. See Robb, *Brave New War*; and J. Fishel and Manwaring, *Uncomfortable Wars Revisited.*

BIBLIOGRAPHY

Abante, Diego. "Uruguay—Democracy: Idea, Practice, and Tradition of Coparticipation." In *Latin America, Its Problems and Its Promise,* edited by Jan Knippers Black, 453–59. Boulder, Colo.: Westview Press, 1984.

Allawi, Ali. *The Occupation of Iraq: Winning the War, Losing the Peace.* New Haven, Conn.: Yale University Press, 2007.

Anderson, Charles W. *Politics and Change in Latin America.* Princeton, N.J.: D. Van Nostrand, 1967.

Anderson, Martin Edward ["Mick"]. *Countries at the Crossroads 2006.* Washington, D.C.: Freedom House, 2006.

———. "Venezuela: Politics in the Military, the Military in Politics." *Inter-American Dialogue* (April 2006): 6–8.

Arana, Ana. "How the Street Gangs Took Central America." *Foreign Affairs* (May / June 2005): 98–110.

———. "The New Battle for Central America." *Foreign Affairs* (November / December 2001): 88–101.

Arms Control and Disarmament Agency. *World Military Expenditures and Arms Transfers, 1968–1977.* Washington, D.C.: ACDA, 1979.

Art, Robert J., and Robert Jervis. *International Politics: Anarchy, Force, Imperialism.* Boston: Little, Brown, 1973.

Asprey, Robert B. *War in the Shadows: The Guerrilla in History.* Garden City, N.Y.: Doubleday, 1975. Reprint ed., New York: William Morrow, 1994.

Azeem, Ibrahim. "Conceptualisation of Guerrilla Warfare." *Small Wars and Insurgencies* (Winter 2004): 112–24.

Baker, James A., III, and Lee Hamilton, co-chairs. *The Iraq Study Group Report: The Way Forward—A New Approach.* New York: Vintage Books, 2006.

Baumgartner, Jose Luis. *Cronica desaforada*. Montevideo: Editorial Fin de Siglo, 2005.

Beckett, Ian F. W. "The Future of Insurgency." *Small Wars and Insurgencies* (March 2005): 22–36.

———. *Modern Insurgencies and Counter-Insurgencies: Guerrillas and Their Opponents since 1750*. London: Routledge, 2001.

———. "The Portuguese Army: The Campaign in Mozambique, 1964–1974." In *Armed Forces and Modern Counter-Insurgency,* edited by Ian F. W. Beckett and John Pimlott, 136–62. New York: St. Martin's Press, 1985.

Bejarano, Ana Maria, and Eduardo Pizarro. "Colombia: A Failing State?" *ReVista: Harvard Review of Latin America* (Spring 2003): 1–6.

Belaunde, Luis Bustamente. "Corrupción y discomposición del estado." In *Pasta basica de cocaina,* edited by Federico R. Leon and Ramiro Castro de la Mata, 301–21. Lima, Peru: Centro de Informacion y Educacion para la Prevencion de Abuso de Drogas, 1990.

Bergen, Peter. *Holy War, Inc.: Inside the Secret World of Osama bin Laden*. New York: Free Press, 2001.

Block, Ludo. "Devising a New Counter-Terrorism Strategy in Europe." *Terrorism Monitor* (Jamestown Foundation) 4, no. 21 (November 21, 2006). http://jamestown.org/terrorism/news/article.php?articleid=2370191.

Boutros-Ghali, Boutros. *An Agenda for Peace*. New York: United Nations, 1992.

———. "Global Leadership after the Cold War." *Foreign Affairs* (March/April 1996): 86–98.

Bridges, Kenneth. *Freedom in America*. Upper Saddle River, N.J.: Pearson/Prentice Hall, 2007.

Brown, Seyom. *New Forces, Old Forces, and the Future of World Politics*. New York: HarperCollins, 1995.

Bruneau, Thomas C. "The Maras and National Security in Central America." *Strategic Insights* 4, no. 5 (2005). http://www.ccc.nps.navy.mil.

———. "Portugal: Problems and Prospects in the Creation of a New Regime." *Naval War College Review* (Summer 1976): 65–83.

Brzezinski, Zbigniew. *The Choice: Global Domination or Global Leadership*. New York: Basic Books, 2004.

———. *Out of Control: Global Turmoil on the Eve of the 21st Century.* New York: Simon and Schuster, Touchstone, 1993.

Bunker, Robert J., and Matt Begert. "Overview: Defending against the Enemies of the State." *Global Crime* (August–November 2006): 309.

Bunker, Robert J., and John P. Sullivan. "Cartel Evolution: Potentials and Consequences." *Transnational Organized Crime* (Summer 1998): 55–74.

Bushnell, David. "Politics and Violence in Nineteenth-Century Colombia." In *Violence in Colombia: The Contemporary Crisis in Historical Perspective,* edited by

Charles Bergquist, Ricardo Penaranda, and Gonzolo Sanchez, 11–30. Wilmington, Del.: SR Books, 1992.

Buzan, Barry. *People, States, and Fear: An Agenda for International Security Studies in the Post–Cold War Era.* London: Harvester Wheatsheaf, 1991.

Carns, Michael P. C. "Reopening the Deterrence Debate." In *Deterrence in the Twenty-first Century*, edited by Max G. Manwaring, 7–16. London: Frank Cass, 2001.

Cassidy, Robert M. "Feeding Bread to the Luddites: The Radical Fundamentalist Islamic Revolution in Guerrilla Warfare." *Small Wars and Insurgencies* (December 2005): 334–59.

Clark, Bruce B. G. "End-State Planning: The Somalia Case." In *Managing Contemporary Conflict: Pillars of Success,* edited by Max G. Manwaring and William J. Olson, 49–69. Boulder, Colo.: Westview Press, 1996.

Clausewitz, Carl von. *On War.* Edited and translated by Michael Howard and Peter Paret. Orig. pub. 1832. Princeton, N.J.: Princeton University Press, 1976.

Comité Central del Partido Comunista del Perú. *Bases de discusión [Bases of Discussion].* Lima: Comité Central del Partido Comunista del Perú, 1987.

———. *Desarrollar la guerra popular sirviendo a la revolución mundial [Developing People's War to Serve the World Revolution].* Lima: Comité Central del Partido Comunista del Perú, 1986.

Contreras Polgatti, Arturo. *Conflicto en la post modernidad.* Santiago, Chile: Mago Editores, 2004.

Corr, Edwin G., and Max G. Manwaring. "The Central Political Challenge in the Global Security Environment: Governance and Security." In *The Search for Security: A U.S. Grand Strategy for the Twenty-first Century,* edited by Max G. Manwaring, Edwin G. Corr, and Robert H. Dorff, 47–61. Westport, Conn.: Praeger, 2003.

———. "The Challenge of Preventive Diplomacy and Deterrence in the Global Security Environment." In *Deterrence in the Twenty-first Century,* edited by Max G. Manwaring, 124–31. London: Frank Cass, 2001.

Corr, Edwin G., and Stephen Sloan, eds. *Low Intensity Conflict: Old Conflicts in a New World.* Norman: University of Oklahoma Press, 1992.

Crawford, William Rex. *A Century of Latin American Thought.* Cambridge, Mass.: Harvard University Press, 1961.

Crenshaw, Martha. "The Causes of Terrorism." *Comparative Politics* (July 1981): 379–99.

———, ed. *Terrorism in Context.* University Park: Pennsylvania State University Press, 1995.

———, ed. *Terrorism, Legitimacy, and Power: The Consequences of Political Violence.* Middletown, Conn.: Wesleyan University Press, 1983.

Crocker, Chester A. "Engaging Failed States." *Foreign Affairs* (September/October 2003): 32–44.

Dahl, Robert A. *After the Revolution? Authority in a Good Society*. New Haven, Conn.: Yale University Press, 1990.

———. *Modern Political Analysis*. Englewood Cliffs, N.J.: Prentice-Hall, 1976.

David, Steven R. "Saving America from the Coming Civil Wars." *Foreign Affairs* (January/February 1999): 103–116.

Della Porta, Donatella. "Left-Wing Terrorism in Italy." in *Terrorism in Context*, edited by Martha Crenshaw, 105–59. University Park: Pennsylvania State University Press, 1995.

D'Oliveira, Sergio Luis. *El Uruguay y los Tupamaros*. Montevideo: Departamento General Artigas del Centro Militar, 1996.

Dorff, Robert H. "Strategy, Grand Strategy, and the Search for Strategy." In *The Search for Security: A U.S. Grand Strategy for the Twenty-First Century*, edited by Max G. Manwaring, Edwin G. Corr, and Robert H. Dorff, 127–240. Westport, Conn.: Praeger, 2003.

Drake, Richard. *The Aldo Moro Murder Case*. Cambridge, Mass.: Harvard University Press, 1995.

Easton, David. *A Framework for Political Analysis*. Englewood Cliffs, N.J.: Prentice-Hall, 1965.

———. *The Political System: An Inquiry into the State of Political Science*. Chicago: University of Chicago Press, 1971, 1981.

Economist. "Survey of Colombia." April 21–27, 2001.

Ellner, Steve. "Revolutionary and Non-Revolutionary Paths of Radical Populism: Directions of the Chavez Movement in Venezuela." *Science and Society* (April 2005): 160–90.

El pais que proponemos construer. Bogota: Editorial La Oveja Negra, 2001.

Esty, Daniel C., Jack Goldstone, Ted Robert Gurr, Barbara Harff, and Pamela T. Surko. "The State Failure Project: Early Warning Research for U.S. Foreign Policy Planning." In *Preventive Measures: Building Risk Assessment and Crisis Early Warning Systems*, edited by John L. Davies and Ted Robert Gurr, 27–38. New York: Rowman and Littlefield, 1998.

Fenzi, Enrico. *Armi e bagagli: Un diario dalle Brigate Rosse*. Genoa: Costa and Nolan, 1987.

Fields, Rona M. *The Portuguese Revolution and the Armed Forces Movement*. New York: Praeger, 1976.

Fishel, John T., and Max G. Manwaring. *Uncomfortable Wars Revisited*. Norman: University of Oklahoma Press, 2006.

Fishel, Kimbra L. "Challenging the Hegemon." *Low Intensity Conflict and Law Enforcement* 11, no. 2/3, special issue (Winter 2002): 285–98.

———. "Challenging the Hegemon: Al Qaeda's Elevation of Asymmetric Insurgent Warfare onto the Global Arena." In *Networks, Terrorism and Global Insurgency,* edited by Robert J. Bunker, 115–28. London: Routledge, 2005.

Fluherty, Vernon Lee. *Dance of the Millions: Military Rule and the Social Revolution in Colombia, 1930–1956*. Pittsburgh: University of Pittsburgh Press, 1957.

Flynn, Stephen E. *The Transnational Drug Challenge and the New World Order*. Washington, D.C.: Center for Strategic and International Studies, 1993.

Frechette, Myles R. R. "Colombia and the United States—The Partnership: But What Is the Endgame?" Carlisle Barracks, Penn.: Strategic Studies Institute, 2006.

———. *In Search of the Endgame: A Long-Term Multilateral Strategy for Colombia.* Miami, Fla.: Dante B. Fascell North-South Center at the University of Miami, February 2003.

Gelb, Leslie H. "Quelling the Teacup Wars." *Foreign Affairs* (November/December 1994): 5.

Giap, Nguyen. *Peoples' War, Peoples' Army*. New York: Frederick A. Praeger, 1962.

Gillespie, Richard. "Political Violence in Argentina: Guerrillas, Terrorists, and *Carapintadas.*" In *Terrorism in Context,* edited by Martha Crenshaw, 211–48. University Park: Pennsylvania State University Press, 1995.

Gilpin, Robert. *War and Change in World Politics*. Cambridge: Cambridge University Press, 1993.

Godfrey, F. A. "The Latin American Experience: The Tupamaros Campaign in Uruguay, 1963–1973." In *Armed Forces and Modern Counterinsurgency,* edited by Ian F. W. Beckett and John Pimlott, 112–35. New York: St. Martin's Press, 2001.

Godson, Roy. "Transtate Security." In *Security Studies for the Twenty-first Century,* edited by Richard H. Schultz, Jr., Roy Godson, and George H. Quester, 81–118. Washington, D.C.: Brassey's, 1997.

Graham, Lawrence S. "The Military in Politics: The Politization of the Portuguese Armed Forces." In *Contemporary Portugal: The Revolution and Its Antecedents,* edited by Lawrence S. Graham and Harry M. Marks, 221–56. Austin: University of Texas Press, 1979.

Gray, Colin S. "Deterrence and the Nature of Strategy." In *Deterrence in the Twenty-first Century,* edited by Max G. Manwaring, 17–26. London: Frank Cass, 2001.

Griffith, Ivelaw Lloyd. *Drugs and Security in the Caribbean: Sovereignty under Siege.* University Park: Pennsylvania State University Press, 1997.

Gross, Lisa. "Uruguay—Movimiento de Liberacion Nacional Tupamaros." In *Handbook of Leftist Guerrilla Groups in Latin America and the Caribbean,* 145–49. Boulder, Colo.: Westview Press, 1995.

Guevara, Ernesto ["Che"]. *Guerrilla Warfare*. New York: Monthly Review Press, 1961.

———. *Obras completas*. Buenos Aires: Ediciones Cepe, 1973.

Guillen, Abraham. "Philosophy of the Urban Guerrilla." In *The Revolutionary*

Writings of Abraham Guillen. Translated and edited by Donald C. Hodges. New York: William Morrow, 1973.

Gunaretna, Rohan. *Inside the al-Qai'da Global Network of Terror.* London: Hurst, 2002.

Guzmán, Abimael. "El discurso del Dr. Guzmán" ["Dr. Guzman's Speech"]. In *Los partidos políticos en el Perú [Political Parties in Peru],* edited by Rogger Mercado U., 85–90. Lima: Ediciones Latinoamericanos, 1985).

Hammes, Thomas X. "Fourth Generation Warfare." *Armed Forces Journal* (November 2004): 40–44.

———. *The Sling and the Stone: On War in the Twenty-first Century.* St. Paul, Minn.: Zenith Press, 2006.

Hanratty, Dennis M., and Sandra W. Meditz, eds. *Colombia: A Country Study.* Washington, D.C.: Federal Research Division, Library of Congress, 1990.

Heffelfinger, Chris. "Al Qaeda's Evolving Strategy Five Years after September 11." *Terrorism Focus* (Jamestown Foundation) 3, no. 35 (September 12, 2006).

Henriquez-Urena, Pedro. *Literary Currents in Hispanic-America.* Cambridge, Mass.: Harvard University Press, 1946.

Hill, James T. Preface to *Building Regional Security Cooperation in the Western Hemisphere: Issues and Recommendations,* by Max G. Manwaring, Wendy Fontela, Mary Grizzard, and Dennis Rempe. Carlisle Barracks, Penn.: Strategic Studies Institute, 2003.

Hodges, Donald C., ed. *Philosophy of the Urban Guerrilla: The Revolutionary Writings of Abraham Guillen.* New York: William Morrow, 1973.

Hoffman, Bruce, and Jennifer Morrison Taw. *The Urbanization of Insurgency.* Santa Monica, Calif.: Arroyo Center / Rand, 1994.

Homer-Dixon, Thomas F. *Environment, Scarcity, and Violence.* Princeton, N.J.: Princeton University Press, 1999.

———. "On the Threshold: Environmental Changes as Causes of Acute Conflict." *International Security* (Fall 1991): 76–116.

Howard, Michael. "The Forgotten Dimensions of Strategy." In Michael Howard, *The Causes of Wars,* 101–15. London: Temple-Smith, 1981.

———. *The Lessons of History.* New Haven, Conn.: Yale University Press, 1991.

Huntington, Samuel P. *The Clash of Civilizations and the Remaking of World Order.* New York: Simon and Schuster, 1996.

———. *The Third Wave: Democratization in the Late Twentieth Century.* Norman: University of Oklahoma Press, 1991.

Iglesias, Carlos Basombrío. "Venezuela: Politics in the Military, the Military in Politics." In *The Military and Politics in the Andean Region,* Inter-American Dialogue, Andean Working Paper, April 2006, pp. 6–8. Available at www.thedialogue.org/publications/2006/spring/basombrio_andean.pdf.

Institute for International Strategic Studies. *The Military Balance, 2005–2006.* London: IISS, 2005.

Inter-American Development Bank. *Annual Report 1999*. Washington, D.C.: Inter-American Development Bank, 2000.

Jamestown Foundation. "GSPC in Italy: The Forward Base of Jihad in Europe." *Terrorism Monitor* 4, no. 3 (February 9, 2006). http://jamestown.org/terrorism/news/article.php?articleid=2369894.

———. "GSPC Joins al-Qaeda and France Becomes Top Enemy." *Terrorism Focus* 3, no. 37 (September 26, 2006). http://jamestown.org/terrorism/news/article.php?articleid=2370144.

Joes, Anthony James. *America and Guerrilla Warfare*. Lexington: University Press of Kentucky, 2000.

———. *From the Barrel of a Gun: Armies and Revolutions*. Washington, D.C.: Pergamon-Brassey's, 1986.

Jordan, Amos A., William J. Taylor, Jr., and Michael J. Mazarr. *American National Security*. 5th ed. Baltimore, Md.: Johns Hopkins University Press, 1999.

Jordan, David C. *Drug Politics: Dirty Money and Democracies*. Norman: University of Oklahoma Press, 1999.

Jordan, Javier, and Robert Wesley. "After 3/11: The Evolution of Jihadist Networks in Spain." *Terrorism Monitor* (Jamestown Foundation) 4, no. 1 (January 12, 2006). http://jamestown.org/terrorism/news/article.php?articleid=2369863.

Judt, Tony. *Postwar: A History of Europe since 1945*. New York: Penguin Press, 2005.

Kaplan, Robert D. *The Coming Anarchy*. New York: Random House, 2000.

———. "The Coming Anarchy." *Atlantic Monthly* (February 1994).

Keegan, John. *A History of Warfare*. New York: Vintage Books, 1993.

Kitson, Frank. *Warfare as a Whole*. London: Faber and Faber, 1987.

Klepak, Hal. "Colombia: Why Doesn't the War End?" *Jane's Intelligence Review* (June 2000): 41–45.

Komer, Robert W. *Bureaucracy Does Its Thing: Institutional Constraints on US-GVN Performance in Vietnam*. Santa Monica, Calif.: Rand, 1972.

Krasner, Steven D., and Carlos Pascual. "Addressing State Failure." *Foreign Affairs* (July–August 2005): 153–55.

Laqueur, Walter. *The New Terrorism Fanaticism and the Arms of Mass Destruction*. Oxford: Oxford University Press, 1999.

———. *No End to War: Terrorism in the Twenty-First Century*. New York: Continuum, 2003.

———. "Postmodern Terrorism." *Foreign Affairs* (September/October 1996): 24–36.

Lee, Rensselaer W., III. *The White Labyrinth*. New Brunswick, N.J.: Transaction, 1990.

Lemke, Douglas. "The Continuation of History: Power Transition Theory and the End of the Cold War." *Journal of Peace Research* 34, no. 1 (1997): 23–36.

———. *Regions of War and Peace*. Cambridge: Cambridge University Press, 2002.

Lenin, V. I. *The Lenin Anthology.* Edited by Robert C. Tucker. New York: W. W. Norton, 1975.

Lessa, Alfonso. *La revolucion imposible.* Montevideo: Editorial Fin de Siglo, 2005.

Lewis, Bernard. "The Revolt of Islam." *New Yorker,* November 30, 2001. www.newyorker.com/FACT/?01119fa_FACT2.

Liddell Hart, B. H. *Strategy.* 2nd rev. ed. New York: Signet, 1967.

Locher, James R., III. *Victory on the Potomac: The Goldwater-Nichols Act Unifies the Pentagon.* College Station: Texas A and M University Press, 2002.

Locke, John. *Of Civil Government: Second Treatise of Civil Government.* New York: Gateway, n.d.

Londono, J., and R. Guerrero. "Violencia en América Latina: epidemiología y costos." IADB Working Paper R-375. Washington, D.C.: Inter-American Development Bank.

Lupsha, Peter A. "The Role of Drugs and Drug Trafficking in the Invisible Wars." In *International Terrorism: Operational Issues,* edited by Richard H. Ward and H. E. Smith, 177–90. Chicago: Office of International Criminal Justice, University of Illinois at Chicago, 1987.

———. "Towards an Etiology of Drug Trafficking and Insurgent Relations: The Phenomenon of Narcoterrorism." *International Journal of Comparative and Allied Criminal Justice* 13, no. 2 (Fall 1989): 60–74.

Machiavelli, Niccolò. *The Art of War.* New York: DaCapo Press, 1965.

Mackinlay, John. "Beyond the Logjam: A Doctrine for Complex Emergencies." In *Toward Responsibility in the New World Disorder,* edited by Max G. Manwaring and John T. Fishel, 114–31. London: Frank Cass, 1998.

———. *Globalization and Insurgency.* London: International Institute for Strategic Studies, 2002.

———. "Warlords." *Defence and International Security* (April 1998): 28–32.

Manwaring, Max G., ed. *Gray Area Phenomena: Confronting the New World Order.* Boulder, Colo.: Westview Press, 1993.

———. "Iberia's Contribution to Western Security." In *European Security Policy after the Revolutions of 1989,* edited by Jeffrey Simon, 590–91. Washington, D.C.: National Defense University Press, 1991.

———. *Internal Wars: Rethinking the Problem and Response.* Carlisle Barracks, Penn.: Strategic Studies Institute, 2001.

———. "An Interview with General John R. Galvin." In *Toward Responsibility in the New World Disorder,* edited by Max G. Manwaring and John T. Fishel, 1–11. London: Frank Cass, 1998.

———. *The Military in Brazilian Politics.* Ann Arbor: University of Michigan Microfilms, 1968.

———. "The New Master of 'Wizard's Chess': The Real Hugo Chavez and Asymmetric Warfare." *Military Review* (September–October 2005): 40–49.

———. *Street Gangs: The New Urban Insurgency*. Carlisle, Penn.: Strategic Studies Institute, 2005.

———. *Uncomfortable Wars: Toward a New Paradigm of Low Intensity Conflict*. Boulder, Colo.: Westview Press, 1991.

Manwaring, Max G., and Edwin G. Corr. "The 'Almost Obvious' Lessons of Peace Operations." In *Toward Responsibility in the New World Disorder,* edited by Max G. Manwaring and John T. Fishel, 196–97. London: Frank Cass, 1998.

Manwaring, Max G., and Edwin G. Corr. "Confronting the New World Disorder: A Legitimate Governance Theory of Engagement." In *Managing Contemporary Conflict: Pillars of Success,* edited by Max G. Manwaring and William J. Olson, 31–47. Boulder, Colo.: Westview Press, 1996.

Manwaring, Max G., and John T. Fishel. "Insurgency and Counter-Insurgency: Toward a New Analytical Model." *Small Wars and Insurgencies* (Winter 1992): 272–310.

Manwaring, Max G., and William J. Olson, eds. *Managing Contemporary Conflict: Pillars of Success*. Boulder, Colo.: Westview Press, 1996.

Manwaring, Max G., and Court Prisk. *El Salvador at War: An Oral History*. Washington, D.C.: National Defense University, 1988.

Mao Tse-Tun. *On Guerrilla Warfare*. Edited by Samuel B. Griffith. Baltimore, Md.: Nautical and Aviation Publishing, 1978.

Marighella, Carlos. *The Manual of the Urban Guerrilla*. Chapel Hill, N.C.: Documentary Publications, 1985.

Maritain, Jacques. *Man and the State*. Chicago: University of Chicago Press, 1963.

Marks, Thomas A. *Colombian Army Adaptation to FARC Insurgency*. Carlisle Barracks, Penn.: Strategic Studies Institute, 2002.

———. "Ideology of Insurgency: New Ethnic Focus or Old Cold War Distortions?" *Small Wars and Insurgencies* (Spring 2004): 107–28.

———. *Maoist Insurgency since Vietnam*. London: Frank Cass, 1996.

———. *Sustainability of Colombian Military/Strategic Support for "Democratic Security."* Carlisle Barracks, Penn.: Strategic Studies Institute, 2005.

———. "Urban Insurgency." *Small Wars and Insurgencies* (Autumn 2003): 100–157.

Maxwell, Kenneth. "The Emergence of Portuguese Democracy." In *From Dictatorship to Democracy,* edited by John H. Herz, 231–50. Westport, Conn.: Greenwood Press, 1982.

———. *The Making of Portuguese Democracy*. London: Cambridge University Press, 1995.

Mercado U., Rogger, ed. *Interview with Chairman Gonzalo*. San Francisco: Red Banner Editorial House, 1998.

Metz, Steven. *The Future of Insurgency*. Carlisle Barracks, Penn.: Strategic Studies Institute, 1993.

Metz, Steven, and Douglas V. Johnson II. *Asymmetry and U.S. Military Strategy: Definition, Background, and Strategic Concepts*. Carlisle Barracks, Penn.: Strategic Studies Institute, 2001.

Metz, Steven, and Raymond Millen. *Future Wars/Future Battle Space: The Strategic Role of American Landpower*. Carlisle Barracks, Penn.: Strategic Studies Institute, 2003.

Mili, Hayder. "Tangled Webs: Terrorist and Organized Crime Groups." *Terrorism Monitor* (Jamestown Foundation) 4, no. 1 (January 13, 2006). http://jamestown.org/terrorism/news/article.php?articleid=2369866.

Miller, David C. "Back to the Future: Restructuring Foreign Policy in a Post–Cold War World." Chapter 2 of *Managing Contemporary Conflict: Pillars of Success*, ed. Max G. Manwaring and William J. Olson (Boulder, Colo.: Westview Press, 1996).

———. "Beyond the Cold War: An Overview and Lessons." Chapter 8 of *Gray Area Phenomena: Confronting the New World Disorder*, ed. Max G. Manwaring (Boulder, Colo.: Westview Press, 1993).

Moran, Sue Ellen, ed. *A Rand Note: Court Depositions of Three Red Brigadists*. Santa Monica, Calif.: Rand, February 1986.

Morgenthau, Hans J. *Politics among Nations: The Struggle for Power and Peace*. Edited by Kenneth W. Thompson. New York: McGraw Hill, 1985.

Moyano, Maria Jose. *Argentina's Lost Patrol: Armed Struggle, 1969–1979*. New Haven, Conn.: Yale University Press, 1995.

Murdock, Clark A., Michele A. Flournoy, Christine E. Wormuth, Christopher A. Williams, Kurt M. Campbell, Patrick T. Henry, Pierre A. Chao, Julianne Smith, and Anne A. Witkowsky. "Beyond Goldwater-Nichols: Defense Reform for a New Strategic Era." Washington, D.C.: Center for Strategic International Studies (CSIS), March 2004, July 2005, and July 2006. http://www.csis.org/isp/bgn/reports.

Oliveira Marques, A. H. de. *A History of Portugal: From Empire to Corporate State*. New York: Columbia University Press, 1976.

Olson, William J. "International Organized Crime: The Silent Threat to Sovereignty." *Fletcher Forum* (Summer/Fall 1997): 70–74.

Organski, A.F.K. *World Politics*. New York: Alfred A. Knopf, 1958.

Orlando, Federico, ed. *Siamo en Guerra*. Rome: Armando, 1980.

Payne, Stanley G. *A History of Spain and Portugal*. Madison: University of Wisconsin Press, 1973.

Perkins, Edward J., and David L. Boren. "Summary, Observations and Conclusions on Preparing America's Foreign Policy for the Twenty-first Century." In *Preparing America's Foreign Policy for the Twenty-first Century*, edited by David L. Boren and Edward J. Perkins, 394–402. Norman: University of Oklahoma Press, 1999.

Picco, Giandomenico. "The Challenges of Strategic Terrorism." *Terrorism and Political Violence* 17 (2005): 11–16.

Pisano, Vittorfranco S. *The Dynamics of Subversion and Violence in Contemporary Italy*. Stanford, Calif.: Stanford University, Hoover Institution Press, 1987.

———. "Libya's Foothold in Italy." *Washington Quarterly* (Spring 1982): 179–82.

Pizarro, Eduardo. "Revolutionary Guerrilla Groups in Colombia." in *Violence in Colombia: The Contemporary Crisis in Historical Perspective,* edited by Charles Bergquist, Ricardo Penaranda, and Gonzolo Sanchez, 169–93. Wilmington, Del.: SR Books, 1992.

Polgatti, Arturo Contraras. *Conflicto y guerra en la post modernidad [Conflict and War in the Postmodern Era]*. Santiago: Mago Editores, 2004.

Porch, Douglas. "Uribes's Second Mandate, the War, and the Implications for Civil-Military Relations in Colombia." *Strategic Insights* 5, no. 2 (February 2006). Available at www.ccc.nps.navy.mil.

Qiao Liang and Wang Xiangsui. *Unrestricted Warfare*. Beijing: PLA Literature and Arts Publishing House, 1999.

Rabassa, Angel, and Peter Chalk. *Colombian Labyrinth*. Santa Monica, Calif.: Rand, 2001.

Restrepo, Luis Alberto. "The Crisis of the Current Political Regime and Its Possible Outcomes." In *Violence in Colombia: The Contemporary Crisis in Historical Perspective,* edited by Charles Bergquist, Ricardo Penaranda, and Gonzalo Sanchez, 273–92. Wilmington, Del.: SR Books, 1992.

Rich, Paul. "Al Qaeda and the Radical Islamic Challenge to Western Strategy." *Small Wars and Insurgencies* (Spring 2003), 45–46.

Rico, Alvaro. *Como nos domina la classe gobernante*. Montevideo: Ediciones Trilce, 2005.

Robb, John. *Brave New War: The Next Stage of Terrorism and the End of Globalization*. Hoboken, N.J.: John Wiley and Sons, 2007.

Rodo, Jose Enrique. *The Motives of Proteus*. Translated by Angel Flores. New York: Brentano's, 1928.

———. *Obras completas*. Buenos Aires: Ediciones Antonio Zamora, 1948).

Rojas Aravena, Francisco. "Nuevo contexto de seguridad internacional: Nuevos desafios, nuevas oportunidades?" In *La seguridad en America Latina pos 11 Septiembre,* edited by Francisco Rojas Aravena, 23–43. Caracas, Venezuela: FLACSO–Chile, 2003.

Rosenau, James. *Turbulence in World Politics*. Princeton, N.J.: Princeton University Press, 1990.

Rousseau, Jean-Jacques. *The Social Contract,* trans. Charles Frankel. New York: Hafner Publishing, 1951.

Rowling, J. K. *Harry Potter and the Sorcerer's Stone*. New York: Arthur A. Levine Books, 1997.

Rubio, Mauricio. "La justicia en una sociedad violenta." In *Reconocer la guerra para construir la paz,* edited by Maria Victoria Llorente and Malcom Deas, 201–235. Bogota: Ediciones Uniandes CERED Editorial Norma, 1999.

Rupp, R. W. "Defense Industrial Assistance to Greece, Portugal and Turkey." *NATO's Sixteen Nations* (October 1987): 81–85.

Sarkesian, Sam C. *U.S. National Security: Policymakers, Processes, and Politics.* Boulder, Colo.: Lynne Rienner Publishers, 1989.

Scheuer, Michael. "Al Qaeda Doctrine for International Political Warfare." *Terrorism Focus* (Jamestown Foundation) 3, no. 42 (November 1, 2006). http://jamestown.org/terrorism/news/article.php?articleid=2370189.

———. "Al-Qaeda's Insurgency Doctrine: Aiming for a 'Long War.'" *Terrorism Focus* 3, no. 8 (February 28, 2006). http://jamestown.org/terrorism/news/article.php?articleid=2369915.

———. "Al Qaeda's New Generation: Less Visible and More Lethal." *Terrorism Focus* 2, no. 18 (October 3, 2005). http://jamestown.org/terrorism/news/article.php?articleid=2369797.

———. "Al-Zawahiri's September 11 Video Hits Main Themes of Al-Qaeda Doctrine." *Terrorism Focus* 3, no. 36 (September 19, 2006). http://jamestown.org/terrorism/news/article.php?articleid=2370135.

———. "Can al-Qaeda Endure beyond bin Laden?" *Terrorism Focus* 2, no. 20 (October 28, 2005). http://jamestown.org/terrorism/news/article.php?articleid=2369820.

———. "Osama bin Laden: Taking Stock of the 'Zionist-Crusader War.'" *Terrorism Focus* 3, no. 16 (April 25, 2006). http://jamestown.org/terrorism/news/article.php?articleid=2369975.

Schoultz, Lars. *National Security and United States Policy toward Latin America.* Princeton, N.J.: Princeton University Press, 1987.

Shifter, Michael. *Hugo Chavez: A Test for U.S. Policy.* Washington, D.C.: Interamerican Dialogue, March 2007.

———. "In Search of Hugo Chavez." *Foreign Affairs* (May/June 2006): 46.

Smith, Edward C., and Arnold J. Zurcher. *The New Dictionary of American Politics.* New York: Barnes and Noble, 1960.

Smith, Paul E. *On Political War.* Washington, D.C.: National Defense University Press, 1989.

Smith, Rupert. *The Utility of Force: The Art of War in the Modern World.* New York: Alfred A. Knopf, 2007.

Sousa Leitao, Antonio Egidio de. "The Portuguese Strategic Triangle." *NATO's Sixteen Nations* (February–March 1986): 87–88.

Spencer, David. *Colombia's Paramilitaries: Criminals or Political Force?* Carlisle Barracks, Penn.: Strategic Studies Institute, 2001.

Spinola, Antonio de. *Ao Servico de Portugal.* Lisbon: Atica/Livraria Bertrand, 1976.

———. *Portugal e o futuro*. Lisbon: Arcadia, 1974.

Steinitz, Mark S. "Insurgents, Terrorists, and the Drug Trade." *Washington Quarterly* (Fall 1985): 147.

Stourch, Gerald, and Ralph Lerner, eds. *Readings in American Democracy*. New York: Oxford University Press, 1959.

Strausz-Hupe, Robert, William R. Kinter, James E. Dougherty, and Alvin J. Cottrell, eds. *Protracted Conflict: A Challenging Study of Communist Strategy*. New York: Harper and Brothers, 1953.

Sullivan, John P. "Maras Morphing: Revisiting Third Generation Gangs." *Global Crime* (August–November 2006): 488–90.

———. "Terrorism, Crime and Private Armies." *Low Intensity Conflict and Law Enforcement* (Winter 2002): 239–53.

Sullivan, John P., and Robert J. Bunker. "Drug Cartels, Street Gangs, and Warlords." In *Nonstate Threats and Future Wars,* edited by Robert J. Bunker, 40–53. London: Frank Cass, 2003.

Summers, Harry G., Jr. *On Strategy*. Carlisle Barracks, Penn.: Strategic Studies Institute, 1989.

Sun Tzu. *The Art of War.* Translated by Samuel B. Griffith. Oxford: Oxford University Press, 1963.

Talmon, J. L. *The Origins of Totalitarian Democracy*. New York: Praeger, 1968.

Toffler, Alvin, and Heidi Toffler. *War and Anti-War: Survival at the Dawn of the Twenty-first Century*. New York: Little, Brown, 1993.

Torres, Vladimir. *The Impact of "Populism" on Social, Political, and Economic Development in the Hemisphere.* FOCAL Policy Paper. Ottawa: FOCAL, 2006.

Trager, Frank N., and Philip S. Kronenberg, eds. *National Security and American Society*. Lawrence: University Press of Kansas, 1973.

Trinquier, Roger. *A French View of Counterinsurgency.* English translation. London: Pall Mall Press, 1964.

Ulph, Stephen. "Mujahideen to Pledge Allegiance on the Web." *Terrorism Focus* (Jamestown Foundation) 2, no. 22 (November 29, 2005). http://jamestown.org/terrorism/news/article.php?articleid=2369835.

Urbina, Andrés Benavente, and Julio Alberto Cirino. *La democracia defraudada [Democracy Defrauded]*. Buenos Aires: Grito Sagrado, 2005.

U.S. Army. Field Manual 90–8, *Counterguerrilla Operations*. Washington, D.C.: Headquarters, Department of the Army, 1986.

———. Field Manual 3–07.22, MCRP 3–33.5, *Counterinsurgency Operations.* Draft. Washington, D.C.: Headquarters, Department of the Army, 2005.

U.S. Department of Defense, Commission on Integrated Long-Term Strategy, Report by the Regional Conflict Working Group, *Supporting U.S. Strategy for Third World Conflict* (Washington, D.C.: Department of Defense, June 1988).

Vergara, Jose Manuel, and Florencia Varas. *Coup! Allende's Last Day*. New York: Stein and Day, 1975.

Verstrynge Rojas, Jorge. *La guerra asimetrica y el Islam revolucionario*. Madrid: El Viejo Topo, 2005.

———. *La guerra periférica y el Islam revolucionario: Origines, reglas, y ética de la guerra asimétrica [Peripheral. Indirect) War and Revolutionary Islam: Origins, Regulations, and Ethics of Asymmetric War]*. Special Edition for the Army of the Bolivarian Republic of Venezuela, IDRFAN, Enlace Circular Militar. Madrid: El Viejo Topo, May 2005.

Wiarda, Howard J. *Corporatism and Development: The Portuguese Experience*. Amherst: University of Massachusetts Press, 1977.

Wilgus, A. Curtis. *Modern Hispanic-America*. Washington, D.C.: George Washington University Press, 1933.

Yin, Robert K. *Case Study Research: Design and Methods*. Thousand Oaks, Calif.: Sage Publications, 1994.

Zuhur, Sherifa. *A Hundred Osamas: Islamist Threats and the Future of Counterinsurgency*. Carlisle Barracks, Penn.: Strategic Studies Institute, 2005.

INDEX